P9-CDC-780

Cruising Guide
to the
Netherlands

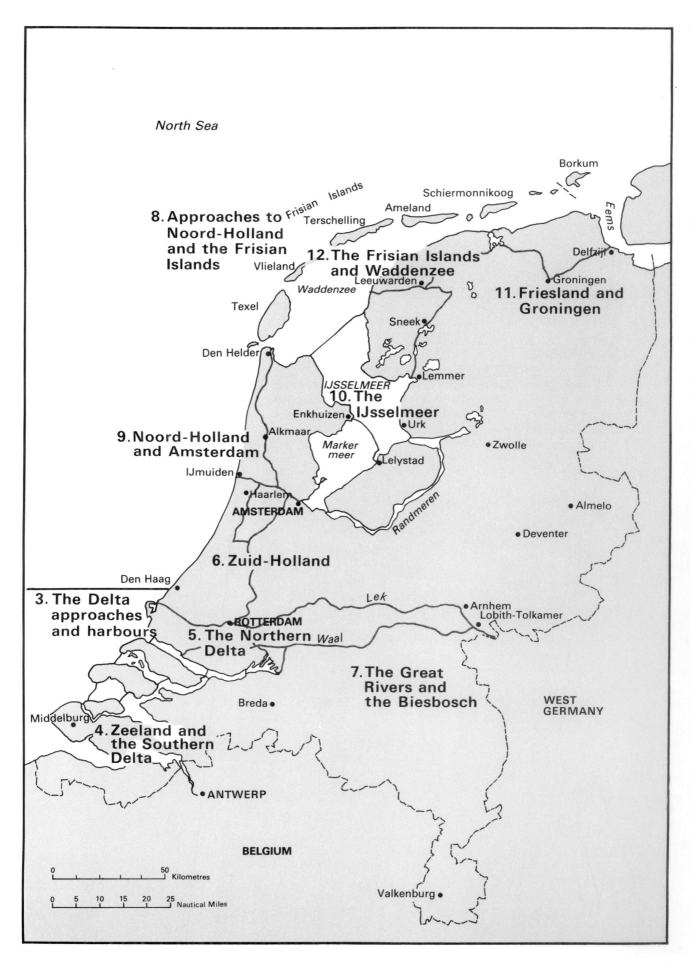

North Sea

Borkum

8. **Approaches to** Frisian Islands
Noord-Holland
and the Frisian Schiermonnikoog
Islands Terschelling Ameland

12. **The Frisian Islands**
and Waddenzee

Eems

Vlieland

Delfzijl

Waddenzee

Leeuwarden

11. **Friesland and**
Groningen

Groningen

Texel

Sneek

Den Helder

IJSSELMEER

Lemmer

10. **The**
IJsselmeer

Enkhuizen

Urk

9. **Noord-Holland** Alkmaar
and Amsterdam

Marker
meer

Zwolle

Lelystad

IJmuiden

Haarlem

AMSTERDAM

Randmeren

Almelo

Deventer

6. **Zuid-Holland**

Lek

Den Haag

Arnhem
Lobith-Tolkamer

3. **The Delta**
approaches
and harbours

ROTTERDAM

5. **The Northern** Waal
Delta

7. **The Great**
Rivers and
the Biesbosch

WEST
GERMANY

Breda

Middelburg

4. **Zeeland and**
the Southern
Delta

ANTWERP

BELGIUM

0   50
Kilometres

0   5   10   15   20   25
Nautical Miles

Valkenburg

Frontispiece

Cruising Guide to the Netherlands

BRIAN NAVIN

Imray Laurie Norie & Wilson Ltd
St Ives Cambridgeshire England

Published by
Imray, Laurie, Norie & Wilson Ltd
Wych House, St Ives, Huntingdon,
Cambridgeshire, PE17 4BT, England.

British Library Cataloguing in Publication Data

Navin, Brian,
    Cruising Guide to the Netherlands
    1. Netherlands. Inland waterways – Pilots' guides
    623.89'229492

    ISBN 0 85288 131 2

CAUTION
Whilst every care has been taken to ensure accuracy, neither the Publishers nor the Author will hold themselves responsible for errors, omissions or alterations in this publication. They will at all times be grateful to receive information which tends to the improvement of the work.

Plans
The plans in this guide are not to be used for navigation. They are designed to support the text and should at all times be used with navigational charts.
    The scales have been chosen to allow the best coverage in relation to page size and consequently on certain small-scale plans numerous buoys and other marks have been omitted for clarity.

The technical data in this work is correct to October 1988.

Set in Plantin by Cromwell Graphics Ltd, St Ives, Huntingdon direct from the Author's and Publishers' disks.
Printed in Great Britain at The Bath Press, Avon

Preface

Ever since my first cruise there in 1973 my interest in the Netherlands has continued to grow. I suppose this stems partly from being a self-adopted East Anglian with a soft spot for friendly people with similar sailing interests, not too far away across the North Sea, all of whom seem to speak English.

I am also fascinated by a country with such a similar landscape to the marshlands of Essex, the Norfolk Broads and the Wash, but whose inhabitants have spent so much time and effort in chiselling it into something different. Nothing in East Anglia can compare with the spectacular Afsluitdijk or with the yachting lock in the Krammersluizen complex, or with the hundreds of lifting bridges in densely populated urban areas which open on the approach of a mast, or with the thousands of historic gabled houses and windmills, magnificently preserved despite Holland's devastation during the Second World War.

Some may argue that this is an excessively artificial cruising landscape where nature is dwarfed by urbanisation and technological marvels, although that in itself provides a sharp contrast to cruising the British coasts. However, for those who prefer to remain close to nature and feel the rhythm of the tides there is still the huge cruising area of the Waddenzee in the north and its Frisian Islands with their 'lost world' character.

Finally, the Netherlands is within a feasible passage range, with just that *soupçon* of adventure in getting there but with convenient ferries nearby. There are a number of alternative routes. For example in 1973 I delivered our small bilge-keeler to Oostende from the Crouch with a strong crew and my young family joined by ferry. From Oostende we unashamedly took time and coast-hopped, creeping along the Flanders coast to the Westerschelde and deep into the Delta to Dordrecht, returning in short stages to Calais and crossing the Dover Strait and Thames Estuary to the Crouch. In the eighties with a deeper, heavier displacement fin-keeler we have usually taken the 'short sharp shock' route – a 1½-day passage from Harwich via IJmuiden to Amsterdam, to slump, dog-tired but happy, over our coffee and *genever* in one of the street cafés near Dam Square knowing that we are in the centre of it all right at the beginning of our holiday.

Acknowledgements

The plans of the harbours on and near the coasts and in the IJsselmeer are based on charts published by the Chef der Hydrografie, 's-Gravenhage, Netherlands.

The plans on the inland waterways are based on charts published by Koninklijke Nederlandse Toeristenbond ANWB.

The author would like to thank the following for their professional help in a number of specific areas: Raymond Bronsgeest and the Rijkswaterstaat Dienst Verkeerskunde for information on railway bridge opening times and on locks operation; Jaap Kuitert and the Watertoerisme department of the ANWB for help with the ANWB catalogues, charts and their interpretation; M.N. Robinson of Observator B.V. for assistance with almanac and chart sources; the staff of the Netherlands Board of Tourism in London for their advice and leaflets; the staff of many provincial VVV offices on the routes covered by this book for the tourist information they provided.

Particular thanks are due from the author to R. Woolhead, P. Skinner, P. Giles, and P. Burton for their time and competence in helping to ferry *Teazle* in so many different directions across the North Sea in 1986 and 1987. Yet again many thanks to A.E. Somers who read through the manuscript. Finally thanks also to B. Thompson for many years' encouragement in a shared obsession.

Once again I am indebted to the staff of Imray, Laurie, Norie and Wilson for their painstaking and meticulous editing, drawing and laying out of what has proved to be a much more complicated reference book than my previous *North Sea Passage Pilot*.

Brian Navin
Southminster, Essex
September 1988

To B.D.N.

Contents

I. General

Introduction

The navigable waterways of the Netherlands are too extensive for a single volume to be comprehensive so this book is selective. It examines the coastal harbours and approaches of the country, overlapping with the author's *North Sea Passage Pilot*, together with 21 waterway tours feasible to vessels with fixed masts up to 17m air draught (in some cases considerably more). However, routes 10, 11 and 12 are limited to vessels up to 12¼, 14 and 12m air draught respectively, possibly a little more in low water conditions. Many motor vessels are of course at an advantage since on some routes they can also pass under those opening bridges or their fixed sections which have sufficient clearance without waiting for the bridge to be opened. However there are only a limited number of these bridges, many having as little as 1m or less clearance when closed.

In Section I, Chapter 1 includes some Dutch waterway history providing a framework of interest for a cruise plan. Chapter 2, together with the appendices at the back of the book, provides a list of information sources and a guide to their interpretation.

Section II covers the southern and Section III the northern part of the country. The first chapter of each, 3 and 8 respectively, covers the approaches and coastal harbours and the remaining chapters give detailed itinerary information on the suggested cruises, moving progressively from south to north. There is ample information for many successive cruising holidays, but if you wish to explore even further afield or elaborate on these routes you can always turn back to Section I and the appendices for help.

Bearings and directions

The bearings given are all in 360° notation and are true. Directions are indicated by the usual abbreviations; W for west, NE for northeast, WSW for west-southwest etc.

Key to abbreviations and symbols

1. General

Throughout the text and plans in this guide familiar abbreviations have been used for convenience. Generally these follow standard conventions, those of the Admiralty are listed in the relevant Admiralty publication (i.e. regarding light or radio information). Admiralty *5011, Symbols and Abbreviations* and a dictionary should be consulted for explanations not listed below. See above for direction abbreviations.

Aero RC	aeronautical radiobeacon
B	black
Ch	channel (radio)
⊖	Customs
F	fixed light
Fl	flashing light
Fl( )	group-flashing light
G	green
HrMr	harbourmaster
hr(s)	hour(s)
ht	maximum clearance height of fixed bridge, or of opening bridge when closed
HW	high water
Iso	isophase light
kn	knot(s)
kph	kilometres per hour
Ldg	leading
LtHo	lighthouse
Lt(s)	light(s)
LtV	light vessel
LW	low water
m	metre(s)
M	nautical mile(s)
max	maximum
No(s)	number(s)
Oc	occulting light
Oc( )	group-occulting light
R	red
RC	marine radiobeacon
RG	radio direction-finding station
RW	red and white
stbd	starboard
t	metric ton weight
TSS	traffic separation scheme
W	white sector (with other colours) no letter if white light only
Wh	white (as of a structure)
Y	yellow/amber/orange

2. Special abbreviations in the route descriptions

KP	*kanaalpeil* (canal water level)
LLWS	lowest low water springs (datum on some charts)

MHW	mean high water (*GHW gemiddeld hoogwater*)
MHWN	mean high water neaps
MHWS	mean high water springs
MLW	mean low water (*GLW gemiddeld laagwater*)
MLWN	mean low water neaps
MLWS	mean low water springs
MR	mean summer river level (*middelbare rivierstand in de zomer* = NR−12 to −20cm)
NAP	*normaal Amsterdams peil* (datum based on mean sea level)
NR	normal river level (*normaal rivierstand* = MR +12 to +20cm)
OLW	agreed low river level (*overeengekomen lage rivierstand*)
WV	*watersport-vereniging* (water sport club)
⌁	fixed bridge (*vaste brug* not annotated on Dutch charts)
⌁	opening bridge (BB or Beweegbare brug on Dutch charts)
≪	locks
⅃	junction
⚓	yacht harbour with extensive facilities
⚓	yacht moorings with walk-on pontoons or direct access to canal or river bank

3. Distances

Distances in *kilometres* and nautical miles, e.g. *5·2km/2·8M*, in the route descriptions are from the previous junction or bridge to the place indicated immediately below.

4. Bridge and lock opening hours in the route descriptions

Day/month Numbered e.g. *1/10-1/4* is 1st October to 1st April.

Time of day 24-hour notation e.g. 0800-1730 is 8:00am to 5:30pm.

Days of the week Abbreviated to m = Monday, t = Tuesday, w = Wednesday, th = Thursday, f = Friday, sa = Saturday, su = Sunday, h = feast days/bank holidays; e.g. m-f is Monday to Friday inclusive, su/h is Sundays and holidays. Feast days/weekday bank holidays are normally Christmas Day, New Year's Day, Easter Monday, Ascension Day, Whit Monday.

Time schedules For road bridges and locks these are based on the January 1988 edition of *Bedieningstijden van sluizen en bruggen* published by Rijkswaterstaat, Dienst Verkeerskunde, ☎ (070) 744893. This does not give times for railway bridges. Although some major road bridges and locks are serviced 24 hours a day the whole year round, most do not operate for varying overnight and lunch-hour periods, and are most restricted in operation on weekends, bank holidays, and where they are next to a railway bridge.

In practice minor time changes are continually being made to these schedules, but if you give yourself plenty of time for your cruise and are prepared for occasional delays the schedules in the route descriptions should provide an adequate guide for several years to come.

Wherever possible a brief general guide is also given to opening times of the railway bridges in the route descriptions, but here you need to obtain the leaflet *Openingstijden spoorwegbruggen* from an ANWB office when you arrive in the Netherlands. This usually covers the year to end May, but is often published late and again you must make allowances for possible variations to these very precise timetables.

The time schedules in the route descriptions are categorised either by day of week or by seasonal period, as in the following examples:

Schiphol bascule bridge (Route 8)
m-f 0500-0630, 1230-1330, 2000-2100; sa *16/4-16/10* 0700-0800, 1230-1330, 1900-2000, *16/10-16/4* 0700-0800, 1230-1330, 1800-1900; su/h *16/4-16/10* 0800-1030, 1830-2100 (on hr and ½hr), su/h *16/10-16/4* closed.

Here days of the week are the basic variable, within which the varying schedules for seasonal periods are listed. Mondays to Fridays have the same servicing hours throughout the year, the Saturday working hours specified are different in summer (16/4 to 16/10) and winter (16/10 to 16/4), and on Sundays and feast days the bridge is open for the specified hours in summer (16/4 to 16/10) but only on the hour and the half hour and closed in winter (16/4 to 16/10).

Prins Hendrikbrug (Route 12)
16/4-1/16/10 m-sa 0900-1200, 1400-1900; su/h 0900-1200, 1500-2000. *16/10-16/4* m-sa 0800-1200, 1300-1700; su/h closed.

Here summer and winter periods are the basic variable within which the varying schedules for days of the week are listed. During the winter period the bridge is not in operation on Sundays and holidays.

Elburg. An old Zuiderzee harbour. Town gate and high street

1. God's water and God's land

'The French once said that God made the world, but the Dutch made their own country. Although this is somewhat of an exaggeration, we consider that the French were right.'

This quotation from a booklet published by the Netherlands Ministry of Transport and Public Works is a classic example of justifiable Dutch pride of achievement in their 1000-year battle with the sea. Throughout the country there are thousands of carefully preserved remnants of this battle – archaeological remains, buildings, machinery, windmills, even reconstructed towns and villages, whilst almost every town and large village has its museum usually with a nautical bias. Many of these places are close by the waterways covered in this book.

Terpen and dykes

Prior to about the year AD 1000, to quote the same source, the Netherlanders 'let God's water flow over God's land', and people in the wettest parts of the swampy deltas of the Rhine, Meuse and Scheldt fled to urban hillocks during flood surges. These hillocks are called *terpen* in Friesland, *wierden* in Groningen, and gradually grew out of deposits of clay and rubbish. Churches and radial villages are now found on them in the northern parts of these provinces. There are over 1000 in Friesland and two good examples are Hogebeintum and Janum north of Birdaard on the Dokkumer Ee (Route 18). In Zeeland an example of another ring village is Dreischor between Bruinisse and Brouwershaven (Route 4) just off the southern Grevelingen shore.

The birth of the Biesbosch

In the 10th and 11th centuries dyke building was developed, and in some cases *terpen* were joined together by dykes and the tidal ebb and flow used to drain the enclosed polders. Extensive dyking and reclamation of this type continued throughout the Middle Ages, but not without repeated disasters which have continued right up to the present day occurring whenever a violent northerly storm coincides with an exceptional spring tide and pushes a growing wave of flood water down the funnel-shaped North Sea. In addition it was not known in the early days that not only was the land around the North Sea progressively sinking but the average sea level was also rising; the net effect of these two slow movements being a 1 metre loss of land per 1000 years.

On the night of the 18–19th November 1421 a storm surge, the St Elizabeth Flood, burst the dykes and submerged the Grote Waard southeast of Dordrecht creating the area now known as the Bies-bosch (the rush woods) which in subsequent centuries was gradually silted up by the outflow of the Waal and the Maas. It was then developed for reed and osier cultivation, and fishing, whilst in recent centuries selective re-dyking has created pasture land between some of the channels. During the Second World War this maze of tree-hung channels made an ideal hideout for the Dutch Resistance. The fascinating Biesbosch Museum is on the south side of the Spieringsluis entrance to the Brabantse Biesbosch on the Nieuwe Merwede (Route 12).

Brabantse Biesbosch. Riverside house, Steurgat

Windmills and the 16th-century polders

The first windmills appeared at the turn of the 15th to 16th century. Previously grain was ground either manually, or by horsepower or water mills. By the early nineteenth century windmills were an integral part of the landscape to be seen in every direction in the flat and windswept countryside. Used for tasks such as milling grain, sawing logs, crushing oilseed, fulling fabrics, pounding hemp and lifting water, at that time there were 9,000 mills. Today just under 1,000 have been preserved. The Zaanse Schans, a 20-acre area on the east bank of the Zaan (Route 14), has a collection of these mills in working order including mustard, saw, paint and oil mills, as well as a variety of other houses and several craft museums (e.g. cheese-making, baking, clog-making) preserving a picture of working life in the Zaan district in the 19th century. There are many other windmills on other routes described in this guide.

Above all the windmill enabled the drainage of wide areas of inland lakes and pools creating much

A beautifully preserved windmill at Gouwsluis

larger polders. In Noord-Holland between Alkmaar and Amsterdam the first three of these to be pumped dry were the Beemster (1612), the Purmer (1622) and the Schermer (1635). These areas and a number of museums are accessible from Routes 14 and 15.

The steam engine and the Haarlemmermeerpolder

Steam-pumping technology imported from Britain heralded the next major stage of land reclamation. In the Middle Ages land sinkage and storm damage created a large inland lake, the Haarlemmermeer, from a number of lakes in the fen lands southwest of Amsterdam, whose growth began to threaten that city as well as Leiden and Haarlem. Like the Zuiderzee which joined it, the Haarlemmermeer was some 4 metres below sea level, subject to similar weather and sea conditions, and had a shipping and fishing industry. As early as 1641 a plan was drawn up to drain the area by use of 166 windmills grouped in threes to obtain the required 4 to 5 metres water-lift but this proved beyond contemporary resources so the fishermen continued to prosper throughout the 18th century.

King William I (1813–40) appointed a commission which decided that the steam engines invented by the British could do the job slightly cheaper than wind power. Although the expression had not yet been invented those early 19th-century Netherlanders certainly knew what cost-benefit analysis was all about, and tried not to underestimate the task. Nevertheless, although the decision was made in 1838, it was not until 1852 after three years nonstop pumping that the three steam-driven pumping stations Leeghwater, Lijnden and Cruquius finished draining the 800 million cubic metres of water out of the lake into the Ringvaart canal on the 60km-long dyke which had been built around the polder. The Cruquius station near Heemstede (Route 9) closed down in 1933 and is preserved as a museum and monument to the project.

The landscape here, created with considerable subsequent trauma is only 125 years old, and Hoofdorp (originally Kruisdorp) the administrative centre, and Nieuwe-Vennep (originally Venneperdorp) are both early new towns. Who would have guessed in 1852 that one of the world's major airports would be sited at Schiphol where once fishing boats were scudding across a choppy lake?

The old pumping station at Cruquius

The Zuiderzee project

The world-famous Afsluitdijk which cuts off the northern end of the IJsselmeer is 30km long. There is a motorway and a restaurant on it from which the gigantic scale of the project can be sensed in looking to the far horizon along the pencil-straight wall. But this was only the beginning, equally awe-inspiring is the thought when standing by the roadside in Zuid Flevoland that every house, hedge, canal, field, garden and road as far as the eye can see is 4 metres below sea level and has come into existence only since the polder was drained in 1967.

During the 12th century, when dyke-building was flourishing, the Zuiderzee emerged as a result of the increasing relative sea level and gradual enlargement of Lake Flevo which covered roughly the present Flevoland area, together with the widening of its northern inlet to the North Sea. By the beginning of the 19th century the Zuiderzee was not only an important fishing region but was heavily used by commercial shipping. Ships from Amsterdam took the Zuiderzee-Waddenzee route from the IJ heading for the island of Urk to avoid the Enkhuizerzand, then heading for the southern end of Breezand, now crossed by the Afsluitdijk, where two routes split off, one to the western world through the Marsdiep between Texel and Den Helder, and the other to northern Europe via the Vlie between Terschelling and Vlieland. On the strength of this trade Amsterdam developed in the 16th century from a mere Zuiderzee fishing village into an international commercial centre whilst towns such as Hoorn, Enkhuizen and Kampen also prospered, as did associated specialist fishing supply ports such as Marken, Volendam, Urk and Spakenburg.

Enkhuizen's Zuiderzee Museum (Route 15), in both its indoor and outdoor sections, shows the type of wealth created by the sea trade, and displays a magnificent collection of Zuiderzee wooden fishing and pleasure craft.

In 1824 the completion of the shorter deep-draught Noordhollands Kanaal route from Amsterdam to Den Helder resulted in the disappearance of larger ships from the Zuiderzee and ended the trade of the small Zuiderzee towns. Amsterdam's trading prospects were further boosted in 1876 by the opening of the even shorter Noordzeekanaal to IJmuiden.

In 1918, the Zuiderzee project was launched to dam off the area in order to reduce the length and cost, and increase the effectiveness of sea defences, as well as increase freshwater supplies and create additional agricultural land. This was one of the first of many difficult environmental decisions to be made by successive governments since it killed off the saltwater marine life of the Zuiderzee. If you occasionally find yourself sailing the IJsselmeer in water which looks like the Dutch *erwetensoep* (thick pea soup which is an enjoyable meal in any case) you will know why. Had they known then what they do today the Afsluitdijk might have been a storm-surge barrier like the one recently completed in the Oosterschelde.

The earliest plan of Hendrik Stevin in 1667 envisaged a Zuiderzee-Waddenzee with dams joining all the Dutch Frisian islands, closing off the IJ near Amsterdam, and digging a short North Sea canal. Dr Cornelius Lely who was Minister of Waterways and Drainage in 1918 had been drawing up and revising plans since the 1890's, but inevitably the final ambitious project took far longer than expected, proceeding in a number of stages with long gaps for each government of the day to make up their minds. Currently the country is in the middle of such a pause before the next stage, as the following chronology shows.

The IJsselmeer Project

- 1920–24 Building of a 2·5km dyke from Noord-Holland to the island of Wieringen.
- 1925–26 A small 100-acre triangular test polder, Andijk, was drained on the peninsula north of Enkhuizen.
- 1927–32 The 30km-long 90m-wide Afsluitdijk between Wieringen and Friesland was built. Work began on an artificial island halfway along the route, and on the sluices and shipping locks at each corner near Wieringen and the Frisian coast, moving to build the dam at six locations in shallow and later progressively deeper water. The controlling sluices have gradually changed the lake from salt to fresh water by progressive outward drainage.
- 1927–30 The draining of the Wieringermeerpolder (50,000 acres) was an integral part of the main dam project.
- 1937–42 The northeast polder (120,000 acres) was being drained when the country was under German occupation.
- 1950–57 Eastern Flevoland (135,000 acres) and in
- 1959–67 Southern Flevoland (107,500 acres) were drained and together now form a new province with an administrative centre at Lelystad.
- 1976 The completion of the Houtribdijk cutting off the southern Markermeer with sluices and shipping locks at each end, and in preparation for draining the Markerwaard polder.

Oost Flevoland near Ketelhaven. It is hard to believe that this land was under the waters of the IJsselmeer in the early 1950s

Flevoland, the Randmeren and the Markermeer

The Dutch cabinet has postponed plans to start draining the Markermeer to create another 125,000-acre polder, in order to allow time for further debate. Time has always been a plentiful commodity in the Netherlands, the project has taken 60 years so far although Lely originally estimated 32, and the next polder will cost at least a billion guilders. After a polder is drained the state reclaims and works the land for five years and then rents it with buildings, mainly on short-term lease, to candidates with appropriate skills, particularly farmers displaced by urban development elsewhere. More recently planned residential and associated industrial development to cater for overspill from the increasingly crowded Randstad region in Zuid-Holland is occurring at Lelystad and Almere.

The latest polders, east and south Flevoland and the planned Markerwaard, have a feature which is useful to cruising yachtsmen: experiment has shown that a continuous band of deep water around the polder maintains the correct ground-water table in the neighbouring 'old' land. The Randmeren (Route 16) lakes have subsequently been developed as recreational areas of water with carefully landscaped banks and many facilities, including those for fishing and cruising, with the ideal combination of old Zuiderzee towns such as Spakenburg, Harderwijk and Elburg on the east and south banks and brand new yacht havens on the west and north banks. The Markerwaard, if, or perhaps merely when, it is complete, will have a similar continuous wide band of encircling water.

South of the PTT tower and the Houtribsluizen by the waterside near Lelystad is 'Information Centre Nieuwe Land' (Route 17) a comprehensive exhibition with all modern aids showing the development of the IJsselmeer and its polders. Lelystad's somewhat mundane precinct shopping centre, if you can find it amongst the leafy suburban sprawl, is nearly 3km east.

Shipwrecks of the Zuiderzee

Ketelhaven Museum is of particular interest to yachtsmen (Route 16), exhibiting ships' inventories and several wrecks exposed by the draining of the polders, including a 26m long, 7m beam, 17th-century cargo vessel. The remains of Second World War aircraft are other 'archaeological' finds on display.

In 1930 the 16 shipwrecks which appeared on the newly drained Wieringermeerpolder took the universities by surprise and despite partial excavation no data at all was recorded. However, since the draining of the northeast polder in 1942 some 350 wrecks have been discovered on the surface of the new polders of which only 140 have so far been systematically investigated; the rest are waiting their turn and are meanwhile being carefully protected from rot in situ.

The value of these wrecks lies in the relatively undisturbed nature of their contents and inventories – cooking utensils, caulking implements, repair tools and materials, armaments – many of which are on show in Ketelhaven. Of even more importance is the fact that this may be an area unique in the world where ships over such a long and continuous period can be investigated; the oldest vessels date from around 1300 when the Zuiderzee was the freshwater Almere (Flevomeer in Roman times) – only in the late Middle Ages does the name Zuiderzee occur, the area only becoming completely saline by the middle of the 17th century.

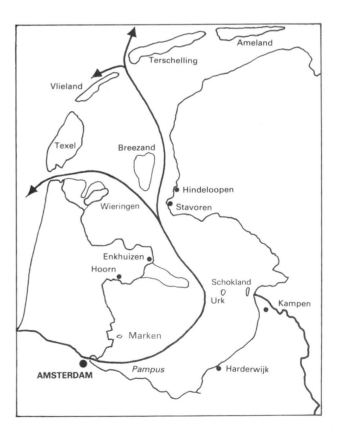

17th-century shipping routes in the Zuiderzee

The Delta Plan

This most recent plan represents the peak of achievement in hydraulic technology. The two remaining projects within the plan were due for completion by end 1987, nearly 30 years after initiation. It has cost 12½ billion guilders (over £4 billion sterling) and created such a huge sustained boost to the Dutch economy that the government are looking

Hollandse IJssel storm surge barrier with lock to left. One of the pillars is being cleaned. The earliest project of the Delta Scheme

for other schemes to fill the gap – a tunnel under the Westerschelde entrance is one possibility.

The main objective again is protection from flooding and cost reduction by reducing the length of sea defences. It also improves the Delta navigations and particularly the Nieuwe (Rotterdamse) Waterweg and the Westerschelde, the world's largest port complexes, as well as improving recreational amenities. The 1953 North Sea storm surge cost Holland nearly 2000 lives and was the driving motivation behind the 1958 Delta Plan Act.

Earlier land reclamation projects on and around the islands of Zeeland left large areas of dyked land below sea level. Dyking reclaimed a huge bay on the southern side of the Westerschelde between Breskens and Terneuzen, and a wide lake/marsh at the east end of the Haringvliet and Hollands Diep south of Dordrecht. This became Dordrecht Island and the Sliedrechtse and Brabantse Biesbosch, whilst several pairs of islands were joined together by dykes.

The Delta Plan aimed at protecting the area from storm surges in two ways. One, by raising and reinforcing the dykes especially along the open tidal navigations of the Rotterdam and Westerschelde waterways, and later when the Plan was amended, also the Oosterschelde. Two, it improved the effectiveness and reduced the cost of protection for long lengths of dyked banks inside the estuaries by the building of outer and inner dams, some with shipping locks and sluice gates, creating inland lakes.

The sluice gates of the Haringvliet 'reservoir' also control the water outflow of the whole Lower Rhine basin. The water in these tideless lakes is penned at levels within a few centimetres of NAP, Normal Amsterdam Standard or mean sea level. This stable water level in turn improves navigation for both commercial and pleasure traffic and improves seaside tourist amenities.

In 1958 there were two small problems: the engineers did not know quite how to do it, and the danger of environmental pollution was low on the politicians' list of priorities. Wisely the public departments involved proceeded by trial and error in increasingly ambitious stages, learning as they went along. When environmental complaints about the earlier projects built up this left plenty of time to redesign the later ones.

The first project was completed in 1958, a simple single guillotine gate storm-surge barrier with a shipping lock on the Hollandse IJssel river between Rotterdam and Gouda (Routes 8 and 9), which helped to remove the flood danger from the most densely populated region. The much later Oosterschelde storm-surge barrier is also on the guillotine gate principle, but with no less than 62 gates designed to last 200 years. The Hollandse IJssel barrier is normally left raised but with a clearance of only 7·5m above MHW, so if you have a higher mast you must go through the lock and the opening bridge on the western side of the barrier.

The second stage, isolating the smallest inlet, originally the Veerse Gat now the tideless Veerse Meer, was also completed rapidly, by 1961, with a simple single shipping lock in the Zandkreekdam at the inland end and the impervious blank wall of the Veersedam at the seaward end, as a result of which the lake is stagnant salt. The level is kept to NAP in summer (*zomerpeil*, April to August inclusive) and NAP −0·7m in winter (*winterpeil*). As in the other 'still-water' estuaries the Veerse Meer has many extremely well designed cruising amenities (see Route 2).

Stage three, isolation of the much bigger Haringvliet, was more difficult, taking until 1971 to complete. Running south of and parallel to the open tidal Nieuwe Waterweg, this provides a huge stopcock for the whole drainage system of the three Rhine tributaries, the Maas, Waal and Lek. The inland Volkerak dam (Route 3) in the tributary on the south side of the Haringvliet, with multiple shipping locks, a yacht lock (a fixed road bridge restricts maximum clearance to NAP +19m) and sluices, cuts off the Haringvliet and all of the northern Rhine tributaries from the southern Delta inlets. The spectacular Haringvlietdam (Chapter 3) at the seaward end has a series of huge inner and outer partially rotating sluice gates worked by hydraulic pistons which are normally kept closed but some of which are swung open at or near LW to control inland water levels and let off Rhine flood water. The Goereesesluis shipping lock through the southern end of the dam has two opening bridges and so is no problem for fixed-mast sailing yachts.

The Delta in 1500

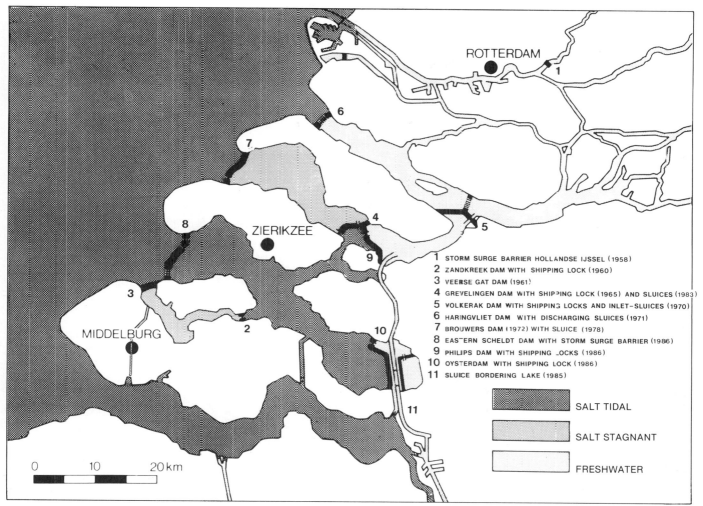

1 STORM SURGE BARRIER HOLLANDSE IJSSEL (1958)
2 ZANDKREEK DAM WITH SHIPPING LOCK (1960)
3 VEERSE GAT DAM (1961)
4 GREVELINGEN DAM WITH SHIPPING LOCK (1965) AND SLUICES (1983)
5 VOLKERAK DAM WITH SHIPPING LOCKS AND INLET-SLUICES (1970)
6 HARINGVLIET DAM WITH DISCHARGING SLUICES (1971)
7 BROUWERS DAM (1972) WITH SLUICE (1978)
8 EASTERN SCHELDT DAM WITH STORM SURGE BARRIER (1986)
9 PHILIPS DAM WITH SHIPPING LOCKS (1986)
10 OYSTERDAM WITH SHIPPING LOCK (1986)
11 SLUICE BORDERING LAKE (1985)

SALT TIDAL

SALT STAGNANT

FRESHWATER

The Delta Plan today

The Haringvliet, Hollands Diep and Amer are now fresh water isolated from the North Sea tides and with a depth dependent on the outflow of the Waal and the Maas as well as the twice daily Haringvliet sluicing programme. During sluicing the whole water level can be reduced by as much as 0·5m in an hour. In general however the current in the Haringvliet is relatively slight but in extreme conditions near the sluices themselves can reach 5·4kn (10kph). Although the sluices are marked by a string of yellow light beacons 2 cables off the dam it is advisable to keep south of the line of red buoys marking the Deltageul channel, linking the lock's Binnenhaven with Hellevoetsluis, particularly when there are red lights on the dam indicating sluicing in progress. There is an interesting exhibition of the Delta Plan combined with a tour of the inside of the sluices accessible from the Aqua Pesch marina on the seaward side of the Goereesesluis (Chapter 3).

Tidal effects of the partial isolation of the Haringvliet vary. Hollands Diep and the whole of the Maas some 30M inland from Dordrecht island to its first weir at Lith has a very small generally downstream current. Beyond the Biesbosch this is of academic interest to fixed-mast vessels of over 9m air draught, due to the fixed bridges. Leaving the Nieuwe Waterweg open at the Hoek has created a strange tidal effect in the four short waterways joining the two main waterway systems – the Spui, Dordtse Kil, Oude Maas and Noord. Here the effect of a double daily tidal stream gradually increases the further north you go approaching the main tidal waterway. It is necessary here to use the appropriate Dutch *stroomatlas* (see Chapter 2, also Routes 5, 6, and 7) since there are 2 to 3 knot maximum mean spring rates in parts especially at the 'T-junctions' of these rivers.

Stage four, the isolation of the Grevelingenmeer took even longer to complete during the heated environmental debate. The inland Grevelingendam and single lock was completed in 1965 and the seaward Brouwersdam with a small sluice in 1978, but sluices in the inner Grevelingendam were only finished in 1983. Penned at a level of NAP −0·2m, but ranging from NAP −0·1 to −0·3m, this is described by Rijkswaterstaat Deltadienst as 'stagnant, salt or fresh', i.e. the smallish 'taps' at each end leave it rather murky. It is virtually free of commercial traffic. Again yachting facilities leave little further to be desired (see Route 4).

For stage five the original intention similarly was to isolate a stagnant Oosterschelde, but in 1976 the scheme was dropped in time to save the shellfish and bird life of the estuary. The outer 'dam' was to

North Sea

Borkum

Frisian Islands

Schiermonnikoog

Terschelling

Ameland

Vlieland

Ee

Lauwersmeer

Reitdiep

Delfzijl

Eems K

Leeuwarden

v. Starken borgh K.

Groningen

Waddenzee

v. Harinxma

Texel

Sneek

Den Helder

Lemmer

IJSSELMEER

Urk

N Holland K.

Enkhuizen

Zwolle

Alkmaar

Marker meer

Lelystad

IJmuiden

Zaan

Haarlem

AMSTERDAM

Max ht 12.5m

Almelo

Randmeren

IJssel

Deventer

Ringvaart

Vecht

Oude Rijn

Gouwe

Utrecht

Den Haag

Neder Rijn

Rott. W

Weg

ROTTERDAM

Lek

Arnhem

Lobith-Tolkamer

Haringvliet

Waal

Max ht 12m

Grevelingen meer

Dordrecht

Maas

's-Hertogenbosch

Max ht NAP+20m

Breda

WEST GERMANY

Middelburg

Oosterschelde

Westerschelde

ANTWERP

Maas

Mast heights up to:
30 Metres
17 Metres
12·5 Metres
9 Metres

BELGIUM

0   50 Kilometres

0   5 10 15 20 25 Nautical Miles

Valkenburg

Routes for four different mast heights

be a 'storm-surge barrier' allowing the tides through and closed only during flood danger. This has meant that as well as spending 5 billion guilders on a complicated open barrier, they have had to spend another 2½ billion plus inflation since 1985 to build two extremely heavy and complicated dams inland. These are the Oesterdam ('Oysterdam') at the eastern end of the estuary which follows the line of the Schelde-Rijn canal that connects Antwerp to the Volkerak, and the Philipsdam (Route 3) which crosses the northern Oosterschelde tributary, the Krammer, and meets the Grevelingendam in a 'T-junction'. These later dams share a single canal-like discharging sluice which leads from the freshwater lakes created behind the dams down to Bath on the Westerschelde. In addition to the commercial locks a special yacht lock, Philipssluis, was being constructed in the Krammersluizen through the Philipsdam in 1987, with a road bridge across restricting maximum clearance to NAP +17·5m. In further recognition of the dangers to sea and inland wildlife the locks in each dam have 'compartmentalised' systems with tanks for flushing out fresh or salt water as vessels come through, to ensure that salt does not get pushed back into the lakes or fresh into the estuary.

The Oosterschelde storm-surge barrier was completed in essence in 1986 but was still being tested in 1987 when the two inland dams and discharging sluice were due to be completed, whilst the road along the top had some considerable time to go to completion. The Delta Expo on the Neeltje Jans harbour complex in the middle of the barrier is well worth visiting, but will be difficult to get to with a yacht until the various harbours on the seaward and inland sides are completed. In late 1987 the cruising man had to cycle or take a taxi to the exhibition from Burghsluis on the north side of the estuary.

In cruising the Oosterschelde (Routes 1, 2 and 3) therefore there will still be tides as far as each dam, so you should use the Dutch *Stroomatlas c, Oosterschelde*, of which an up-to-date version was published in 1987. At the entrance the many pillars and islands of the Oosterschelde barrier, have constricted the width of outlet for the tidal streams, whilst the range of tide has been slightly reduced. So keep well away from all parts of the barrier and use the buoyed channels leading to the Roompotsluis lock which must always be used for entrance, with both gates closing even though the water level inside hardly changes. The motorway across the dam also crosses a fixed bridge over the lock, which is NAP +20m, so it is hard luck if your mast is much over this since the maximum spring range of tide is only about 1·7m above and below NAP. On the western edge of the lock is a control tower with a customs office on one of the higher floors inside for clearance while going through. However, there was some doubt whether this customs facility would be continued beyond November 1988, so do check in advance before you need to use this facility.

For further advice on the Delta works, tide tables, etc., contact:

Rijkswaterstaat Deltadienst
Afd. Voorlichting Oosterscheldewerken
Van Veenlaan 1
4301 NN Zierikzee
Netherlands
☎ (01110) 8000 or 7058 (daily information)

The profit and loss account

The Dutch Ministry of Transport and Public Works have produced some interesting estimates of land reclamation illustrating just how difficult the struggle has been.

	Hectares	Acres
1200 to 1900		
Sea coast reclamation	380,000	951,000
Lakes reclamation	140,000	350,000
Losses	−567,000	−1,417,000
1900 net	−47,000	−116,000
1900 to date		
Wieringermeer	20,000	50,000
Northeast polder	48,000	120,000
Eastern Flevoland	54,000	135,000
Southern Flevoland	43,000	108,000
1987 net	118,000	297,000
Markerwaard (not begun)	50,000	125,000

Whilst the net gain amounts to only about 3% of the total Netherlands' land area, a gross reclamation of 20% was needed to overcome the inexorable increase of 1 metre in sea level. Governments cannot afford to sit back complacently now that the sea-defences are complete. Even though the 1-metre battle over the next 1000 years, backed by the Delta works, will be a little easier at the beginning it will become increasingly expensive to maintain the vast structures created in the 20th century. But it all makes work for the working man, and the Netherlanders have been continuously hard at it ever since they decided that their *terpen* mounds were just not good enough.

Ringvaart van de Haarlemmermeerpolder near Buitenkaag

Zaanse Schans

Goes. Head of Havenkanaal

Goes. Building at head of Havenkanaal

Typical scenery of Flevoland bank of Randmeren

Traditional barge yacht (*aakjacht*) on IJsselmeer

2. Information sources

Telephoning

From the Netherlands If you use a public call box make sure you have plenty of 1 guilder, 25 cent and also in a few places 2½ guilder coins. Telephoning the UK from the Netherlands the dialling code is 09 44 (09 being Netherlands international code and 44 the UK country code), followed by the area code without its first 0, then the local number.

To the Netherlands Dialled from the UK, Netherlands telephone numbers given in this chapter are exactly as listed, the number in brackets (010 31) being the international code, 010, and the country code for the Netherlands, 31. The area code without its first 0 follows, then the local number.

Within the Netherlands As in the UK, the area code has an initial 0. Within the Netherlands, telephone numbers given in Chapters 3 to 12 should be dialled exactly as listed, except within the local dialling district when the code numbers in brackets at the beginning (including the first 0) should be omitted. On the many occasions I telephone Dutch numbers, to my shame, the recipient usually speaks good English.

Addresses for tourist information

Sailing is as integral a part of the Netherlands tourist scene as motoring, cycling and walking. Tourist offices, therefore, are an extremely useful source of information for yachtsmen.

In the United Kingdom for information about sailing and tourism in the Netherlands contact:

Netherlands Board of Tourism
Egginton House, 25–28 Buckingham Gate
London SW1E 6LD. ☎ (01) 630 0451

The Netherlands is covered by a network of separately administered tourist information offices, subsidised by local authorities and the government. They provide advice and literature on their local areas, book tickets, and help find accommodation. Called VVV (Vereniging voor Vreemdelingenverkeer – an old Dutch expression which translates literally as 'club for foreign traffic') they are organised under a number of provincial information offices (see diagram). Of course if writing from the UK add 'Netherlands' to the address.

VVV Groningen
Naberpassage 3, 9712 JV Groningen
VVV Friesland
Stationsplein 1, 8911 AC Leeuwarden

The Dutch Provinces

VVV Drenthe
Postbus 95, 9400 AB Assen
VVV Overijssel
Postbus 500, 7600 AM Almelo
VVV Gelderland
Postbus 988, 6800 AZ Arnhem
VVV Flevoland
Postbus 548, 8200 AM Lelystad
VVV Utrecht
Maliebaan 79, 3581 CG Utrecht
VVV Noord-Holland
Rokin 9–15, 1012 KK Amsterdam
VVV Zuid-Holland
Markt 85, 2611 GS Delft
VVV Zeeland
Postbus 123, 4330 AC Middelburg
VVV Noord-Brabant
Postbus 90, 5260 AB Vught
VVV Limburg
Postbus 811, 6300 AV Valkenburg

VVV Amsterdam
Postbus 3901, 1001 AS Amsterdam
VVV Rotterdam
Stadhuisplein 19, 3012 AR Rotterdam
VVV Den Haag
Groot Hertoginnelaan 41, 2517 EC Den Haag

The above are only the provincial centres, in addition almost every small town has a VVV office which can help in finding suitable accommodation should the boat become too claustrophobic. These offices are open at least from Monday to Friday 0900 to 1700, and Saturdays 1000 to 1200, and in the season often in the evenings and on Sunday afternoons. If you wish to write in advance for advice then you can make up the address – 'VVV', name of town, name of province, Netherlands – and your letter should get there.

The Dutch equivalent of our UK Automobile Association (membership of the UK AA entitles one to certain privileges from the Dutch organisation when in the Netherlands) is the ANWB – Algemeen Nederlandse Wegbruickers Bond, the 'general association for Netherlands road and waterway users'. This organisation produces road and waterway maps sold through the VVV offices listed above. The ANWB also has offices in all the large towns, providing information and selling its maps and books. The head office address is:

ANWB
Wassenaarseweg 220, 2596 EC Den Haag
Netherlands. ☎ (010 31) 70 141440

Addresses for charts and almanacs

In the UK most Admiralty chart agents can obtain Dutch charts. Some may be prepared to obtain almanacs and tables as well. The larger agents are:

Kelvin Hughes
145, Minories, London EC3
☎ (01) 709 9076

Stanfords International Map Centre
12–14 Long Acre, Covent Garden, London WC2
☎ (01) 836 1321

Captain O.M. Watts Ltd
45, Albemarle Street, London W1
☎ (01) 493 4633

London Yacht Centre
13, Artillery Lane, London E1
☎ (01) 247 0521

Brown & Perring Ltd
Redwing House
36–44 Tabernacle Street, London EC2
☎ (01) 253 4517

Imray Laurie Norie & Wilson Ltd
Wych House, The Broadway
St Ives, Huntingdon, Cambs PE17 4BT
☎ (0480) 62114

In the Netherlands the three main agents for yachting charts, almanacs and tables are:

Observator B.V.
Vasteland 18–26, 3011 BL Rotterdam
☎ (010 31) 10 4130060
L.J. Harri B.V.
Prins Hendrikkade 94/95, 1012 AE Amsterdam
☎ (010 31) 20 248035/248036
Datema-Delfzijl B.V.
Oude Schans 11, 9934 CM Delfzijl
☎ (010 31) 5960 13810

As in Britain many of the Dutch chandlers sell charts and books, particularly members of the 'Nauticring' buying group located in most parts of the country.

Almanacs and tables

Almanac, ANWB

The two volumes of the ANWB *Almanak voor watertoerisme, deel 1* and *deel 2*, are obtainable from most Dutch sources listed above. *Deel 1* includes copies of the various waterway regulations which waterway users are legally required to carry aboard. The latest edition, 1987, will last you for several years and is not frequently re-published. *Deel 2*, published annually in March, is not legally required aboard but is more useful than *deel 1*.

Both volumes of the *Almanak* are in Dutch. However the 1988 edition of *deel 2* now has a 4-language introductory section, list of abbreviations and glossary of terms used. The English translations now provided are far more enlightening than the average pocket dictionary, which one may still find helpful on occasion. Certainly *deel 2* which is filled with lists of figures and data under alphabetical place name is not difficult to use but can be very time-consuming. Do remember that 'IJ' (double capitals when beginning a place name) or 'ij' (pronounced 'ay' as in 'tray') takes the place of the English 'Y' in the alphabet, i.e. it comes just before 'Z'.

Deel 2 lists most information under the name of the nearest town or village, but a significant, non-overlapping part of the information, where the nearest town or village is not so obvious, is listed under the name of the appropriate waterway, also in the alphabetical order.

Extensive information is provided, including road bridge and lock opening times, essential addresses and telephone numbers, marinas, moorings, lifting facilities, laundrettes, customs facilities, port signals and regulations, limited tidal information and some harbour sketches.

It includes tide tables for Den Helder, Hoek van Holland, Zierikzee and Vlissingen, with time but not height differences for various secondary ports.

Railway bridge opening times are not given, but a form is provided to mail order the ANWB *Openingstijden spoorbruggen* (opening times for railway bridges) which is published annually in June (see below).

Railway bridges, opening times, ANWB

A free leaflet, *Openingstijden spoorbruggen*, obtainable from the ANWB and its main regional offices, covers the year between 1st June and 31st May and is based on the annual railway timetable. It gives the much more restricted daily times of openings of the railway bridges over the waterways, many of which are alongside major motorway bridges. Often the timing of an inland cruise over several days including a weekend is dictated by the availability of a single railway or motorway bridge. Since the leaflet is published well after the beginning of the timetable year you will often be working on slightly out-of-date information, but it does not change extensively.

Locks, road and railway bridges, service times

The two official annuals, *Bedieningstijden van sluizen en bruggen* and *Bedieningstijden spoorbruggen*, from which the ANWB derive the almanac and leaflet information on bridge opening times described above, can be obtained direct from:

Dienst Verkeerskunde van de Rijkswaterstaat
Onderafd. Binnenscheepvaart, Postbus 20906
2500 EX 's-Gravenhage, Netherlands
☎ (010 31) 70 744887/744893

Alternatively you may be able to obtain these two official sets of tables from one of the three Dutch nautical book suppliers listed above. Once again the railway bridge booklet is issued well after the beginning of the railway year since the national water authority needs time to scour through the railway timetables.

Tide tables

A small annual booklet, *Getijtafels voor Nederland*, published by the Ministrie van Verkeer en Waterstaat is available from Dutch nautical book shops. The 1988 edition gave tide tables for 23 standard ports, considerably more than in the UK Admiralty tide tables or in any other English nautical almanac. Times of HW (*hoogwater*) and LW (*laagwater*) are in Middle European Time (MET) which is GMT +1 hour, the same as British Summer Time, so 1 hour must be subtracted to obtain GMT. In the Netherlands yet another extra summertime hour is added so that local time becomes GMT +2 hours, so you must add 1 hour to the MET times in the *Getijtafels* during Netherlands Summertime (ZT) from roughly the end of March to the end of September.

Tidal heights in the tables are in centimetres plus (+) NAP for HW and in centimetres minus (−) NAP for LW. NAP datum is *normaal Amsterdam peil* (standard) which is close to mean sea level unlike the Admiralty's chart datum (lowest astronomical tide). However, for Dordrecht which is well inland, LW heights are plus (+) NAP so a weather eye should be kept for such exceptional items. Most Dutch Hydrographic chart soundings are given to LLWS (lowest low water springs), so at the bottom of the *Getijtafels* pages the depth of LLWS below NAP is also listed (e.g. LLWS = NAP −256cm).

Consequently working out soundings needs a little thought, and offshore the tables in the next paragraph below are easier to use.

The days of new moon (NM), first quarter (EK), full moon (VM) and last quarter (LK) are also marked. There are sketch charts showing times of HW and LW at places in the Waddenzee and inland on the great rivers. Unlike Admiralty tide tables, however, there is no graphical means of working out tidal heights and times between HW and LW, although tidal ranges are small.

Tidal levels and streams

Waterstanden en Stromen, published by the Chef der Hydrographie, does the coast tidal calculations for you and includes tidal atlases. It is available from Dutch nautical book shops. It covers 16 places in the coastal areas and Westerschelde, including Europlatform (N of the Eurogeul approach), and Pennzoil K13A platform (60M WNW of Den Helder) – see Admiralty *List of Lights Volume B* for characteristics of both platforms. It gives tidal heights in decimetres above LLWS at 1-hourly intervals for every day of the year at each of these places. At the back it gives tidal atlas plans at 1-hourly intervals for 4 areas: the southern North Sea including the British, Frisian and W Danish coasts; the Westerschelde; the Waddenzee W; and the Waddenzee E, together with a HW timetable for the standard port appropriate to each.

Times are in local time i.e. MET (GMT +1 hour) and Netherlands Summertime, ZT (MET +1 hour) depending on appropriate dates, so you do not even have to correct for this if you are working in local time. If you are working in English time approaching the coast then be extremely careful to convert the times, and do not forget to do this in the HW tables accompanying the tidal atlases. It must be stressed, however, that the 1988 edition did not cover the Oosterschelde nor any of the waterways inland of the Hoek. Nevertheless it is extremely useful approaching from offshore to be able to extract two simple figures from the tables for the time and height of tide which can be directly applied (or after easy interpolation in the unlikely event you need to work to the nearest 5 or 10 minutes) to the Dutch charts to reduce soundings.

Charts

The Netherlands is probably the world's best charted country. All of the necessary charts, tidal atlases and ANWB maps are listed at Appendix I. The country is covered partially by UK Admiralty and yachtsmen's charts which draw a lot of information from the Dutch charts, and it is covered comprehensively by Dutch hydrographic department charts and ANWB waterway charts. In the Netherlands all of the Dutch charts can be bought at most chandlers and yachting booksellers, and usually at the main ANWB offices.

UK Admiralty charts

There are 22 of relevance, of which 4 are passage charts of 1:250,000 scale or more, and the rest vary from 20,000 to 75,000 scale some with inset plans of 10,000 to 25,000 scale. The approach and smaller-scale charts are good and useful for the initial passage, but it is better to use Dutch large-scale charts rather than Admiralty for the more detailed cruising. The large-scale charts are in any case usually directly derived from Netherlands charts, but with a correction delay. Do not forget many of these still give soundings in fathoms to Admiralty chart datum, which does not coincide with the Dutch datum in the *Getijtafels* and *Waterstanden en Stromen* (see above).

Dutch sea charts

Like the UK charts the Dutch sea charts (*zeekaarten*) are only of use if read in conjunction with or with a knowledge of the Dutch symbols and abbreviations booklet (chart *1*). As in the UK the Dutch hydrographer publishes a weekly and 3-monthly list of chart corrections (*Berichten aan Zeevarenden*) which covers both the sea charts and the small-craft charts, and is obtainable at Dutch authorised chart agents, including the three listed above.

There are 23 charts of relevance, of which 3 are passage charts of 1:375,000 scale or more, 3 are approach charts of 100,000 to 150,000 scale and the rest of 20,000 to 75,000 scale, with some extremely useful harbour plan insets. The outstanding chart in this series is *1351 IJsselmeer* which has no less than 17 plans. The series is generally more economical than the Admiralty series. For example the single chart *1443 Westerschelde tot Antwerpen met Kanaal van Terneuzen naar Ghent* requires two UK charts. *1448 Noordzee, Westkapelle tot Stellendam en Maasvlakte* covering the Slijkgat approach to the Haringvliet is also a useful chart of an area not properly covered by the UK Admiralty.

Dutch small-craft charts

This series of eight sets of charts (*kaarten voor kust-en binnenwateren*) each in 38 by 54cm booklet form to fit the small chart table are excellent value for the yachtsman and cover all the coastal areas, the Waddenzee, the IJsselmeer and all the Delta inlets.

In the tidal areas soundings, as on the sea charts, are in metres based on LLWS, heights on some are based on mean sea level and on others on MHWS so read the legend, which is in English as well as Dutch, under the titles.

In the non-tidal areas the sounding and height data are shown under the titles. They vary from special levels in completely enclosed 'still' waters such as the Grevelingenmeer (NAP −0·2m), to NAP (OLW, agreed low river level) and MHW (heights) in flowing/semi-tidal areas such as the Haringvliet. Again, read the legend.

There is a plethora of detailed harbour charts with least depths marked, and there are miniature coloured drawings of many of the landmarks, churches and lighthouses, usually easily recognisable from offshore. It is always better to use these hydrographic office charts where available in preference to the more fragile and often less detailed ANWB *Waterkaarten*.

ANWB charts

This series of 18 charts/maps, *Waterkaarten A to S* (excluding Q), covers all the Netherlands' navigable waterways, with the exception of the sea coasts, the Westerschelde, the IJsselmeer (parts are done only), and a small area in the northeast essentially empty of waterways. It covers most of Drenthe, Overijssel and E Gelderland. All of these charts were last published in 1986 or 1987 thus including most recent major road alterations.

The legend is unfortunately only in Dutch, but a translation can be obtained from the ANWB. Soundings and heights are in decimetres, and in the inland 'still' waters relate to local canal, polder or weir water levels and on the flowing inland rivers to MR (mean summer river level). In the tidal areas soundings relate to MLW and bridge heights to MHW, and these, expressed in decimetres + or − NAP, are given at intervals in boxes alongside selected reaches of the inland rivers. You can use the *Getijtafels* (see above) to work out approximate times of HW and LW inland.

Tidal atlases

Nine atlases, *Stroomatlassen*, in booklet form, 30 by 42cm, also ideally fitting a small chart table, cover the areas of coast and tidal rivers roughly coincident with the small-craft charts. There are additional atlases for deeper-draught vessels where the hydrographer has measured the direction and strength of average tidal currents across two different surface depths (0–5m and 0–10m). Each has 13 pages of hourly streams based on a local port HW, and there are insets which make the whole series economical. In addition to tidal arrows an extremely useful feature is the pecked line across each plan to show the boundary between rising and falling water; the rising area coloured blue and the falling area white.

Formalities and regulations

Customs formalities

On arrival in the Netherlands you are required to report to the nearest port with customs facilities, and go to them not wait for them to board. The customs office addresses are listed under the appropriate ports later in this book. It is also advisable to fly the yellow code flag Q until clearance is obtained.

The customs officer will ask for information about the vessel and owner, completing a form for you to sign, the *Verklarung*, a copy of which will be given to you exempting you from import duties and taxes on the vessel for up to a 12-month period. You should check and sign this statement. During its period of validity you can leave and return to the

Netherlands. If you require an extension you must apply for it before the certificate expires. You are not allowed to sell, rent or loan out the boat in the Netherlands without paying the appropriate taxes.

When obtaining customs clearance you will also be required to obtain immigration clearance, showing the crew's passports to the officers with the gun-holsters! Usually they accompany the customs officials, but in some ports, such as IJmuiden you will be sent by the customs official to another office.

Licences and insurance

There are few licensing or legal restrictions on pleasure vessels visiting any part of the Netherlands. Only motorboats capable of 16kph (approximately 8½kn) need a licence which can be obtained at most large post offices, showing your passport and ship's registration and insurance documents and paying a modest fee.

In 1988 the government was considering the introduction of a navigation licence for vessels longer than 15 metres and motorboats capable of a speed greater than 20kph (just under 11kn) regardless of length. If your vessel comes into these categories please remember to contact the Netherlands Board of Tourism (address above) for advice before sailing.

Before travelling to the Netherlands you should contact your insurance company to ensure that you are adequately covered for third-party accidents and for the inland waterways as well as coastal areas in the Netherlands. It is also advisable to check the personal insurance of crew members, and take out some form of travel/accident insurance. It is also worth checking at a UK tourist office about any vaccination regulations and EEC health services requirements in order to qualify for free medical treatment.

It is advisable not to carry firearms aboard, and this includes signalling pistols, unless you have a special licence and clearance. Again make sure you contact the Netherlands Board of Tourism in London to enquire about this in advance if you intend to take such things with you, or you may find yourself in serious difficulties when you arrive. Better still, like the Dutch, stick to normal smokes, flares, parachute signals and your VHF radio telephone for sending distress signals.

To minimise any potential legal problems it is advisable for the boat to be UK-registered, be appropriately marked and numbered, and carry aboard the registration documents. Either type of registration is useful – the RYA-administered Small Ships Register, or the more expensive Part 1 Register for larger vessels and special cases.

Speed limits

In coastal waters, on the wider rivers (excluding the Maas), the Waddenzee, and the IJsselmeer there are no speed limits. There is a limit of 6kph (3½kn) on canals through towns and on very narrow canals, increasing to 12–15kph (6½–8kn) on larger canals and waterways.

There are speed limits for parts of the Grevelingenmeer, the Haringvliet and the Hollands Diep of 9kph (5kn), and for busy stretches of larger rivers of 16kph (8½kn). On some of the lakes there are limits as well as exemptions in places for water-skiing. Watch out for the speed signposts. *Deel 2* of the *Almanak* gives details of all these limits by locality. *Deel 1* as well as the small-craft charts' legend illustrates the signposts you can expect to find.

Shipping regulations

Creative bureaucracy on a worldwide, EEC, national and local basis has produced a minefield of waterways regulations. In the Netherlands in addition to the many local waterway regulations and bylaws, four major sets of shipping regulations apply.

1. International Regulations for Preventing Collisions at Sea, the *Zeeaanvaringsreglement* (ZAR), familiar to all nationalities of yachtsmen, cover all of the coastal areas on the seaward side of the Frisian Islands, the North Sea coast, and on the seaward side of the Delta estuaries. They apply everywhere else in the Netherlands except where they may interfere with the special local regulations below. In any case the local regulations generally conform as closely as possible with the international regulations. No cruising man should be unaware of Rule 1 (a), (b) or (c) nor the rest of the international regulations.

2. Inland Waters Police Regulations, the *Binnenvaartpolitiereglement* (BPR), cover most of the inland waterways, the Waddenzee, IJsselmeer, and Zeeland estuaries and waterways except the Westerschelde.

3. *Scheepvaartreglement Westerscheide* covering this river are joint rules agreed with the Belgian government.

4. International Rhine Waterways Police Regulations, the *Rijnvaartpolitiereglement* (RPR), apply on the Lek, Waal and Rhine inland of Rotterdam and Dordrecht.

All of these, as well as many of the local rules are included in *deel 1* of the *Almanak*, in Dutch of course, and the BPR rules alone total some 50,000 words. Now that visiting waterway tourist traffic is building up there is a very strong case for the Netherlands government via the ANWB to publish these rules in other languages including English.

The first advice to the visitor unfamiliar with Dutch is to carry the rules aboard and obey religiously the International Collisions Regulations, particularly those relating to narrow channels and vessels restricted in their manoeuvrability. Observe carefully all the local traffic signs, a pictorial list of which translated into English is included at the front of each of the Dutch small-craft charts and look out for the speed-limit boards (in kph after an indicated distance in metres to which they apply).

Take particular care in manoeuvring in congested waterways, at waterway and at lake junctions, and proceed under sail alone only when there is plenty of sea room and few other vessels nearby, keeping well away from other traffic. Make sure you keep to starboard and always have a 'supporting' engine in readiness as this is a legal necessity in many places particularly on the big rivers between Hoek van Holland, Rotterdam and Tolkamer/Lobith on the German border, and between Lobith and Wijk bij Duurstede SE of Utrecht. Also make sure you have a large properly mounted radar reflector.

At the back of *deel 1* under *Bijlagen* is an extremely useful list in Dutch, but illustrated with coloured drawings and therefore not difficult to interpret, applying to both the BPR and RPR regulations, which includes: lights and shapes, sound signals, waterside traffic signs, bridge and lock entry signals and lights, and buoyage/withies. Many of these conform to the International Collision Regulations but there are additional ones amongst them. A few of the more unusual ones to the UK yachtsman are:

- Various combinations of blue lights on vessels means they are carrying dangerous cargo.
- A green over white light is carried by a ferry boat.
- A white flashing light and a blue board carried on the starboard side of a vessel means that it wishes to pass starboard to starboard of oncoming vessels, possibly because of its draught, restricted manoeuvrability, the depths or the current (e.g. on a bend).
- Red, white, red horizontally striped sign board on a bridge span or weir-gate means banned to traffic. Two yellow diamonds (or yellow lights) horizontally disposed on a span means it is the recommended span to go under, with opposing traffic forbidden. One yellow diamond (or yellow light) means it is the recommended span but you may meet opposing traffic which is also allowed.
- Two sets of sign boards with, confusingly, very similar meanings: a white and green diamond (green pointing inwards) on each side of a lock or bridge passageway means it is recommended to stay inside the limits indicated; a white and red diamond (red pointing outwards) on each side of an entrance means prohibited to pass outside the limits indicated.
- On opening bridges and locks single or double red lights alone have the obvious meaning and similarly single or double green lights, however a red over a green means no entry but the span or lock is about to open. If the green light is flashing and the span or lock is still open, then entry is forbidden unless it is too late to stop.
- Important sound signals ('−' long, 4 second blast; '·' short, 1 second blast)
  - −   Attention!
  - ·   I am going to starboard
  - ··   I am going to port
  - ···   I am going astern
  - ····   I am unable to manoeuvre
  - ······ There is danger of collision
  - −·−   I require service at an opening bridge or lock

Buoys and marks

Special double-colour green and red lateral system spherical and spar topmarked buoys are found frequently in the inland waters (not in the Waddenzee where the IALA 'A' system is followed with double-colour conical, can and spar buoys indicating preferred channels at channel junctions). They are found particularly in the IJsselmeer and Randmeren near beginning of channels. Red over green with a red can topmark means channel is to port of the buoy heading inwards (i.e. leave to starboard entering – not what one would expect with a red can topmark). Green over red with a green conical topmark means channel is to starboard of the buoy. Several red, green and red horizontal bands with a spherical red and green topmark means channels of equal importance on each side.

Opening bridges and locks

Passing through opening bridges and locks is usually free, but occasionally in the case of groups of bridges and important locks (which often have bridges at each end) you have to pay something up to 5 guilders, usually at the first of the group; the price will probably be displayed on a board. In some places be ready to place the money into a *klomp* (Dutch clog) suspended on the end of a fishing line by the bridgekeeper, but often this merely means the operator is asking for an unofficial tip.

Give yourself plenty of time for journeys with several locks and bridges, and try to start early in the morning. Be ready for tying up and waiting, and do not always expect published timetables to be sacrosanct. Plan your day's journey around the times of opening of the main railway/motorway bridges en route as these have the tightest schedules. Use the telephone to warn the *wachter* of your plans if this is recommended.

Where bridges are marked BB (*beweegbare brug*) on the charts, they are opening bridges, and the

The magnificent lift bridge at Waddinxveen

height in decimetres given on the chart (preceded by H on the ANWB charts) is the height above the water when closed. If BB is not indicated this means they are fixed (*vaste brug*) so the height figure is the fixed headroom.

Opening bridges come in a number of forms. Most common is the drawbridge, *ophaalbrug*, with supporting lifting arms. Swing bridges are *draibruggen*, despite the sound of the word. Lifting bridges, *hefbruggen*, have single spans which slide upwards between pillars, often on railway bridges. The floating bridge, *vlotbrug*, is found only occasionally, for example on the Noordhollands Kanaal to Den Helder, and consists of two floating spans which slide across the water and meet. Finally the bascule bridge, almost as frequent as the drawbridge, is an unsupported span whose fulcrum swings the span upwards.

Many rail and motorway bridges, despite their weight, are bascules, and if the wind is over Force 6 be prepared for the opening of this type of bridge to be cancelled until conditions moderate. In fog conditions bridges often, particularly on motorways, remain closed. Frequently there are also pairs of similar or different bridges alongside each other, and bridges at each end of a lock, as well as twin-facing bridges with draw, swing or bascule spans which meet.

There are two main types of lock. One is the *keersluis*, which is left open (*staat open* on the chart) for most of the time and closed only in times of flood danger. There are many of these in Friesland, Groningen and in approach canals to inland harbours such as Zierikzee and Stavenisse. The other is the *schutsluis*, where you are locked through and need to be prepared for tying up smartly with large fenders and long warps. Many of the big sea locks do not have special yacht locks, and with heavy barge traffic are daunting; for example the Oranjesluizen on the IJ/Noordzeekanaal near Amsterdam. Yachts usually go in after the commercial traffic, and are often invited to come out first.

Some of the large lock complexes, like the Volkeraksluizen (with a special *jachtensluis*), have loudspeaker systems where you press a buzzer on the pontoon and speak into the microphone to the lock-keeper (English always works), so watch for these.

VHF radio is always useful approaching the large locks. I will never forget speaking to the Roompotsluis *brugwachter* on VHF and he shouting in reply to me from the window in his tower which was directly alongside my aerial. Cleating systems vary from bollards on the top of the walls, to rows of inset cleats at different levels on the walls, to bights of warp or vertical chains along the walls. When mooring, I have found it easiest to moor on the lee side of the lock to be held against the wall by the wind rather than chance missing a hold on the windward side and swinging out awkwardly and unmanoeuvrably bow or stern first. In most conditions it pays to make sure to fasten your stern warp first or you may swing uncontrollably out and be unable to fasten your stern to the wall, particularly if the wind is from astern.

Above all with locks and bridges be prepared for frustration and adversity. One evening I paid 3½ guilders to lock through at Spaarndam with a SW near gale astern blowing straight into the lock from across the wide lake behind. My wife and I sighed with relief after just managing to tie stern first without scraping the topsides. We then found the motorway bridge beyond the lock was closed because of the wind strength so had to return through the lock again to the only accessible moorings (other than a post out in mid-river) paying a second 3½ guilders. Next morning we paid another 3½ guilders to lock through again in only slightly more moderate wind conditions. Spaarndam did prove a lovely village, and underlined the benefits of the leisurely approach in Holland.

Fixed bridges and clearance scales

In the UK a knowledge of your boat's exact draught is taken as read, but how many yachtsmen know their air draught? In the Netherlands this overall height above the waterline must be known accurately if you wish to explore the estuaries, lakes, and rivers. Many of the bridges are fixed whilst the short opening spans on many of the high bridges are opened with reluctance if your vessel appears of a viable height – and this is often far more apparent to the bridge-keeper looking down at you, than to yourself staring tremblingly upwards as the masthead rapidly closes with the approaching bridge span.

Do not worry too much about those confusing variations in height data on the various charts, nor about working out clearance to the nearest decimetre at a precise time on a certain day. Every significant bridge has a clearance scale (*hoogteschaal*). However, you will obviously need to work out an approximate best time for clearing the bridge if your height is very close to the charted clearance. Make sure your engine is adequate for the job so that you are not going to be swept uncontrollably by the current through the bridge when you have decided to turn back.

Simply approach the recommended span of the bridge (usually charted, and easy to sight since the recommended through route is marked by a yellow triangle or two triangles in the middle of the span), read off the clearance from the scale on either or both sides (binoculars help), and continue on or turn back. The scale rises from the water usually on a supporting pillar on the starboard side or on both sides of the recommended channel through a fixed bridge or the fixed part of an opening bridge. It is painted in alternating 1-metre yellow and black bands each with large figures showing the metric clearance of the span above the water level, with non-numbered decimetre sub-divisions. Always be sure to pass under the highest recommended part of the span. Sometimes scales are painted black and white. Occasionally, particularly on the big rivers, there is a separate scale about a kilometre before the bridge on the starboard side of the channel in each direction, named and marked on the ANWB chart (e.g. Baanhoek railway bridge on chart *K*).

To work out approximations of clearances and times, *deel 2* of the *Almanak* (as well as this guide for the bridges covered) gives full details of the clearances of all bridges in metres above NAP for tidal waters, and above other appropriate datum points for bridges on the inland waters.

Clearance of fixed bridges in tidal waters

In tidal waters it is better to use the *Almanak deel 2* figures in conjunction with the *Getijtafels* for working out close estimates rather than the heights quoted on the Dutch small-craft charts which are of minimum likely clearance.

Here is an example of the use of the data for the Zeelandbrug in the Oosterschelde. *Deel 2* (and this guide) shows that between pillars 3 and 52 each span of this bridge has a clearance above NAP of 15·1m in the middle of the span. HWS is NAP +1·8m so must be subtracted from the NAP clearances to obtain clearance at HWS, and LLWS is NAP −1·8m so must be added to the clearances to obtain clearance at LLWS. The resultant clearances in the middle of the span range from 13·3m at HWS to 16·9m at LLWS.

To do the calculations for HW and LW on a particular time and date simply extract the appropriate HW and LW NAP figures from the Zierikzee table in the *Getijtafels* and subtract or add these to the *Almanak* data for the bridge. For times in between you need to interpolate using the twelfths rule, but treat the approximations with caution, give yourself plenty of room for error, and always read the scale on the recommended traffic spans towards the northern and southern ends of the bridge.

Apart from the Zeelandbrug there are only a few other significant tidal bridges, mainly in small-craft chart *1809* which covers the rivers from the Hoek to Dordrecht.

Clearance of fixed bridges in semi-tidal and non-tidal waters.

Estimation of clearance for the bridges on the ANWB charts must be even more approximate because of the lack of any accurate timetables of water heights. The ANWB charts cover the semi-tidal rivers as well as the canals and dammed rivers and estuaries. They give soundings and bridge heights in decimetres, so do not forget to divide by 10 to work in metres. Soundings are preceded by D (*diepte*), heights by H and widths of locks and spans (also in decimetres) by W. It helps to cross-check the clearance figures on the charts with those in the *Almanak deel 2*. Always pay attention to the scale beside the span, whatever your own calculations show.

The ANWB use three types of datum for bridge clearances depending on whether waterways are 'still' (e.g. canals), semi-tidal or non-tidal flowing rivers (see also Appendix II).

1. *Still inland waters such as lakes and canals*
   Both soundings and bridge heights relate to a single local datum: canal, weir or polder water level (*kanaalpeil*, *polderpeil*, or *stuwpeil*). Here the figures on the charts and in the *Almanak* solve the problem, but there can always be exceptional water level conditions so use each span's scale as well.

2. *Semi-tidal waters and waters subject to the Haringvliet and main rivers sluicing programme*
   The clearance problem here is complicated by a small tidal range, so bridge heights on the ANWB charts are given to MHW giving a small safety margin at most other states of tide. The range varies from 1½m at Rotterdam, to around 1m at Vianen on the Lek where the weirs and sluices take over. It peters out rapidly eastwards on the Merwede/Waal from 1m near Dordrecht to around 0·2m at Heesselt where the downstream current takes over.

   On the Haringvliet the sluicing programme (as mentioned in Chapter 1) can create a daily range of 0·25m and as high as 1m in exceptional conditions, so you must use the scale on the Haringvlietbrug. If your height is marginal time yourself close to LW Haringvlietsluizen from the *Getijtafels* and keep the engine running.

   On the Lek and Merwede/lower Waal if your height is marginal you can work out a very approximate time and clearance for HW or LW from the tables and diagrams in the *Getijtafels*, or the *Almanak*, together with the *Almanak* clearances and MHW/MLW NAP heights of tide, and go through near LW. Again there are sometimes exceptional water levels, so always use the scale.

3. *The Waal*
   On the inland Waal (the Maas is of no interest to fixed-mast vessels since the bridges are too low) the 1½ to 4kn river stream swamps the tidal effect, and bridge clearances above Heesselt are based on MR (*middelbare rivierstand*), mean summer river level, May to October. This is 12 to 20 centimetres less than NR (*normaal rivierstand*). As the actual levels can vary around this average use of the scales (*hoogteschaals*) is critical, as well as having a powerful reliable engine. Local advice from yacht clubs, barge skippers etc. helps. A good tip is to estimate the difference between the MR charted clearance and the actual clearance from the scale at a preceding higher bridge in advance of passing through the problem bridge.

II. THE SOUTH

3. The Delta approaches and harbours

Charts Admiralty *110, 120, 122, 325, 1406, 1872*
Imray *C30*
Dutch small-craft *1801, 1803, 1805, 1807, 1809*
Dutch nautical *1014, 1035, 1349, 1350, 1442,
1443, 1448, 1449, 1533*

Tidal atlases Admiralty *North Sea – southern portion*
Dutch *Stroomatlassen a, c, e, f, n*

Tidal streams
Westerschelde approaches
(based on HW Vlissingen and HW Dover)

Position	Start times			
	VLISSINGEN		DOVER	
	East	*West*	*East*	*West*
4M NE Kwintebank By	−0230	+0330	−0030	+0530
Neths/Belg. frontier[1]	−0400	+0215	−0200	+0415
Westerschelde ent. (Nieuwe Sluis)	−0500	+0115	−0300	+0315
Oostgat (N end)	+0540	−0130	−0445	+0030

Note
[1] NE and SW-going

Westerschelde river
(based on HW Vlissingen and HW Antwerp)

Position	Start times			
	VLISSINGEN		ANTWERP	
	In	*Out*	*In*	*Out*
Vlissingen Road	−0515	+0100		
Terneuzen	−0430	+0130		
Hansweert	−0400	+0200	−0610	−0010
Antwerp	−0230	+0300	−0440	+0050

Oosterschelde estuary (based on HW Zierikzee and *Stroomatlas c* 1987 'interim' edition[1])

Position	Start times	
	ZIERIKZEE	
	In	*Out*
Westgat[2]	−0430	+0130
Roompotsluis, both sides	+0615	−0015
Zierikzee, off ent.	+0615	+0030
Wemeldinge, off ent.	+0600	HW
Tholensche Gat, off lock[3]	+0530	+0030
Zijpe[3]	+0600	+0030

Notes
1. Based on computer-generated predictions of the effects of the Oosterschelde works after basic completion in April 1987. Tidal atlas contains strong warning that the reality may differ considerably.
2. Strong SW-going (in) and NE-going (out) offshore.
3. In both cases a rising tide tends to run southwards across lock entrances, and falling tide northwards.

North of Oosterschelde
(based on HW Hoek van Holland and HW Dover)

Position	Start times			
	H. VAN HOLLAND		DOVER	
	NE	SW	NE	SW
Offshore N of Oosterschelde to close S of Europoort	−0305	+0310	HW	−0530
	In	*Out*	*In*	*Out*
Mid Brouwershavensche Gat	−0305	+0255	HW	+0600
SW point of Goeree[1]	−0550	+0115	−0245	+0320
In Slijkgat	−0330	+0330	−0025	−0550
Off Maasmond ent.	−0200	+0430	+0105	−0450

Note
1. Flood SSE, ebb NNW

Nieuwe Waterweg, Nieuwe Maas, Oude Maas: Hoek van Holland to Dordrecht
(based on HW Hoek van Holland and HW Dover)

Position	Start times			
	H. VAN HOLLAND		DOVER	
	In	*Out*	*In*	*Out*
In Maasmond entrance	−0230	+0215	+0035	+0520
Maassluis	−0215	+0230	+0050	+0535
Rotterdam	−0145	+0300		
Dordrecht, Oude Maas W	HW	+0430		
Dordrecht, Noord	+0030	+0500		

Tidal differences and ranges
(based on HW Dover)

Place	HW (time)	Springs/Neaps (range in metres)
Vlissingen	+0200	4.4/3.0
Terneuzen	+0225	4.7/3.3
Hansweert	+0300	5·0/3·5
Antwerp	+0342	5.4/4.0
Zierikzee	+0305	3.3/2.4
Wemeldinge	+0340	3.9/2.7
Hoek van Holland	+0310	1.8/1.5
Rotterdam	+0435	1.8/1.6
Dordrecht	+0505	1·0/0·8

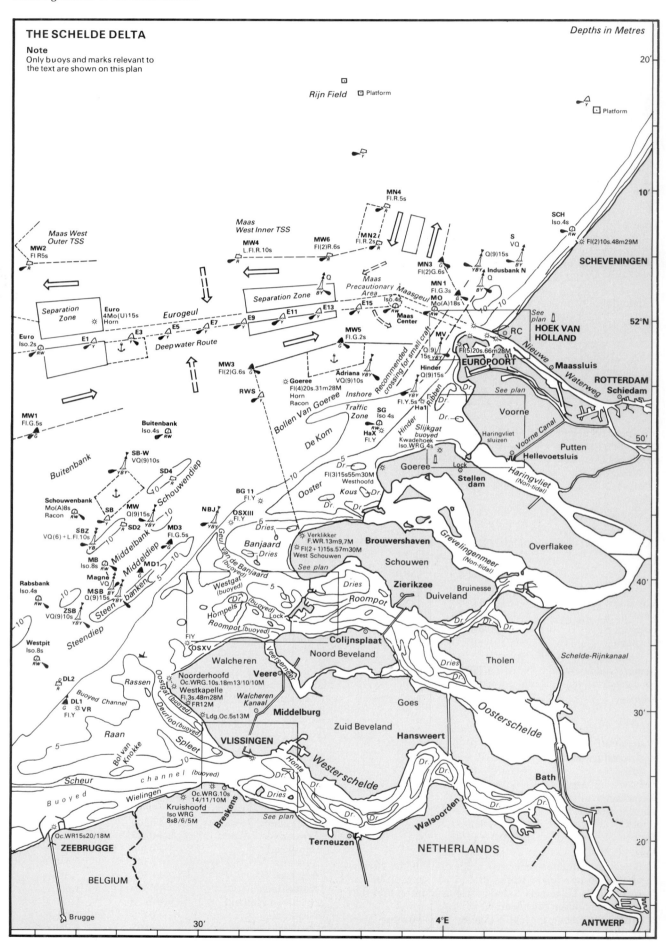

THE SCHELDE DELTA

Depths in Metres

Note
Only buoys and marks relevant to
the text are shown on this plan

Rijn Field   Platform

Platform

Maas
West Inner TSS

MN4
Fl.R.5s

SCH
Iso.4s

SCHEVENINGEN

Fl(2)10s.48m29M

Maas West
Outer TSS

MW2
Fl R5s

MW4
L.Fl.R.10s

MW6
Fl(2)R.6s

MN2
Fl.R.2s

MN3
Fl(2)G.6s

S
VQ

Q(9)15s

Indusbank N
Q

MN1
Fl.G.3s

MO
Mo(A)18s

HOEK VAN
HOLLAND

52°N

Euro
4Mo(U)15s
Horn

Separation
Zone

Eurogeul

E9   E11   E13

Q

Maas
Precautionary
Area

E15

Iso.4s

Maasgeul

RC

Separation Zone

Deep water Route

Maas
Center

MV
Q(9)
15s

EUROPOORT

Maassluis

Euro
Iso.2s

E1   E3   E5   E7

MW5
Fl.G.2s

Fl(5)20s.66m28M

Nieuwe

ROTTERDAM
Schiedam

MW3
Fl(2)G.6s

Adriana
VQ(9)10s

Hinder
Q(9)15s

Voorne

Waterweg

MW1
Fl.G.5s

Buitenbank
Iso.4s

RWS

Goeree
Fl(4)20s.31m28M
Horn
Racon

Inshore

Recommended
crossing for small craft

Ribben

See plan

Haringvliet
sluizen

Voorne Canal

Putten

Buitenbank

SB-W
VQ(9)10s

SD4

Bollen Van Goeree

Traffic
Zone

SG
Iso 4s

Fl.Y.5s

Ha1

Hinder

Kwadehoek
Iso.WRG.4s

Hellevoetsluis

Haringvliet
(Non-tidal)

Schouwenbank
Mo(A)8s
Racon

SB

MW
Q(9)15s

Schouwendiep

BG 11
Fl.Y

HaX
Fl.Y

Slijkgat
buoyed

Goeree

Lock

Stellen
dam

Overflakee

Grevelingenmeer
(Non-tidal)

SBZ
VQ(6)+L.Fl.10s

SD2

MD3
Fl.G.5s

NBJ
YBY

OSXIII
Fl.Y

Dries

Verklikker
F.WR.13m9,7M

Fl(3)15s55m30M
Westhoofd

Kous

Ooster

Brouwershaven

MB
Iso.8s

MD1

Banjaard
Dries

Fl(2+1)15s.57m30M
West Schouwen

See plan

Schouwen

Duiveland

Rabsbank
Iso.4s

Magne
VQ

MSB
Q(9)15s

Steenbanken

van de Banjaard
(buoyed)

Westgat
(buoyed)

Dries

Zierikzee

Bruinesse

Roompot

Tholen

Schelde-Rijnkanaal

ZSB
VQ(9)10s

Middeldiep

Middelbanken

Dries

Hompels

Roompot (buoyed)

Lock

Colijnsplaat

Dries

Oosterschelde

Westpit
Iso.8s

Steendiep

FlY

OSXV

Walcheren

Noord Beveland

Veerse Meer

Dries

DL2

Rassen

Noorderhoofd
Oc.WRG.10s.18m13/10/10M
Westkapelle
Fl.3s.48m28M
FR12M

Veere

Walcheren
Kanaal

Goes

DL1

VR
Fl.Y

Buoyed Channel

Deurloo (buoyed)

Ldg.Oc.5s13M

Middelburg

Zuid Beveland

Hansweert

Bath

Raan

Oostgat (buoyed)

VLISSINGEN

Honte

Westerschelde

Bol van Knokke

Spleet

Scheur

channel (buoyed)

Wielingen

Oc.WRG.10s
14/11/10M
Kruishoofd
Iso WRG
8s8/6/5M

Breskens

Dries

See plan

Walsoorden

Dries

Oc.WR15s20/18M

ZEEBRUGGE

Terneuzen

NETHERLANDS

ANTWERP

BELGIUM

Brugge

30'   4°E

Major lights

Name of light	Characteristics	Position	Structure
Nieuwe Sluis	Oc.WRG.10s27m14-10M	51°24'·5N 3°31'·3E	B 8-sided metal tower, Wh bands 055°-R-084°-W-091°-G-132°-W-238°-G-244°-W-258°-G-264°-R-292°-W-055°
	Horn(3)30s	51°24'·4N 3°30'·4E	Wh metal framework tower, B bands
Westkapelle	Fl.3s48m28M	51°31'·8N 3°26'·9E	Sq stone tower, R metal superstructure
West Schouwen	Fl(2+1)15s57m30M	51°42'·6N 3°41'·6E	Grey round stone tower, R diagonal stripes on upper part
Westhoofd	Fl(3)15s55m30M	51°48'·8N 3°51'·9E	R sq stone tower
Goeree	Fl(4)20s31m28M	51°55'·5N 3°40'·2E	RW chequered tower on platform on piles, RC, Racon, helicopter platform
	Horn(4)30s		
Hoek van Holland			
Maasvlakte	Fl(5)20s66m28M	51°58'·2N 4°00'·9E	B 8-sided concrete tower, orange bands, 340°-vis-267°
Maasmond Ldg Lts 112°			
Front	Iso.4s29m21M	51°58'·9N 4°04'·9E	Wh concrete tower, B bands, 101°-vis-123°
	By day 11M		
Rear	Iso.4s46m21M	51°58'·5N 4°06'·0E	Wh concrete tower, B bands, 101°-vis-123°
	By day 11M		
Maasmond Ldg Lts 107°			
Front	Iso.R.6s29m18M	51°58'·6N 4°07'·6E	R tower, Wh bands, 099·5°-vis-114·5°
	By day 7M		
Rear	Iso.R.6s43m18M	51°58'·5N 4°08'·0E	R tower, Wh bands, 099·5°-vis-114·5°
	By day 8M		
Europoort Calandkanaal			
Ldg Lts 116° Front	Oc.G.6s29m16M	51°57'·6N 4°08'·8E	Wh concrete tower, R bands, 108·5°-vis-123·5°
	By day 7M		
Rear	Oc.G.6s43m16M		Wh concrete tower, R bands, 108·5°-vis-123·5°
	By day 7M		
Noord Hinder LtV	Fl(2)10s16m27M	52°00'·1N 2°51'·2E	R hull, Wh upperworks, RC, Racon
	Horn(2)30s		

Radiobeacons

Name	Freq. (kHz)	Ident.	Range (miles)	Seq.	Position
Marine radiobeacons					
Smith's Knoll Group	287·3				
Smith's Knoll LtV		SK	50	1	52°43'·5N 2°18'·0E
Goeree Lt		GR	50	2	51°55'·5N 3°40'·2E
Dudgeon LtV		LV	50	3	53°16'·6N 1°17'·0E
Outer Gabbard LtV		GA	50	4	51°59'·4N 2°04'·6E
Cromer Lt		CM	50	5	52°55'·5N 1°19'·1E
Noord Hinder LtV		NR	50	6	52°00'·2N 2°51'·2E
IJmuiden Group	294·2				
IJmuiden		YM	20	1,4	52°27'·8N 4°34'·6E
Hoek van Holland		HH	20	2,5	51°58'·9N 4°06'·8E
Eierland Lt (fog only)		ER	20	3,6	53°11'·0N 4°51'·4E
Aero beacon					
Valkenburg/ Scheveningen	364	GV	25	Cont	52°05'·7N 4°15'·2E

Coast radio stations

Scheveningen Radio covers the whole of the Netherlands via nine separate VHF transmitting/receiving relay stations. You simply tune in to the appropriate channel of the nearest station and call *Scheveningen Radio*. The stations relevant to the routes in the southern part of the country covered in Section II of this book are listed here. Those for the northern area, Section III, are listed in Chapter 8 on page 89. Also listed below (page 24) are the details for MF radiotelephony at Scheveningen.

Station	VHF Channel	Position
Goes	Ch 16,23[1],25,78,84	51°31'N 3°54'E
Rotterdam	Ch 16,24,27,28,87[1]	51°56'N 4°28'E
Scheveningen	Ch 16,26,83[1]	52°06'N 4°16'E
Haarlem	Ch 16,23,25[1],85	52°23'N 4°38'E

Station RT (MF)	Transmits (kHz)	Receives (kHz)	Freq⁴ (kHz)	Traffic lists (times)	Storm warnings (times)	Weather messages (times)	Navigational warnings (times)
Scheveningen (PCG)(PCH)	1764^2, 1862^5, **1890**, **1939**, $2182^{2,5}$, **2600**, 2824^2, **3673**	2049^3 2182^3 2520^3	1862^5	odd H+05	On receipt	0340, 0940, 1540, 2140	0333, 0733, 1133, 1533, 1933, 2333
			1890	odd H+05	On receipt	0340, 0940, 1540, 2140	0333, 0733, 1133, 1533, 1933, 2333
			1939		On receipt		
			2600		On receipt		
			2824	0105, 0305, 0505, 2305		0340	0333, 2333

Notes

1. VHF Channel for traffic lists at every H+05; storm warnings at every H+05; weather messages at 0605, 1205, 1805, 2305 (in Dutch). Broadcasts given 1hr earlier when DST is in force. Ch 16 and all working VHF channels (bold) have 24hr watch.
2. 24hr service.
3. 24hr watch. Use 2049 when 2182 is distress working. 2520 is calling frequency, alternative is 2182.
4. Frequency (kHz) on which traffic lists, storm warnings, weather messages and navigational warnings are given as listed (in English and Dutch).
5. 1862 located at Nes only 53°24'N 6°04'E. 2182 located at Scheveningen and Nes.

Major fixed daylight marks

Belgian frontier to Breskens
Isolated hotel (conspic) at Wielingen close E of the frontier
Nieuwe Sluis Lt (22m, B octagonal tower, Wh bands)
Breskens grain silo between Westhaven and Oosthaven

N bank of Westerschelde – Vlissingen to Noorderhoofd
Vlissingen: 2 chimneys (125m) 1M inland on Kanaal door Walcheren, a windmill, St James Church spire, and Vlissingen main Lt (10m, brown metal framework tower at entrance to Koopmanshaven)
Kaapduinen: radio mast and two Ldg Lt towers (14 & 13m, yellow square stone, R bands)
Westkapelle Lt (52m, square stone tower, R metal superstructure)

Walcheren coast – Noorderhoofd to Roompot
Noorderhoofd Lt (16m, R round metal tower, Wh band)
Domburg church spire and nearby water tower
Oosterhoofd, chimney
Veere church tower (square with dome) and town hall spire

Schouwen coast (S to N)
Concrete lookout tower
West Schouwen Lt (50m, grey round stone tower, R diagonal stripes on upper part)
Westhoofd Lt (52m, R square stone tower)
Goedereede church tower
Kwade Hoek Lt (4m, B mast, Wh bands)

Voorne coast (S to N)
Radio mast (75m, R Lts) NE of Zwarte Hoek
Brielle church tower
Oostvoorne church tower

Maasvlakte and Hoek van Holland
2 chimneys (175m, R Lts)
Maasvlakte Lt (62m, B octagonal tower, orange bands)
Europoort entrance Lts
Nieuwe Zuiderdam & Nieuwe Noorderdam entrance towers to Maasmond (31m, orange towers, B bands, helicopter landing platforms on top)
Church towers of 's-Gravenzande, Monster and Ter Heijde

Offshore approaches

The Delta has two freely open entrances at its northern and southern extremities leading to two of Europe's largest port complexes: Europoort/Nieuwe Waterweg, and Westerschelde/Antwerp and in between two entrances with lock access, the Haringvliet and the Roompot. Customs clearance can be obtained at Maassluis (but not at Berghaven), at the Roompotsluis and at Vlissingen (or Breskens) but not at the Haringvliet's Goereesesluis. There was some doubt at time of publication whether the Roompotsluis customs facilities would be continued beyond 1988. The three major problems for pleasure craft approaching any of these four entrances are sandbanks, weather and shipping.

Inshore areas of less than 5 metre soundings and drying shallows stretch westwards and southwards from the point of each of the main islands – Voorne (near Europoort, the Bollen), Goeree (the Ooster), Schouwen (the Banjaard) and Walcheren (the Rassen/Raan). Offshore the Delta is screened by three broken longitudinal banks generally with 7 to 8-metre depths and of danger to yachts only in winds upwards of Force 4. The outer northernmost is the Schouwenbank, then a string of banks, Thorntonbank, Rabsbank and Middelbank, stretch from the Westerschelde approaches to Schouwen Island. Finally the Steenbanken off the Roompot has some patches of less than 5 metres which are definitely to be avoided.

Weather

Because of the lie of the islands and banks the prevailing southwesterlies and also northeasterlies tend to blow parallel with the coast across the entrances and along the outer banks, but southwesterlies do tend to funnel and strengthen into the entrance channels on the southern sides of the Westerschelde, Oosterschelde and Haringvliet (i.e. the Slijkgat) estuaries. Entrance to Maasmond, Hoek, can be extremely uncomfortable in ground swell from cross seas in bad weather particularly with a southwesterly against an ebb out of the entrance, whilst entrance in strong northwesterlies should be avoided at all times. Unfortunately the best time of entrance, from 2hrs before up to local HW, is often when the big ships are entering. Approach to the outer banks to enter the Oosterschelde or Haringvliet should also be avoided in strong coast-parallel and onshore winds, although once inside the outer banks there is some protection. Standing well offshore in bad weather or fog can also provide problems from the heavy shipping in and near the traffic separation schemes, so pick your weather.

Fog is infrequent, tending to occur early in season, but is extremely dangerous given the heavy traffic, but if unavoidable it is definitely advisable in moderate wind/sea conditions to anchor inshore in as shallow water as possible away from shipping – there are many areas in the Delta and on the Belgian coast where this is possible.

Traffic separation schemes, marks and lights

Heavy shipping traffic is a benefit as well as a danger since navigationally the area is the world's best-provided. Offshore to guide traffic into and past Europoort are the two major precautionary areas at Noord Hinder Junction and round *Maas Center*, the latter with a radar surveillance area stretching for a 6 to 7-mile radius from Hoek van Holland. It is critical that pleasure craft should if at all possible keep out of the traffic separation schemes and particularly the precautionary areas since shipping can be moving in many directions, and of course when crossing the traffic separation schemes should do so at a right-angled aspect to the traffic whether under sail or engine. It is easy to take such navigational precautions since the whole offshore and inshore area is profusely buoyed and lighted. There are offshore lights and long distance onshore lights on the point of each island. There are many lit buoys along the banks and there is also a screen of Fl.Y.5s beacons at varying, but frequently 3 to 5 mile intervals strung from island point to island point across the closed Delta estuaries usually not far from the 5 metre contour.

Maas precautionary area – recommended yacht route

Yachts heading from the north for the Hoek or across the outer Delta coast cannot avoid crossing part of the Maas precautionary area, which is the crossing point outside Europoort for the Maas North and Maas West inner traffic separation schemes, the latter with its deep water route heads direct from offshore into the Hoek (Maasmond) entrance. In the middle of the precautionary area is charted a one mile diameter circle which is a prohibited area for all except deep-draught vessels, *Maas Center*, marked on its southern side by an Iso.WR.4s light buoy and acting as a roundabout.

Yachts are recommended to keep to a special route on the landward side of the precautionary area so there is no question of entering from direct across the North Sea, a vessel must approach from along the coast either from the inshore traffic zone south of Europoort or from the north east and Scheveningen outside the Maas North TSS, and must either enter Europoort direct when permitted or cross the traffic at the roadstead into Europoort at as close to a right angle as practicable following a specially charted (on Dutch small-craft chart *1801*) route 1½M wide for small craft. The officially recommended procedure is formidable: call Maasmond (VHF Channel 3) before crossing, give name of vessel, position, course, maintain listening watch, follow a track close west of a line joining buoys *MV*, *MVN* (south of the entrance) and *Indusbank N* (north of the entrance), and cross under power and in company when possible.

Radio aids and weather forecasts
See also Appendix III

Although the area has good Decca coverage it is only modestly provided with radiobeacons which you should check are still transmitting since in the next few years it is possible that they will be phased out. Of the two groups listed above, four, Scheveningen (also with a nearby aero beacon), Hoek, Goeree and Noord Hinder LtV are in an approximate line, difficult for three-point fixes, and the other five are well outside the area. However, Scheveningen Radio close north of the Delta is the centre of an exceptional network of VHF radio transmitters and is one of NAVAREA 1's special stations feeding frequent local weather, hazard and other navigational information into the NAVTEX network. Advice can always be sought in English from this source. It transmits weather forecasts in Dutch on VHF and in Dutch and English on medium wave, whilst the BBC shipping forecasts for Thames area are also adequate.

Rescue services
See also Appendix IV

VHF Ch 16 of course provides immediate access to the rescue services. In addition to coastguard watch posts the area is provided with 4 offshore lifeboats at Breskens, Burghsluis inside the N end of the Oosterschelde barrier, the Buitenhaven of the Goereesesluis/Haringvlietdam, and Hoek van Holland and most of these have mobile inshore lifeboats as well. Additionally there are inshore lifeboats only at Cadzand near the Belgian border and Ouddorp inside the N end of the Brouwersdam.

Tidal streams and river currents

Well offshore north of the Westerschelde tidal streams are simple but inshore are more complicated.

Offshore streams run NE from 2hrs before HW Hoek van Holland and turn SW about 4hrs after HW Hoek although there is a prolonged period of slack or turning tide around these two approximate times.

Inshore streams out of Maasmond entrance and out of the now blocked channels north of the Oosterschelde entrance tend to be dammed up by the offshore streams for 4 to 5hr periods, delaying the times of the turns of tides and giving considerable periods of slack water. At Hoek van Holland this results in a prolonged double LW with only a 4½hrs rise of tide and 7½hr ebb from Rotterdam. At the Maasmond/Hoek entrance ingoing starts only 2½hrs before HW Hoek, whilst outgoing starts at 2½hrs after HW Hoek and at Rotterdam at 3hrs after HW Hoek. In the Slijkgat off the Haringvliet dam and the Brouwershavensche Gat off the Brouwersdam timings are similar to Maasmond, ingoing starting 3 to 3½hrs before HW Hoek and outgoing 2 to 3hrs after HW Hoek.

Westerschelde In the Westerschelde streams are similar to those in any large seagoing river – at Nieuwe Sluis on the S side of the entrance the ingoing stream starts 8hrs before the outgoing stream starts at Antwerp, 45m upstream, so the upriver passage is simplified, but there are only 4½hrs for travelling downriver. Offshore the tidal approach is almost the reverse of this, with a 9hr favourable outward stream from the entrance to the *Kwintebank* buoy 30M away but only 3½hrs favourable on the flood tide.

Oosterschelde In the Oosterschelde, which is a wide estuary throughout and only 25M long, streams tend to turn almost simultaneously within a ½hr of HW and LW Zierikzee, whilst round the 'pools' off the two new inland dams (Oesterdam and Philipsdam) after April 1987 the Hydrographer is predicting prolonged periods of slack water throughout the tidal cycle, with cross-entrance tides at the locks. But read the *Caution* in the 'interim' Oosterschelde *Stroomatlas c* (1987) – these are computer estimates and practical experience could turn out different.

The net effect of the inshore streams is that it is easier to coast hop from north to south across the Delta than from south to north since more tide can be carried in the southerly direction. For example, the 30M passage between Goereesesluis in the Haringvlietdam round Goeree and Schouwen to the Roompotsluis can carry a full 7hrs of tide with a continuing stream into the Oosterschelde if started around HW Hoek +0330. In the opposite direction it is only possible to carry about 5hrs stream at best, say by starting at 2 to 3hrs before HW Zierikzee and initially pushing 2 or 3hrs of tide out of the Roompot. Try working out tidal timing for both directions between Vlissingen and the Roompot, and Haringvliet and Hoek, or indeed for the whole of the outer route between Vlissingen and Hoek.

The Westerschelde approaches and entrance

Distance 32M *Kwintebank* buoy to Breskens.

Apart from a coastal approach with the flood along the Belgian coast a good North Sea crossing route from the Harwich area direct to the West Hinder LtV crosses the Noord Hinder south and West Hinder traffic separation schemes at right angles and follows the outer edge of the latter scheme to the *Kwintebank* buoy. The simplest of all the deep-water approach routes to the Delta is from this buoy S of the abundantly buoyed Scheur/Wielingen channels as far as Zeebrugge. Crossing the outer entrance of the new Zeebrugge harbour at right-angles it enters the Westerschelde close to the Nieuwe Sluis Lt, continuing along the well-buoyed river, or into Breskens, or into Vlissingen. The outward route can be the reciprocal or alternatively N of the Scheur channel and along the northern edge of the West Hinder TSS.

Nieuwe Sluis at the Westerschelde entrance is 30M from Kwinte Bank, a good single tide's sail, but streams off the Sluis turn some 2½hrs earlier than near Kwinte Bank. The outward passage therefore is easier than the inward passage; starting 1hr after HW Vlissingen gives 9hrs of favourable stream to get well beyond the *Kwintebank* buoy and start the crossing to Harwich or the Essex rivers. The inward passage cannot avoid some adverse tide, since E-going tide starts near Kwinte Bank at −2½hrs and W-going at Nieuwe Sluis at +1¼hrs on HW Vlissingen giving only 3 to 4hrs of fair tide, but always plan to have some flood into the entrance since the ebb is very strong.

Because of the constricted neck of the estuary between Vlissingen and Breskens tidal streams at springs can average 4 knots, i.e. they can run even faster. At Nieuwe Sluis the ingoing stream starts at HW Vlissingen −0500.

The river entrance is deep (10–20m soundings), and a buoyed (lit) shipping entrance channel leading to a precautionary area traffic scheme off Vlissingen delimits the Wielingen N and S anchorage areas on each side of the channel. There is heavy seagoing shipping and barge traffic, and large numbers of ingoing ships anchor off the entrance in the recommended anchorages. Yachts approaching Vlissingen from seaward normally enter through the S anchorage area past Nieuwe Sluis Lt, then cross the traffic lanes at right angles to enter the harbour. Two chimneys inland, St James Church spire and a windmill (see *Major fixed daylight marks* above) are unmistakable landmarks. The Breskens–Vlissingen ferry also crosses the river at this point.

Finally, it cannot be stressed enough that a good lookout should be kept for ships from both directions. If you are sailing – and the banks are not heavily built-up except for occasional factory installations – then be ready with the engine.

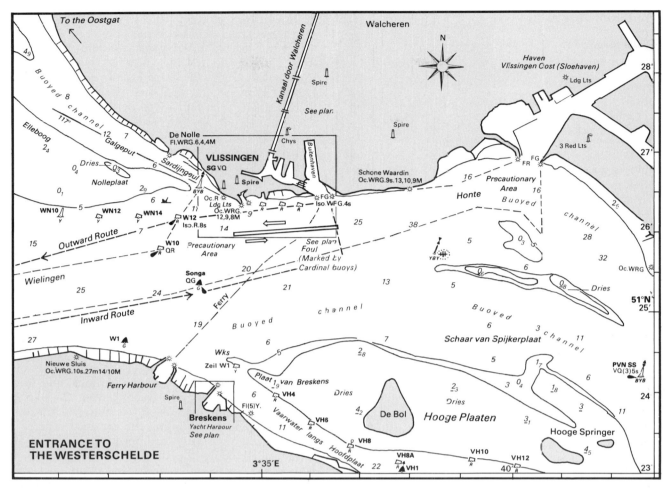

Westerschelde entrance

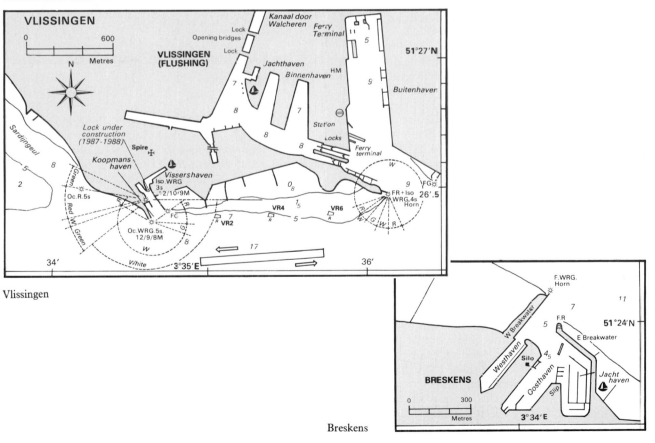

Vlissingen

Breskens

VLISSINGEN

Tidal range
MHWS 4·8m, MLWS 0·4m, MHWN 3·9m, MLWN 1·0m

Port radio (VHF)
River Schelde Information Service, Vlissingen port radio Ch 09
Vlissingen locks Ch 22 ☎ (01184) 1 23 72
Vlissingen radio, HrMr Ch 14 (broadcasts H+50)

Entry signals
VHF contact is desirable for entry.
Signal station on S pier R flag/R Lt – port closed; R and G flag/R and G Lt – port closed to vessels over 6m draught.

Customs
Westerhavenweg near the lock, ☎ (01184) 6 00 00.

Entrance and facilities
Pass between the port and starboard entrance Lts (2¼ cables apart) into the main E harbour (Buitenhaven). Watch out for the Breskens and the larger Olau Line (from Sheerness) ferries which tie up N of the locks. The locks are serviced throughout the day, have traffic signals and a megaphone, and whilst waiting it is possible to tie up to pilings on the S wall, although it is preferable to motor around or tie alongside any suitably sized commercial vessel which is waiting at the pilings. Locks do not operate if the water level outside is above NAP +3·20m or the fall is greater than 3·25m. Inside carry on past the two Binnenhavens, turn to starboard into the Kanaal door Walcheren and to starboard again before the bridge into the yacht harbour (VVW Schelde Vlissingen ☎ (01184) 6 59 12). 3 to 4m deep.

At VVW Schelde mooring is bow and stern to pontoons and posts. It is a small marina and busy in season but usually places are found and there are all facilities – showers, toilets, slipway, diesel, boat-lift/crane (10t max), a chandlery across the road, and a laundrette near the harbour. The town centre itself is a good half hour's walk. The harbour is very convenient for meeting crew from the ferry, and for continuing on along the Kanaal door Walcheren to the Veerse Meer, through a usually open lock (*keersluis*) and several opening bridges (times can be found out in the yacht harbour). Vlissingen succeeds in being a pleasant seaside and fishing town with a 14th-century church and 16th-century gate, as well as being a large shipbuilding centre.

Late in 1987 a major redevelopment of Koopmans Haven and Vissershaven, the fishing harbour complex at the western end of the Vlissingen waterfront near the town centre, was in progress. The Vissershaven to the north of this small complex was being converted into a yacht harbour with full facilities including a repair yard and a theatre on the southern quayside. The current lock entrance is to be rebuilt with an opening bridge. But this could take 2 years to complete, so watch out for progress, as this will be a very convenient harbour with up-to-date facilities much closer to the town and promenade than the current facilities to the east.

If you wish to make passage round Walcheren from Vlissingen to the Neeltje Jans and its Roompotsluis via the Sardijngeul, Galgeput and Oostgat channels and then well offshore round into the Roompot, tidal timing can be difficult and a fair tide throughout is impossible for a normally-powered yacht, so use *Stroomatlassen a* and *c* and be prepared to push the tide at some point. In the reverse direction it is possible to take a fair tide all the way.

BRESKENS

No entry signals or port radio.

Customs
Deltahoek 7, ☎ (01172) 2610, open 0700 to 2100.

Entrance and facilities
A large building with a silo tower is the main landmark in the centre of the harbour, which can be seen well offshore. Past the Veerhaven (ferry harbour) entrance on the S bank of the estuary there is a simple starboard turn into the harbour, and then to port into the municipal yacht haven, ☎ (01172) 19 02, 1–3m minimum depth, taking care to keep clear of fishing vessels using the entrance. This is a sophisticated and fully equipped marina with all facilities, including the yachting wife's paradise, a laundrette. There are boat-lifts and cranes available nearby for most craft (yard, Standfast Construction B.V. ☎ (01172) 17 97). The nearby town has a good shopping street and a suburban aspect.

The Oosterschelde approaches and entrance

Distance 16M *Middelbank* buoy to Roompotsluis.
Apart from the coastal approaches from the Haringvliet and Vlissingen following the buoys, approach from direct across the North Sea is also possible. This is emphatically a fair weather route. Approach is from the Noord Hinder south TSS, taking care of course to cross the latter scheme at right angles to the traffic, then picking up one or more of the group of buoys marking the outer banks.

The best approach is to aim for *Middelbank* buoy, the middle of a NW–SE string of 5 Lt buoys stretching just over 7M from the S end of Schouwenbank to the Steenbanken and straddling Middelbank. At night it is very difficult to miss all of these buoys, from N to S: *Schouwenbank* (RW, Mo(A)8s), *SBZ* (S card, lit), *Middelbank* (RW, Iso.8s), *Magne* (N card, lit, 9·6m swept wreck marker) and *MSB* (W card, lit). Westkapelle Lt (Fl.3s28M) and Noorderhoofd Lt (Oc.WRG.10s13-10M, and white in this sector) on the end of Walcheren are leading lights (149·5°) which line up with all 5 of these buoys, with some slight deviations.

The estuary approach is 14M wide so it is essential to pick up the buoyed channels. The only significant marks on each shore to help in good visibility in daylight are the West Schouwen Lt (a R diagonally striped tower like a helter-skelter, 50m high) to the N, and to the S the Noorderhoofd Lt (a R tower with Wh band just in front of the sea wall but only 16m high), and the Westkapelle Lt (a square stone tower with a R metal superstructure, 52m high but peeping over the sea wall). At night in reasonable visibility with their 30, 13, 28M ranges respectively they are most useful, particularly the transit mentioned above. There are also a number of prominent churches on Walcheren and particularly the church spire and its neighbouring water-tower on the coast at Domburg N of Westkapelle.

From *Middelbank* buoy head along the leading line (taking care to miss the buoys) for the southernmost of the 5 buoys, *MSB*, near which the Steenbanken can be crossed (6m at this point so the weather must not be much more than Force 4 to 5, otherwise a detour may be necessary depending on wind direction). E of this there is a choice of two routes (in daytime, only one at night) around each side of the Hompels bank direct to the Roompot lock entrance, and each with closely spaced G, and R channel-marking buoys and occasional cardinal buoys and Y beacons:

1. The Westgat and Oude Roompot channel in which many of the marks are lit.
2. The Roompot proper in which the marks are not lit and at the end of which there is a short buoyed dogleg N to the lock.

From 16M offshore after a North Sea passage about 3hrs are needed to get to Roompotsluis. The flood into the Roompot starts at HW Zierikzee −0615 (Dover −0315), so ideal arrival timing at Middelbank is between HW Zierikzee +0300 and +0600 (Dover −0600 and −0300), giving from a full to a half flood start at the Roompot, depending on how far into the Oosterschelde you wish to sail and whether or not you wish to push some tide initially in the Roompot approaches. During the whole of this period the offshore tide is running SW, continuing to do so until HW Dover, so the last part of the passage from the TSS is port-bowing into the tide.

Leaving the Roompotsluis on the return journey across the North Sea, the outgoing tide starts at HW Zierikzee +0115 (HW Dover +0415), and depending again on whether or not you wish to push some tide from Zierikzee or Colijnsplaat best timing to reach the lock is between HW Zierikzee and HW +0300 and reaching the Middelbank 3 hours later when the tide is running SW giving a good quartering tidal stream across to the Noord Hinder S TSS.

The stream rates after the inland dams are completed are predicted to reduce from previous levels which were in places as fast as on the Westerschelde: 2·4kn is now the maximum hourly mean spring ebb predicted for the Oude Roompot where previously it was nearer 4kn, and 1kn maximum in the Keeten, Mastgat and Zijpe where previously it was 3kn to over 4kn. If the predictions are right then if weather and tidal conditions in the estuary entrance are adverse it should now be much easier to break out an anchor against the stream than it used to be, so anchoring behind the offshore banks in such conditions is even more tempting. But such tactics need to be carefully judged until firmer evidence is published in the tidal atlases.

ROOMPOTSLUIS AND NEELTJE JANS

Port radio (VHF)
Roompotsluis Ch 18

Entry signals
VHF contact with the locks is desirable. No entry signals other than traffic light signals into the locks.

Customs
Clearance can be obtained at the Roompotsluis lock *1/4-1/11* 0800-1600. Closed rest of year. ☎ (01115) 1630. At time of going to press consideration was being given to closing this facility altogether in November 1988.

Entrance
Entrance to the Noordland Buitenhaven of the Roompotsluis is assisted by a number of Lt buoys and beacons at the end of the Oude Roompot channel, as well as by leading Lts (each Oc.G.5s, 73·5°), and having passed between the port and starboard-hand Buitenhaven entrance Lts on the ends of the high curving walls, there is a turn to starboard and S to round the Q.R Lt into the lock, which has traffic lights. There are pontoons for waiting on each side of the locks. Entrance is available on a 24-hour basis, and there are two telephones for reporting to the lock-keeper. There are also small harbours of refuge on each side of the lock, with good protection on the seaward side.

Colijnsplaat

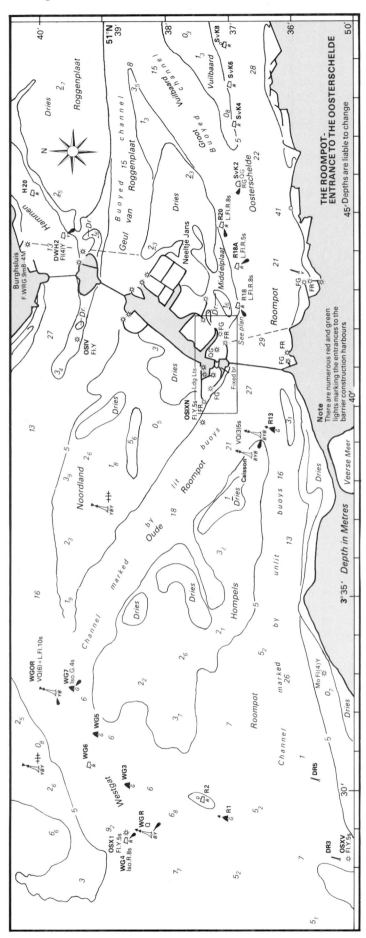

THE ROOMPOT-
ENTRANCE TO THE OOSTERSCHELDE

Depths are liable to change

Note
There are numerous red and green
lights marking the entrances to the
barrier construction harbours

3°35' *Depth in Metres*

Oosterschelde entrance

Approaching the dam from either side, however, it cannot be stressed enough to keep in the buoyed channels and keep well out of the charted and buoyed danger areas, over ½M and in some cases over 1M wide, on each side of the storm-surge barriers. There are also separate artificial harbours on each side of the Neeltje Jans island complex in the middle of the barrier upon which the Delta Expo (see Chapter 1) is located, but at time of going to press much building work was still to be done, especially on the motorway across, so if you want visit the exhibition it may be worth discussing the question with the lock-keeper whilst you are at the lock. You have to climb up the tower on the lock to clear customs in any case.

It is essential for vessels with high air draught to note that there is a fixed bridge over the Roompotsluis lock, shown on the Dutch charts as having 18·2 to 18·6m minimum clearance and in *deel 2* of the *Almanak* with a clearance of NAP (Normal Amsterdam Standard) +20m. At time of going to press clearance scales (*hoogteschaals*) were being completed, so if you have a marginal air draught above 18m it is essential to work out the NAP height of tide from Dutch tide tables. Mean range of tide at the lock is 2·49m, i.e. MHW = NAP +1·23m and MLW = NAP −1·26m, so the average range (the actual range can exceed this average of course) of clearance is 21·2m to 18·7m.

Once through the lock, then past the Binnenhaven with its Q.G Lt and between the inland entrance Lts into the estuary. The route is then S of the buoys marking the shoals behind the central dam and either N or S around the Vuilbaard shoal along the buoyed channels to Zierikzee (the Groot Vuilbaard and the Roompot) or Colijnsplaat (Schaar van Colijnsplaat).

ZIERIKZEE AND COLIJNSPLAAT
See Chapter 4, Routes 2 and 3.

Haringvliet approach and the Slijkgat

Admiralty charts do not cover the Slijkgat so the Dutch small-craft chart *1801* is needed. There is no tidal atlas coverage of this particular area but streams start running into and out of the Slijkgat at −0330 and +0330 on HW Hoek van Holland, but can be affected by sluicing operations through the dam which occur particularly when there is a heavy discharge from the Rhine and Maas. Red Lts are shown on the Haringvlietdam when sluicing operations are in progress. It is essential to keep to the buoyed channels on either side of the dam and keep well away from the sluices and the buoyed and beaconed danger areas at least 300m wide on the W side and 500m on the E side of the sluices.

Since customs clearance is not available it is unlikely that entrance to the Slijkgat is made after a North Sea crossing; it is more likely to be after a coasting passage. The channel is 7½M long from the offing Lt buoy, *SG* (RW) close to a Fl.Y beacon, and is simple and well buoyed with closely spaced R

and G buoys, some lit, and a Fl.Y beacon at the southward turn towards the final buoys leading up to the Buitenhaven entrance.

STELLENDAM

Port radio (VHF)
Goereesesluis Ch 20.
☎ locks and HrMr (01879) 10 00.

Entry signals
Contact with the locks on VHF is desirable. No entry signals other than traffic light signals into the locks.

Customs
Clearance cannot be obtained here or at Hellevoetsluis. The nearest ports of clearance are at the Roompotsluis, Vlissingen and Maassluis.

Entrance and facilities
Entrance is past the starboard Lt at the end of the high west wall, then following the wall and a sharp swing to port round the port Lt on the S breakwater and through the Buitenhaven to the lock (traffic lights). On the other side follow the N wall and a sharp swing to port through the entrance following the buoyed channel out and then E along the S side of the R buoys (some lit) across to Hellevoetsluis.

On each side of the locks there are waiting pilings, and across each end of the lock an opening bridge. The seaward main road bridge has NAP +14·3m clearance and is, where possible, left closed, so do not hesitate to ring up the bridge and state your height if you are in doubt. The inland bridge has only NAP +6·14m and has to be opened; service hours are m-th 24hrs, f 0000-2200, sa 0800-2000, su/h *1/4-1/11* 0800-2000, *1/11-1/4* 0800-1000, 1700-1900.

On the seaward side in the Buitenhaven (4·7m least depth) at the Goereesesluis is Aqua Pesch marina, so if you want to pay a visit to the Delta Exhibition (see Chapter 1) near the lock, together with a film (in several languages) and a guided tour inside the *spuisluizen* then this is your chance. At Aqua Pesch there are toilets, showers, a laundrette and a 20t boat-lift, ☎ (01879) 2600, but Stellendam town is 3km away. At weekends only it is possible to lie in the Binnenhaven fishing harbour (5m least depth) on the inland side of the lock probably alongside a fishing boat.

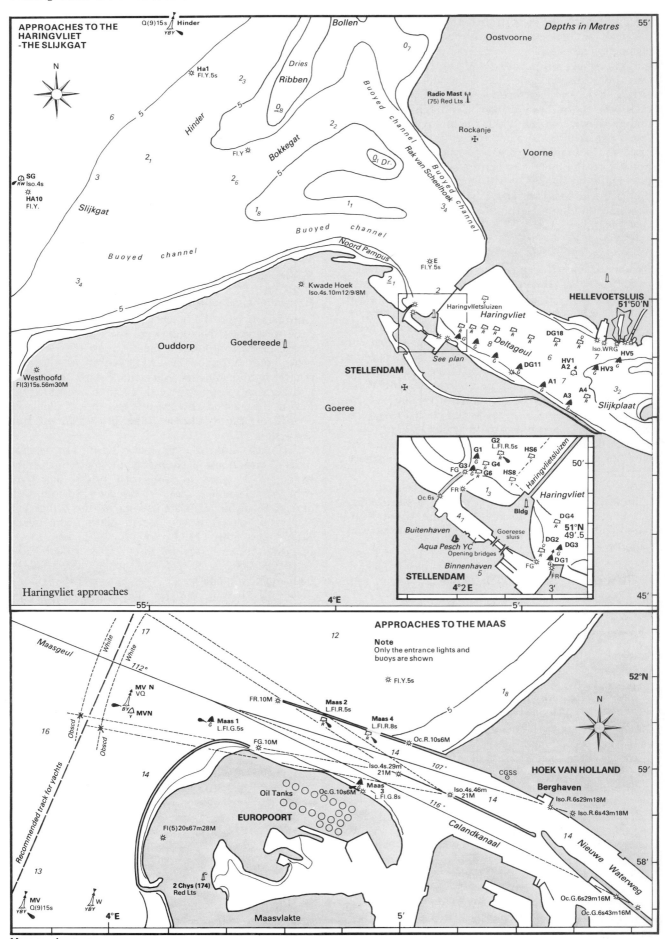

APPROACHES TO THE HARINGVLIET -THE SLIJKGAT

Depths in Metres

55'

Q(9)15s Hinder
YBY

Bollen

Oostvoorne

N

Ha1
Fl.Y.5s

Dries
Ribben

Bokkegat
Fl.Y.

2₃

0₇

Radio Mast
(75) Red Lts

Rockanje ✠

Voorne

SG
RW Iso.4s

HA10
Fl.Y.

Hinder

2₁

Q₁ Dr.

2₆

0₈

5

5

6

5

5

2₂

3

Slijkgat

Buoyed channel Rak van Scheelhoek

3₄

Buoyed channel

1₈

1₁

HELLEVOETSLUIS
51°50'N

Buoyed channel

Noord Pampus

E
Fl.Y.5s

2₁

2

Haringvlietsluizen

Haringvliet

Kwade Hoek
Iso.4s.10m12/9/8M

See plan

Deltageul

DG18

Iso.WRG

HV5

3₄

5

Ouddorp

Goedereede

STELLENDAM

8

6

HV1
A2

DG11

HV3

Westhoofd
Fl(3)15s.56m30M

✠

A1

7

A3

A4

Slijkplaat

3₂

Goeree

50'

G2
L.Fl.R.5s

HS6

G1

G3 G4

HS8

FG G6

Haringvlietsluizen

Haringvliet

FR

1₃

Oc.6s

Bldg

DG4

4₁

Goereese sluis

51°N
49'.5

Buitenhaven

DG2

DG3

Aqua Pesch YC
Opening bridges

FG

DG1

Binnenhaven

5

FR

STELLENDAM
4°2 E

3'

45'

Haringvliet approaches

55'   4°E   5'

APPROACHES TO THE MAAS

Maasgeul

White

17

12

Note
Only the entrance lights and
buoys are shown

White

112°

MV N
VQ

Fl.Y.5s

52°N

BY
Y

MVN

FR.10M

Maas 2
L.Fl.R.5s

Maas 4
L.Fl.R.8s

16

Obscd

Maas 1
L.Fl.G.5s

Oc.R.10s6M

107°

HOEK VAN HOLLAND

59'

Obscd

FG.10M

14

CGSS

Recommended track for yachts

14

Oil Tanks

Iso.4s.29m
21M

Iso.4s.46m
21M

Berghaven

Iso.R.6s29m18M

Oc.G.10s6M

Maas
3
L.Fl.G.8s

116°

Iso.R.6s43m18M

EUROPOORT

Calandkanaal

14

Nieuwe Waterweg

58'

Fl(5)20s67m28M

13

2 Chys (174)
Red Lts

5'

Oc.G.6s29m16M

MV
Q(9)15s
YBY

W
YBY

4°E

Maasvlakte

Oc.G.6s43m16M

Maasmond entrance

Tidal range

MHWS 2·1m, MLWS 0·3m, MHWN 1·7m, MLWN 0·3m

Traffic control and port radio

Four traffic offices control Hoek van Holland approaches and the waterways inside Hoek (see Dutch charts for exact location).

Haven Coordinatie Centrum (HCC) 51°54'·8N 4°25'·9E
Harbour office to the N of VCS Centre (see below) between Rotterdam and Schiedam.
☎ (010) 4251400/4251410, VHF Ch 11, 14.

Traffic Centre, Hoek v Holland (TCH) 51°58·9'N 4°06·8'E
Signal station on the N bank at the Hoek at km 1030·7.
☎ (01740) 38801/38811, 2182kHz, VHF Ch 13.

Traffic Centre Botlek (VCB) 51° 53·5'N 4° 18·9'E
Radar station on W side of the Oude Maas entrance on S bank of the Nieuwe Waterweg at km 1013·3.
☎ (010) 4724601/4724611, VHF Ch 13.

Traffic Centre Stad (VCS) 51° 54·3'N 4° 25·9'E
Radar station on N bank of Nieuwe Maas between Rotterdam and Schiedam at km 1005·2.
☎ (010) 4251701/4251711, VHF Ch 13.

The approaches and waterways are divided into sections, each with a specific VHF channel and with boundaries very clearly marked on the Dutch small-craft charts, *1801* and *1809*. Groups of channels are handled by each of the three Traffic Centres above. If you have a VHF radio, whether you are a small pleasure vessel or a large ship, HCC recommend that you keep watch on sector frequency and report in to each channel as you cross the boundary. They will tell you what to do. The radio channels, which also cover the harbours as well as the km-posted sections of the rivers, are as follows.

Call	Ch	Centre	Area
Maasaanloop,			
Maas Approach	01	TCH	Outer Radar area
Pilot Maas	02	TCH	Outer Precautionary Area
Maasmond/Maas			
Entrance	03[1]	TCH	Inner precautionary area/entrance
Waterweg	65[1]	TCH	TCH to KM 1023
Europoort	66	TCH	Europoort S of ent.
Maassluis	80[1]	VCB	km1023-1017
Botlek	61[1]	VCB	km1017-1011 (km1005 Oude Maas)
Oude Maas	62[1]	VCB	km1005-999
Hartel	05	VCB	Hartelkanaal (part of)
Eemhaven	63[1]	VCS	N Maas km1011-1007
Waalhaven	60[1]	VCS	N Maas km1007-1003
Maasbruggen	81[1]	VCS	N Maas km1003-998
Brienenoord	21[1]	VCS	N Maas km998-993
Opening bridges	13[1]		Service in above areas.

Note

1. These are the only channels likely to be used by yachts, unless they accidentally stray (not recommended) into the Maas Approach and Pilot Maas areas.

A 55-channel VHF radio is certainly advisable, but if not you must have Ch 3, since crossing, entering and leaving Maasmond entrance you must report in to *Maasmond*. If in any doubt in advance ring Haven Coordinatie Centrum (HCC) who speak English.

Entry signals

N mole tidal signals, G over Wh Lt – rising; Wh over G Lt – falling.

Traffic signals for Europoort, Nieuwe Waterweg and Oude Maas are shown from the radar station at Noorderhoofd, and give the yachtsman an idea of what is happening around him, but he must obey the instructions of port control on VHF.

From seaward

W   station in operation

RRR
W   no entry Europoort nor Waterweg
RRR

RR
W   no entry Europoort
RR

RR
W   no entry Waterweg
RR

RR
W   no entry Oude Maas
RR

From upstream (Rotterdam)

W   station in operation

RRR
W   navigation to sea prohibited
RRR

RR
W   departure via Nieuwe Waterweg prohibited
RR

RR
W   departure via Calandkanaal prohibited
RR

R
W   departure via Beerkanaal prohibited
R

Customs

Clearance cannot be obtained at Berghaven (Hoek van Holland) which is only a harbour of refuge, so you must continue upriver to Maassluis (Buitenhaven), or Vlaardingen (Buitenhaven), or Schiedam (Spuihaven), or Rotterdam (Veerhaven). See Route 7 for telephone numbers.

Approach and entrance

Approaching from offshore, and if you intend to bypass Berghaven which is uncomfortable for yachts, this route is better attempted from Scheveningen and the N. Arriving at Maasmond entrance at slack water, 2hrs before HW Hoek, follows a long period of SW-going tide offshore, and precedes the full 4 to 5hrs of ingoing tide to Rotterdam.

Approaching Maasmond from the S requires either pushing a complete foul tide to obtain the full ingoing stream at the above time at the entrance or taking a fair tide offshore and accepting a hard push up the Nieuwe Waterweg. If you are making the journey outwards, the tide is outgoing along the Waterweg for about 7½hrs, starting at Rotterdam at +0300 on HW Hoek. Leaving Rotterdam about 4½hrs later at around −0500 HW Hoek gives time to reach the entrance before the tide turns ingoing and just catches the start of the N-going tide offshore, convenient if you are heading N towards Scheveningen. Alternatively starting at HW +0100 and pushing the tide for 1½hrs for part of the way means reaching the entrance on an outgoing tide with the offshore tide just turning S, nicely placed for a 6½hr push southwards.

Entrance after permission from the harbour control can be confusing by day or night, since there are three sets of daylight intensity leading lights (as well as the many other harbour lights and ship lights at night), so make sure you are thoroughly familiar with them. They are in fact very simple; the middle set are white marking the direct line of the Splitsingsdam (112°) separating the Nieuwe Waterweg and Europoort, the port set are (naturally) red (107°) leading into the Waterweg, which is what you want, and the starboard set green (116°) lead into Europoort, which you definitely do not want.

Once inside this is a straightforward deep water route with typical 10m to 15m depths in the main channel with generally very steep edges, but beware boulders very close to the edges as well as a few narrow shoal banks between the entrance and the Oude Maas junction.

BERG HAVEN, HOEK VAN HOLLAND
Depth 3·1 to 4·5m.

The harbour entrance is on the north side of the Nieuwe Waterweg between port and starboard Lts just before reaching the front leading mark of the Waterweg (a R tower). This is a working harbour in frequent use by patrol boats, so apart from picking up and dropping crew from the ferries, or in emergency it is not recommended for yachts. If you do enter consult one of the clearly marked patrol boats for a berth, and never leave the boat unattended. Harbour office ☎ (01747) 37 51.

See Chapter 5, Route 7 for other harbours and facilities on the Nieuwe Waterweg.

4. Zeeland and the Southern Delta

Route 1
Vlissingen to Yerseke via Breskens, Terneuzen and the Kanaal door Zuid Beveland

Commentary
This is a quick passage route to the Oosterschelde and not a recommended scenic route. The minus points are that traffic is busy in the Westerschelde where the tides run hard and seas run high in strong winds funneled along the reaches. The Westerschelde has industrial shorelines or high dykes with little of interest, the canal runs through low-lying, bleak pasture areas and the last part of the route in the Oosterschelde is some distance off a similar flat shoreline. There are however plus points en route. Vlissingen has beaches and a boulevard, a memorial to Admiral de Ruyter, the 17th-century scourge of the Medway, a 14th-century church and a 16th-century town gate. Breskens although a basic modern town has an excellent yacht harbour with a good club/restaurant. Terneuzen is a picturesque Dutch canal town with an interesting labyrinth of narrow shopping streets. Wemeldinge is a village where you can rest up in relative peace away from the madding crowd. Finally, the rather plain little town of Yerseke sells good fish, particularly the speciality of mussels and oysters, and has a teeming fishing harbour where you can stare to your heart's content at people messing about in boats.

Distance 57km/32M

Bridges 3 opening

Locks 2

Tides, heights and soundings
Tidal except in Kanaal door Zuid Beveland. In tidal areas soundings to LLWS (lowest low water springs), and heights to MHWS (mean high water springs), soundings and heights to KP (*kanaalpeil*, canal level) in the Kanaal door Zuid Beveland. See Chapter 3 for tidal streams in the Westerschelde and Oosterschelde. Streams are fast in the Westerschelde and definitely need to be worked, easy for the distances involved here. In the Oosterschelde the Delta works are expected to substantially reduce tidal rates, but the final effects are not yet known, so again try to work the tides.

Minimum depths en route
2·7m in Springergeul. 1·7m in entrance to Yerseke.

Charts
Dutch small-craft charts *1803, 1805. Stroomatlassen a* and *c.*

Route description

VLISSINGEN (entrance) See Chapter 3.

WIELINGEN CHANNEL (crossing)
6m depth min. Cross precautionary area at right angles. Approaching Breskens' entrance take care to clear Plaat van Breskens spit (0·4m depth to drying), marked on S side by Y unlit buoy *Zeil W1*. At night the sector Lt on the W molehead of Breskens entrance helps in approach. Note unmarked wreck (3m) close E of Wh sector.

5·9km/3·2M
BRESKENS (entrance) See Chapter 3.

VAARWATER LANGS HOOFDPLAAT
5m depth min. *VH* buoys. Daytime route only, for strangers. Unlit buoyed channel. Take care to clear drying spit N of Hoofdplaat.

SPRINGERGEUL
2·7m depth min. *SPR* buoys. Continuation, unlit buoys, between Hooge and Lage Springer drying shoals.

10·9km/4·9M
Close N of G unlit buoy *SPR5*.

PAS VAN TERNEUZEN
8m depth min. Lit buoys, Ldg Lts 125° to just N of tanks of Dow Chemical works. Beware of big ships, pass carefully entrances of Braakmanhaven, and W and E Buitenhavens of Terneuzen (all well lit).

8·9km/4·8M
⚓ **TERNEUZEN** (entrance)
Tidal range
MHWS 5·1m, MLWS 0·4m, MHWN 4·2m, MLWN 1·0m
Port radio (VHF)
Post Terneuzen Ch 11. ☎ (01150) 12161
Radio/Radar Terneuzen Ch 03
Entry signals to Veerhaven
R flag at W molehead or R Lt under R Lt at E molehead – entry prohibited. Use VHF if entering locks and Oost Buitenhaven or requiring information.
Customs
Ambtenarenwacht on the Middensluis ☎ (01150) 12377.

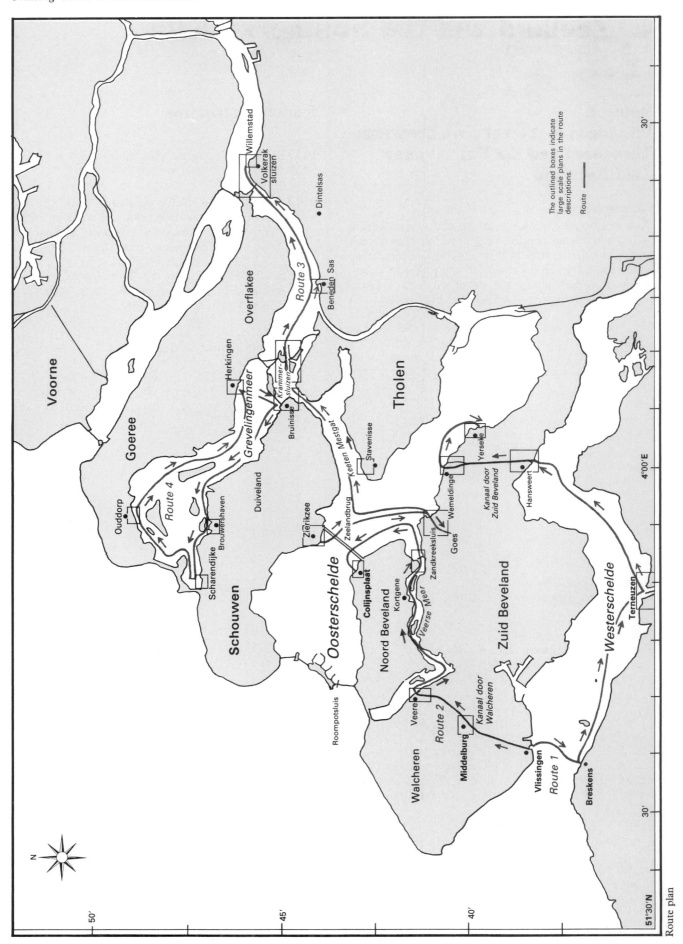

The outlined boxes indicate
large scale plans in the route
descriptions.

Route ———

Voorne

Willemstad

Volkerak
sluizen

Dintelsas

Goeree

Overflakee

Route 3

Beneden Sas

Herkingen

Grevelingenmeer

Krammer-
sluizen

Tholen

Ouddorp

Route 4

Bruinisse

Keeten Mestgat

Stavenisse

Yerseke

Scharendijke

Brouwershaven

Duiveland

Zierikzee

Wemeldinge

Kanaal door
Zuid Beveland

Hansweert

Schouwen

Oosterschelde

Zeelandbrug

Goes

Zandkreeksluis

Colijnsplaat

Noord Beveland

Kortgene

Zuid Beveland

Roompotsluis

Veerse Meer

Veere

Route 2

Kanaal door
Walcheren

Westerschelde

Walcheren

Middelburg

Terneuzen

Vlissingen

Route 1

Breskens

N

50'

45'

40'

51°30'N

30'

4°00'E

30'

Route plan

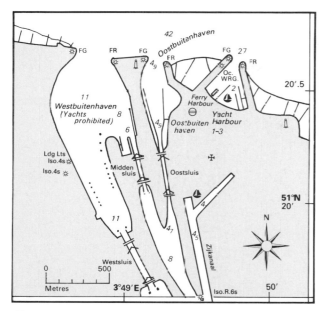

Terneuzen

Entrance and facilities

Ebb can run 3kn and more across entrance. Slack water is usually ½ hour after HW and ¾ hour after LW. Make sure to pass the two Buitenhaven entrances to the Veerhaven/Jachthaven entrance Lts, F.R&G, backed on W pier by Oc.WRG.5s sector Lt. Westbuitenhaven is forbidden to yachts. Yachts bound for Gent-Terneuzen canal use Oostsluis in Oostbuitenhaven.

Jachthaven Terneuzen is in the SE corner of the Veerhaven (toilets, showers, laundrette machines, drying grid) ☎ the secretariat, Grand Hotel Rotterdam (01150) 12041.

There are two clubs, Royal Belgian SC and WV Honte. On the east pontoon is Jachthaven WV Neusen with toilets and washing facilities. WV Neusen also has moorings inside the locks in the Binnenhaven, with 15t crane, ☎ (01150) 96331, and Vermeulen's Jachtwerf B.V. nearby, also has a 12t crane and a 50t boat-lift, ☎ (01150) 12716/13115/12866. Shopping centre close to Veerhaven.

PAS VAN TERNEUZEN/OVERLOOP VAN HANSWEERT

7m depth min. Lt buoys, also 21·5° Ldg Lts along Overloop. Beware big ships, keep clear of Everingen and Hansweert drying shoals to stbd, and Ossenisse drying spit on S of Hansweert bend.

18·3km/9·9M
HANSWEERT (entrance)

Tidal range
MHWS 5·3m, MLWS 0·3m, MHWN 4·5m, MLWN 0·9m

Port radio (VHF)
Post Hansweert Ch 22 (locks). ☎ (01130) 1486.
Post Hansweert Ch 71 (harbour entrance).

Entry signals
None, it's essential to call locks on VHF.

Customs
On locks ☎ (01130) 1723 (e.g. bound from Antwerp).

Entrance and facilities

Ebb can run 3kn plus across entrance. A very large eastern extension to the harbour across the old Zijhaven and with its own entrance and a new Oostsluis was completed in November 1987 with provisional moorings in the harbour to be replaced by permanent arrangements in 1988, so watch out for changes in Lts and pilotage instructions. The present entrance Lts are Oc.RWG.10s on W pier, F.G on E pier. The W pier Lt is on a R metal framework tower with Wh band, and in fog has F.Y Lt and Horn(4)30s.

« Entrance channel to Oostsluis. Serviced at all hours, except when river level is above NAP +3·65m. The Westsluis is scheduled to come into full operation in 1990.

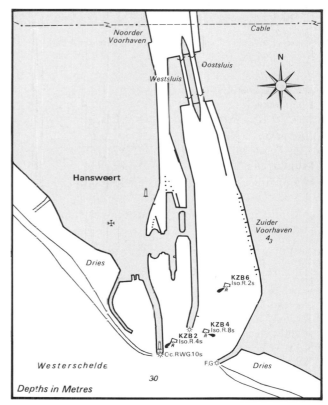

Hansweert

KANAAL DOOR ZUID BEVELAND

5m depth min. Maximum speed 15kph (8·1kn) up to 20m, 12kph (6·5kn) to 30m, 8kph (4·3kn) over 30m. Cable over canal ht is KP +33m. Radar reflector essential. Keep to edges of channel but use echo sounder.

3·2km/1·7M
⌐ Vlake rail and road bridge (ht KP +7·5m)

Service hours See *Openingstijden spoorbruggen* or ☎ Hansweert or Wemeldinge locks. Go through only on 2 G Lts. Normally opens once per hr for a few minutes, occasionally half hourly. ☎ (01130) 1366.

3·3km/1·7M
⌐ Postbrug (ht 1·5–3·6m KP) is serviced at all times.

Kanaal door Zuid Beveland, the Postbrug open for a barge

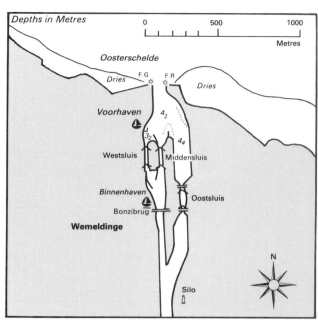

Wemeldinge

WEMELDINGE
Tidal range
MHWS 3·4m, MLWS 0·4m, MHWN 3·0m, MLWN 0·5m
Port radio (VHF)
Sluis Wemeldinge Ch 18 ☎ (01192) 1491.
Municipal HrMr ☎ (01192) 1463/2093.
🚢 **Bonzijbrug** *Service hours* m-sa 0600-2200, su/h closed.
⚓ Binnenhaven moorings near Westsluis. Toilet portakabin.
≪ **Middensluis** (Westsluis rarely used).
Service hours m-sa 0600-2200, su/h closed. Only opened when outer level is higher than canal level. When Middensluis unavailable **Oostsluis** is alternative avoiding Bonzijbrug.
Service hours all times. None of the locks are opened when river level is above NAP +1·9m or below NAP −1·9m, or a difference in level of over 2m. KP = NAP +2·6m.
⚓ **Voorhaven** 3·2m depth min. Municipal yacht harbour, floating pontoons.
MHW NAP +1·61m, MLW NAP −1·52m. Variation may occur in these levels with completion of the Delta Plan.

Voorhaven at Wemeldinge. Yacht moorings

1·4km/0·8M
Depart entrance to Voorhaven between F.R&G Lts. *Fog signals* Horn 30s and F.Y Lt on E molehead. Fl.Y on W molehead when ship leaving. R flag or 2 R Lts on W molehead – inward traffic only.

OOSTERSCHELDE
3m depth min. Unlit buoys *SvI* (Schaar van Yerseke) series. A single GR offing Lt buoy *SvI2*, so daylight route for visitors. Take care to clear spit and underwater mole NE of Wemeldinge entrance, rounding N of G unlit buoy *O15*. Keep clear of drying bank to S and also, nearer to Yerseke, bank to NE with R buoy off spit. Narrows to half a cable wide near Yerseke entrance; Ldg Lts 155°, Iso.4s, on NE wall of Yerseke.

Binnenhaven at Wemeldinge. Windmills and moorings

5·2km/2·9M
⚓ YERSEKE (entrance to Oude Vissershaven)
Tidal range
MHWS 3·5m, MLWS 0·4m, MHWN 3·1m, MLWN 0·5m
Port radio (VHF)
Municipal HrMr VHF Ch 9.

Entrance and facilities
Minimum depth channel 1·7m, 1·2m in all three harbours, so you may sit in the mud at LW. Cross the entrance to Nieuwe Vissershaven (Kon. Julianahaven) which is banned to yachts and round G buoy into Pr. Beatrixhaven (Oude Vissershaven) between F.R&G entrance Lts. Floating pontoons S corner. Toilets and showers. HrMr ☎ (01131) 1726. WV Yerseke has 10t crane.

Alternatively cross Oude Vissershaven entrance rounding into Prins Willem-Alexanderhaven between F.R&G Lts. This is a harbour for long stay only by arrangement.

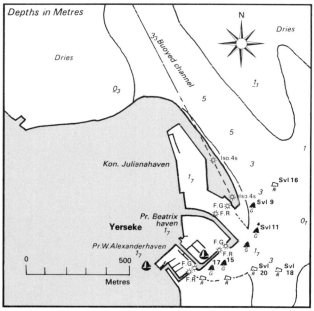

Yerseke

Yerseke. Koningin Julianahaven, the largest of the fishing harbours

Route 2
Vlissingen to Colijnsplaat via the Walcheren canal and the Veerse Meer

Commentary

This is a scenic route with easy, mainly non-tidal navigation through picturesque Zeeland towns and villages with their minaret spires, church domes, gabled buildings, cobbled squares and narrow streets. Middelburg, capital of Zeeland, was badly bombed in the Second World War but has been beautifully restored and in some cases replicas of old buildings have been built. There is a 15th-century town hall, and an abbey with an 85m tower to climb, which also houses the Zeeland Museum with its local costumes, jewellery and historic artifacts.

Veere was once the thriving major sea port on the originally open Veerse Gat handling the import of Scottish wool in the 15th to 18th centuries. The merchants' houses are still known as the 'Scots Houses' and now house a museum. The Grote Kerk contains the tomb of a 15th-century Lord of Veere and his wife Mary Stuart, daughter of King James of Scotland. There is also a Gothic town hall.

Colijnsplaat and Kortgene are more modest but pleasant large villages, the former with a fishing harbour where fresh fish can be obtained.

The route has first-class yachting facilities, but tends to be crowded in summer, although in the tideless Veerse Meer there are many quiet moorings and anchorages away from the crowds.

Distance 46km/25M
Bridges 7 opening
Locks 1 open keersluis, 2 locks
Tides, heights and soundings
Non-tidal except in Oosterschelde where streams do not run fast (see Chapter 3). Soundings and heights in the Walcheren Canal to canal level (KP = NAP +0·9m), and in the Veerse Meer to summer level (VZP = NAP, Sept–Oct level is NAP −0·3m, and winter level in Nov–April is NAP −0·7m). In Zandkreek/Oosterschelde soundings to LLWS (mean lower low water springs), and heights to MHWS (mean high water springs).

Minimum depths en route
Generally 3m, but as little as 2m in some of the yacht harbours on the Veerse Meer.

Charts
Dutch small-craft charts *1803, 1805. Stroomatlas c.*

Route description

VLISSINGEN (entrance to VVW Schelde (see Chapter 3)
⚓ «**Keersluisbrug** and open sluice. VHF Ch 22.
Service hours m-sa 0600-2200, su/h 0700-1100, 1700-2100, depending on train service.

KANAAL DOOR WALCHEREN
Depth 6m, shallow at edges. Maximum speed 15kph (8·1kn) up to 20m, 12kph (6·5kn) to 30m, 8kph (4·3kn) over 30m. Some barge traffic between the Westerschelde and northern delta. Keep engine ready.

1·2km/0·7M
🚤 **Sloebrug** (ht 5·0m). VHF Ch 22.
Service hours See Keersluisbrug above.

0·8km/0·4M
🚤 **Draaibrug Souburg**. VHF Ch 22.
Service hours See Keersluisbrug above.

3·6km/1·9M
MIDDELBURG
🚤 **Schroebrug** (ht 0·6m). VHF Ch 22.
Service hours See Keersluisbrug above. Not during rush hours *1/6-1/10* 0730-0830, 1230-1330, 1630-1730.

0·4km/0·2M
🚤 **Stationsbrug** (ht 1·4m). VHF Ch 22.
Service hours See Schroebrug above. Also closed approximately 10 minutes past ½hr in conjunction with train service.

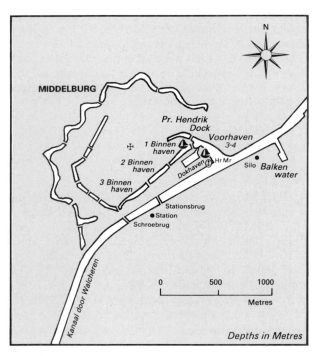

Middelburg

0·7km/0·4M
⚓ To port into Voorhaven (depth 3–4m) temporary moorings. For overnight stay port again through opening Spijkerbrug (ht 2·7–3·2m) into 1st Binnenhaven, pontoons of WV Arne, toilets, showers, laundrette, 5t crane ☎ (01180) 12878/27180.

5·8km/3·1M
⚓ **Veere schutsluis** (large and small lock), VHF Ch 22, waiting posts each side.
Service hours Daily 0500-2330 (su/h to 2300 only).

⚓ Pontoons of Marina Veere on N bank, toilets, showers, 25t boat-lift, ☎ (01181) 223.

0·8km/0·4M
⚓ **Entrance to Veerse Meer** between F.R&G Lts. To port keeping ½ a cable off E of port-hand withies (unbound).

VEERSE MEER
15kph (8·1kn) max. Withies, bound N side, unbound S side mark 2m contour round lake, depth outside varies to 25m.

1·9km/1·0M
VEERE
⚓ To port into Stadshaven (depth 2·6–3·4m) between F.R&G Lts. JC Veere, toilets and showers.
⚓ 1·5km NW along shore of Veerse Meer is entrance (F.R&G Lts) to Jachthaven Oostwatering (depth 3–5m). 15t boat-lift. WV De Arne, ☎ (01181) 484/929, toilets, showers, 12t crane. Jachtwerf Oostwatering has a laundrette.

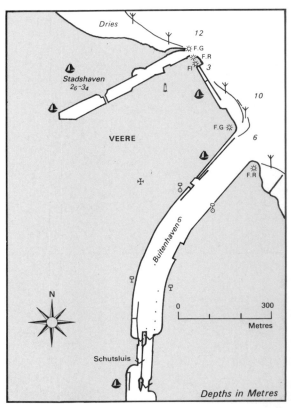

Veere

VEERSE MEER
Channel S and W of the islands.

⚓ There are pontoons and recommended anchoring places on edges of the islands, but many are shallow to 1m or less.

4·0km/2·2M

Iso.R.4s beacon close to stbd. Stbd into channel to Oranjeplaat channel marked with unlit posts and withies. 2·5m depth min. Beware Lemmerplaat spit E of entrance, particularly on outward passage NE.

0·8km/0·5M

ORANJEPLAAT (Arnemuiden)

⚓ Jachthaven Oranjeplaat entrance. End of withied channel. Showers, toilets, 10t crane, De Arne ☎ (01182) 1419/1709. HrMr (01182) 1248.

VEERSE MEER

⚓ Schenge channel NE and E of the islands. More pontoons and recommended anchorages on E edges of the islands, some to 2m depth. On E shore of lake is a crescent-shaped channel in the bank, De Omloop, with pontoons 2·5m depth min. Haven de Piet, depth 3–4m, 350m NE is a harbour reserved for fishermen.

5·0km/2·7M

⚓ **Vluchthaven Geersdijk**. Entrance N bank close E of beacon, Iso.G.4s, between R&G unlit posts with topmarks. 1·5–3m depth. Pontoon, toilet. Exposed in easterlies.

VEERSE MEER

⚓ Channel E and N of the islands. More pontoons and recommended anchoring places on S edges of the islands, some to 2m depth. Withies mark edges of wide shoals N and S bank as well as approaches to moorings of Schelphoek and Sabbingeplaat.

3·9km/2·1M

KORTGENE

⚓ Jachthaven Delta Marina. ☎ (01108) 1315. N bank, F.R&G entrance Lts. 2·1–3·5m depth. Toilets, showers, laundrette, 16t crane. 600m to village.

⚓ **WOLPHAARTSDIJK**

HrMr (3 harbours including Schorhaven) ☎ (01198) 1525. Complex of 6 harbours on S bank opposite Kortgene. The largest, Schorhaven has 2·5–3·2m depth. WV Wolphaartsdijk in the Schorhaven has toilets, showers, laundrette, 5t crane, ☎ (01198) 1562. 2½km to the village.

VEERSE MEER

Channel eastwards, wide shoals 2m and less N and S.

3·9km/2·1M

《 ⌁ **Zandkreeksluis and opening bridge** (ht 5·5m). VHF Ch 18. Waiting posts each side. Serviced all times. F.R&G entrance Lts tidal side.

ZANDKREEK (tidal)

4m depth min. Buoyed, lit. MHW NAP +1·54m, MLW NAP −1·47m. Variation may occur with completion of Delta Plan.

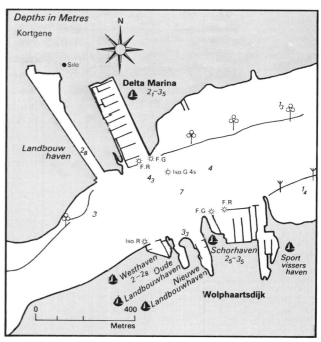

Delta Marina and Wolphaartsdijk

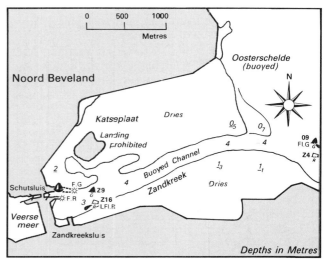

Zandkreeksluis

OOSTERSCHELDE

6m minimum depth in channel to Colijnsplaat.

3·7km/2·0M

Clear Zandkreek spit, G Lt buoy *O9*, heading N.

6·8km/3·7M

⌁ **ZEELANDBRUG**

VHF Ch 18, ☎ (01110) 13237/(01199) 262. 52 pillars. Between 3 and 52 each symmetrical span has clearance of NAP +15·1m in middle and NAP +11·5m at corners. HWS is NAP +1·8m and LLWS is NAP −1·8m giving average clearance range of 13·3m to 16·9m, but greater range at certain exceptional tides. If you have worked out clearance from NAP-based tide tables for Zierikzee (*Getijtafels*) and remain in doubt then:

Either ring up bridge and ask for the clearance.

Or making sure you can make way against wind and tide, consult the height gauges (lit at night) on the ingoing pillars of the recommended traffic spans marked on the Dutch charts. There is an ingoing and outgoing span in the northern and southern halves of the bridge for each channel leading N and S of the Vuilbaard shoal, and each span has a Y Lt in the middle on the side facing the oncoming traffic. If clear of shipping use the appropriate span.

Or use the opening bridge at the northern end, calling the bridgekeeper at least ½hr before.

Service hours 16/3-1/11 m-f 0700-0707, 0723-0737, 0853-0907, 0923-0937 and then each hour 53-07, 23-37 until 2107 then 2123-2130; sa/su/h 0900-0907, 0923-0937, 0953-1007, 1023-1037 and then each hour 53-07, 23-37 until 2107 then 2123-2130. *1/11-16/3* m-f 0700-0900[1], 0900-1700, 1700-2130[1]; sa/su/h 0900-2130[1].

1. 2 hours notice required.

3·2km/1·7M

⚓ **COLIJNSPLAAT** (entrance)
MHW NAP +1·43m, MLW NAP −1·26m.

Entrance and facilities
Harbour entrance F.R&G Lts on metal poles, very narrow. Tide runs across the entrance. Fishing harbour only at E end of haven (2·9m depth). WV Noord Beveland at W end has 2·4m depth but extreme W end pontoons are shallow. Showers, toilets, ☎ (01199) 762. Delta Yacht, 35t boat-lift, ☎ (01199) 776/769. Village shops nearby.

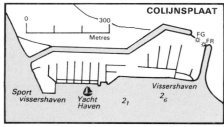

Colijnsplaat

Route 3
Zierikzee to Willemstad via Goes, Stavenisse, and Dintelsas

Commentary

This is another scenic passage, partly tidal and partly non-tidal with two very large sea-locks and the associated barge traffic. Zierikzee, Goes and Willemstad are three of the most picturesque Zeeland towns, with cobbled streets, town halls, churches, museums, restaurants, and interesting harbours.

Zierikzee is the only tidal harbour but visitors lie at floating pontoons well away from the estuary. This originally fortified town has three 14–16th-century town gates, a municipal museum in a beautiful town hall, a maritime museum in a 16th-century prison, and the 58m unfinished Monstertoren which is worth climbing.

Goes has a pretty tree-hung yacht harbour, delightful municipal moorings in the midst of a gabled town with an 18th-century mock Gothic town hall and a 14th-century Grote Kerk.

Willemstad is a moated fortress town built towards the end of the 16th-century to guard the entrance to the Hollands Diep to Dordrecht. The earlier fortifications and the Second World War German bunkers and gun positions, the Maurits-huis, originally governor's residence and now the town hall, the arsenal, and the Protestant church are all worth visiting.

All three towns are crowded in high season so it pays to go early or late, but a place can usually be found rafted alongside other vessels. Stavenisse, Benedensas and Dintelsas are small less fashionable places, where it may be easier to find moorings, calling in the other towns for short visits.

The Krammersluizen's yacht lock, Philipssluis, was completed in the second half of 1987 and locking through previously meant using the big ship lock. If required to use this, follow in, but keep well out of the way of the barges. Take care to see who leaves first, it is sometimes the yachts.

At the Volkeraksluizen's yacht lock, if you are alone locking through, do not contact them on VHF but climb onto the pontoon, press the buzzer and speak into the microphone (they will reply in English).

The locks at Benedensas and Dintelsas off the now tideless Volkerak were still operating in May 1987 and it may be a considerable time before water conditions on each side are balanced sufficiently to leave these locks permanently open and stop charging lock dues in each direction.

Distances 73km/40M

Bridges 3 opening (Goes Havenkanaal), and 3 which have high fixed clearances or an opening bridge alternative.

Locks 3.

Tides, heights and soundings

Tidal to the Krammersluizen (Philipsdam) but not fast streams, and non-tidal beyond. In the tidal areas soundings are to LLWS (lowest low water springs), and heights to MHWS (mean high water springs). Soundings and heights in the inland waters are to: Goes Havenkanaal, KP is NAP +0·7m but can reach 1·2m; Volkerak, Volkerak level is NAP; Hollands Diep, OLW (agreed low river level) is NAP.

Minimum depths en route

2·4m Zierikzee Havenkanaal, 1·4–1·5m in parts of Goes, Stavenisse dries, 2·2m near Benedensas, and 1·5m parts of Willemstad.

Charts

Dutch small-craft charts *1805, 1807*. *Stroomatlas c.*

Route description

⚓ ZIERIKZEE (entrance)

Tidal range

MHWS 3·0m, MLWS 0·3m, MHWN 2·7m, MLWN 0·4m

5kph (2·7kn) max beyond the Keersluis. Municipal HrMr ☎ (01110) 13174. Assistant HrMr/bridge-keeper ☎ (01110) 14716. No entry signals or port radio.

Entrance and facilities

From offshore the conspicuous landmark is the huge square Sint Levens Monstertoren, a belfry which would have also had a spire had the money not run out. The stream runs across the entrance which is from SE between F.R&G Lt Bns on the breakwaters. In addition, on the W molehead is a sector Lt, Oc.RWG.6s, on a 6m R round pedestal with a Wh band. NW winds across the entrance can cause uncomfortable seas because of the fetch. The Havenkanaal (2·4m depth min) leads through an open *keersluis* (closed when water is NAP +1·99m). Immediately to port is a yacht haven with 2·5m depth, and WV Zierikzee with toilets and showers ☎ (01110) 14700. Next to port before the opening

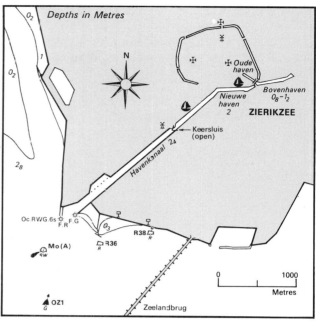

Zierikzee

bridge is the Stadshaven, or Nieuwe Haven, 2m depth, with a floating pontoon (☎ above). 40t crane at Fa. Burcksen, ☎ (01110) 12595. 18t crane at Vrijland Watersport ☎ (01110) 14223. Laundrette at Ria Geluk, Nieuwe Haven 141. Shopping centre and town close by.

Course SE through Zeelandbrug.

1·7km/0·9M

⌑ ZEELANDBRUG

See Route 2 for description of passage.

ENGELSCHE VAARWATER/OOSTERSCHELDE

EV and *O* series of buoys, some lit. 5·3m depth min. Keep clear of steep-to Vondelingsplaat and Galgenplaat drying shoals and their shelving northern spit, and watch for traffic across entrance of Zandkreek.

9·4km/5·2M

SAS VAN GOES

MHW NAP +1·55m, MLW NAP −1·47m.

« Entrance to Schutsluis of Goessche Sas between F.R&G Lts. Keep well clear of drying shoal N of entrance marked by *O13* unlit G buoy.

⚓ Moorings on N side of Binnenhaven after lock.
Lock service hours m-f 0600-2200; *1/5-1/10* sa/su/h 0800-1200, 1600-2000; *1/10-1/5* sa/su/h 0700-0900, 1200-1300, 1700-1800.
Bridgekeeper VHF Ch 18, ☎ (01100) 16744

HAVENKANAAL

3·2m depth but shallow at edges, 6kph (3·2kn) max.

Zierikzee, the gate house at the head of the Nieuwe Haven

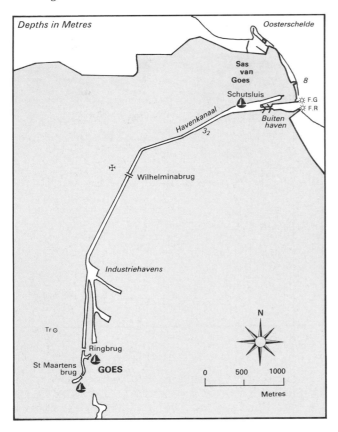

Goes

St Maartensbrug, Goes, the entrance to the municipal yacht moorings at the head of the Havenkanaal

Goes, head of the Havenkanaal and municipal moorings

2·5km/1·2M

 **Wilhelminabrug** (ht 0·2m). Moorings before bridge.
Service hours m-sa 0600-2400, su/h 0700-2200.

2·3km/1·3M
GOES
Ringbrug (ht 1·7m)
Service hours 1/5-1/10 m-f on the hr (except at 1200) 0700-2100; sa 0800, 0900, 1000, 1100, 1700, 1800, 1900, 2000. *1/10-1/5* daily on request 0600-2200.
WV De Werf. HrMr ☎ (01100) 16572. Port side of small LtHo. 1·4m depth, and stbd side 2m. Showers, toilets, clubhouse.

Yacht haven of WV de Werf, Goes, with its tiny lighthouse

0·4km/0·2M
St Maartensbrug drawbridge (ht 2·2m)
Service hours See above for Ringbrug.
Municipal moorings, showers, toilets, laundrette, 1·5–2m depth. HrMr ☎ (01100) 27857. 20t crane in Industriehaven N of the Ringbrug.

Return along Havenkanaal same route as above.

5·2km/2·8M
OOSTERSCHELDE (entrance at Sas van Goes, tidal)

Follow reciprocal of outward route, Engelsche Vaarwater, northward rounding spit, keeping in at least 3m and heading E near R Lt buoy *EV6*.

7·8km/4·2M
R Lt buoy *EV6*

KEETEN, MASGAT, ZIJPE, KRAMMER

Tidal, 6m minimum depth in channel. Wide steep-sided drying 'shelves' on each side *Kt* and *K* series buoys, some lit.

6·0km/3·3M

Kt9 G Lt buoy close to stbd. Course direct for Stavenisse.

0·5km/0·3M

➥ STAVENISSE (entrance)

Tidal range

MHWS 3·1m, MLWS 0·3m, MHWN 2·8m, MLWN 0·4m

HrMr ☎ (01663) 2815. Oc.RWG.5s sector Lt on a black framework on E side of entrance which is difficult to sight as channel turns E inside entrance. Open *keersluis* 200m down entrance channel, closed if level above NAP +2·3m. Channel dries, outside sluice NAP −1·8m, inside sluice NAP −1·5m. The harbour itself almost dries at LLWS so vessels sit on the ground. Entry dependent on draught but usually for visitors advisable after half tide rising. Jachthaven Stavenisse SW end of haven, toilets and showers. 4·5t mobile crane at Garage T.J. Struik, ☎ (01663) 2330.

Anna Jacobapolder Veerhaven Ferries only.

Zijpe Veerhaven Ferries only.

Zijpe Vluchthaven Yachts must not be left un-attended.

Bruinisse Nieuwe/Oude Vissershavens Fishing vessels only.

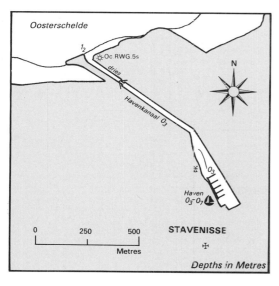

Stavenisse

See Route 4 for Grevelingen locks and lake.

12km/6·5M

≪ PHILIPSDAM and KRAMMERSLUIZEN
(Krammer entrance)

W side MHW is NAP +1·54m, MLW is NAP −1·49m. E side VK = NAP. VHF Ch 22 *Krammersluizen*.

Krammersluizen. The ship locks in the incomplete Philipsdam

Krammersluizen. Northern ship lock

Krammersluizen. In May 1987 the *jachtensluis* and the fixed motorway bridge were not finished. These yachts are waiting to go through the ship locks

Small craft must use the new yacht lock, Philipssluis, with a N-facing outer entrance 1·2km (0·7M) along N wall of the main lock. Entrance to main lock between F.R&G Lts.

Service hours Main lock at all times. Yacht lock hours *1/4-1/10* 0600-2200; small craft have to use the main lock at night and in winter.

⌒ **Fixed bridge** E side of yacht lock (ht NAP +17·8m). Clearance in metres is shown on an automatic board.

⌒ **Opening bridge** N main lock (ht NAP +13·5m).

⌒ **Fixed bridge** S main lock (ht NAP +14·5m).

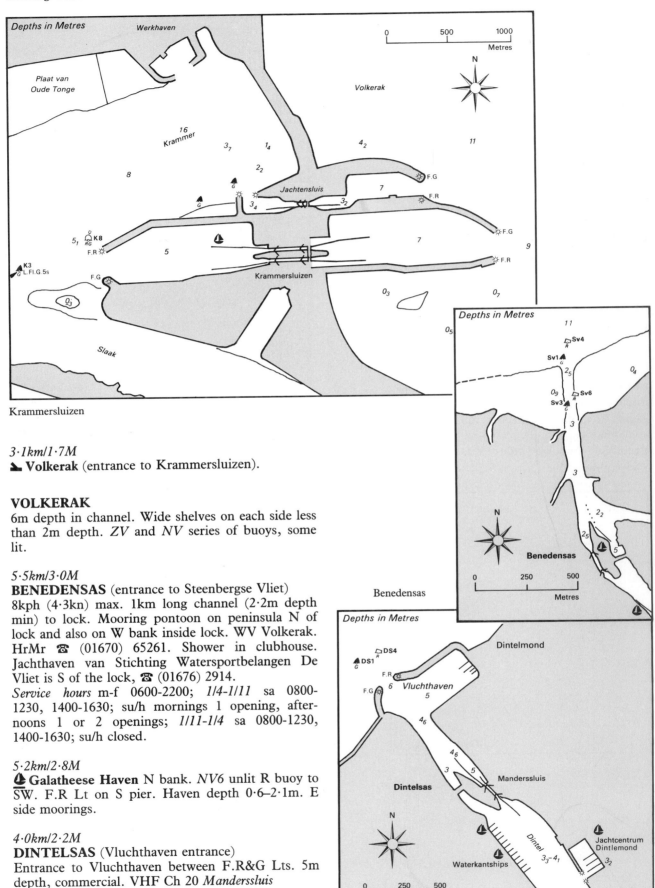

Krammersluizen

Benedensas

Dintelsas

3·1km/1·7M

⚓ **Volkerak** (entrance to Krammersluizen).

VOLKERAK
6m depth in channel. Wide shelves on each side less than 2m depth. *ZV* and *NV* series of buoys, some lit.

5·5km/3·0M
BENEDENSAS (entrance to Steenbergse Vliet)
8kph (4·3kn) max. 1km long channel (2·2m depth min) to lock. Mooring pontoon on peninsula N of lock and also on W bank inside lock. WV Volkerak. HrMr ☎ (01670) 65261. Shower in clubhouse. Jachthaven van Stichting Watersportbelangen De Vliet is S of the lock, ☎ (01676) 2914.
Service hours m-f 0600-2200; *1/4-1/11* sa 0800-1230, 1400-1630; su/h mornings 1 opening, afternoons 1 or 2 openings; *1/11-1/4* sa 0800-1230, 1400-1630; su/h closed.

5·2km/2·8M
⚓ **Galatheese Haven** N bank. *NV6* unlit R buoy to SW. F.R Lt on S pier. Haven depth 0·6–2·1m. E side moorings.

4·0km/2·2M
DINTELSAS (Vluchthaven entrance)
Entrance to Vluchthaven between F.R&G Lts. 5m depth, commercial. VHF Ch 20 *Mandersluis*

⋘ Manderssluis Lock-keeper VHF Ch 20, ☎ (01672) 2385.

Service hours m-f 0600-2200; *1/4-1/11* sa 0800-1230, 1300-2100; su/h 0800-1100, 1500-2100. *1/11-1/4* sa 0800-1230, 1300-1630; su/h closed.

⚓ Jachtcentrum Dintelmond, 3·2-3·5m depth. F.R&G entrance Lts. N side of Dintel are showers, toilets, 10t crane, ☎ (01672) 2894/2372. S side of Dintel are Waterkant Ships (25t boat-lift) and WV De Dintel moorings.

VOLKERAK/HELLEGAT
NV and *HG* series of buoys, some lit, northwards keeping W and clear of Oost Hellegat shoal.

4·8km/2·6M
⋘ VOLKERAKSLUIZEN
Entrance to yacht lock, F.R&G Lts. VHF Ch 18 for use of the 3 ships locks. VHF Ch 69 otherwise. Yacht lock is operational *1/4-1/11* at all times of day. For rest of year small craft use main locks to SE. Pontoon at yacht lock has two-way speaker system, and VHF should only be used if going through opening bridge on S ship lock.

⌒ **Fixed bridge over yacht lock** (ht NAP +19m). Clearance in metres is shown on an automatic board.

⌒ **Fixed bridge N main lock** (ht NAP +14·8m)

⌒ **Fixed bridge middle main lock** (ht NAP +14·8m)

⌒ **Opening bridge S main lock** (ht NAP +14m). Through Hollands Diep entrance to Volkeraksluizen.

Dintelsas off the Volkerak. Jachtcentrum Dintelmond on the N side of the Dintel

2·8km/1·5M
WILLEMSTAD (Voorhaven entrance)
HrMr (E arm of Voorhaven) ☎ (01687) 2576/3262. Keep clear of traffic when crossing main locks and Willemstad Werkhaven. Narrow entrance round single F.G Lt N pier. Voorhaven channel, 2-4·5m depth. Binnenhaven, 1·6-2·8m depth, picturesque but crowded. Municipal yacht haven, 1·5-3·2m depth, and WV Willemstad. Toilets, showers in each haven. 1½t crane in Binnenhaven, M. Wierckx, ☎ (01687) 2855. Ship crane, Fa. Grubo.

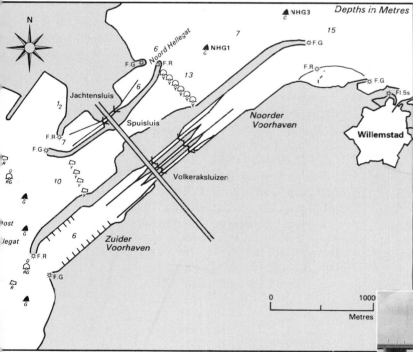

Volkeraksluizen

Volkeraksluizen. Jachtensluis waiting pontoon on the N side, with a push button loud speaker on it for communicating with the English speaking lock-keeper

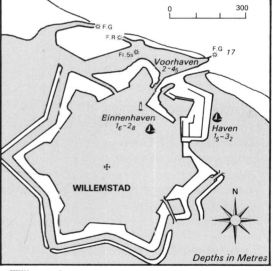

Willemstad

Route 4
A tour of the Grevelingenmeer

Commentary

This is easy non-tidal cruising, with no commercial traffic, plenty of open space for sailing and high-quality yachting facilities. At the Jachthaven Aquadelta, Bruinisse, there is a complex of shops, restaurant, club, flats, and repair facilities. Like Veere, Brouwershaven used to be a major seaport on an open Grevelingen. There is a market square with the statue of the 16th-century poet Jacob Cats, a 16th-century town hall, a large 13th-century church, and of course a windmill. The charming little triangular fishing harbour of Ouddorp is a long walk from its town which is the centre of Goeree. Goeree used to be a small island out on the periphery of the Delta but is now joined to Over-flakee and the mainland. The roomy unpopulated artificial refuge harbours behind the Brouwersdam, with their wildlife and nearby sea-beaches, are also worth a visit.

Distance 57km/31M

Bridges and locks 1 lock and opening bridge at the Grevelingensluis.

Tides, heights and soundings

On tidal side of Grevelingendam soundings are to LLWS (lowest low water springs) and heights to MHWS (mean high water springs). Throughout the lake both heights and soundings are to GP (*Grevelingenpeil*) NAP −0·2m.

Minimum depths en route

2m Brouwershaven Havenkanaal, 1·4m E side of Ouddorp haven, 1·5m Herkingen Haven but 2·1m in yacht harbour.

Charts

Dutch small-craft chart *1805*.

Route description

GREVELINGENDAM

Grevelingensluizen seaward side.

Tidal range

MHWS 3·2m, MLWS 0·2m, MHWN 2·8m, MLWN 0·3m

From the Krammer, approach to lock is via Zuid Grevelingen channel, *ZG* buoys unlit, 3m depth min. Iso.WRG.4s sector Lt on point to the S. Entrance to lock is between F.R&G Lts.

《 ⌒ **Grevelingensluis and drawbridge** (ht 6·4m)

VHF Ch 22 *Grevelingensluis*, ☎ (01113) 1473.

Service hours 15/6-1/9 0700-2200. *1/9-15/6* 0800-2200.

GREVELINGENMEER

No speed limit except 9kph/4·9kn in narrow channels between islands. Wide shelf areas around shores and islands marked with withies at 1·5m depth. From SE to NW: unbound withies/R buoys to port, bound withies/G buoys to stbd. At NW end

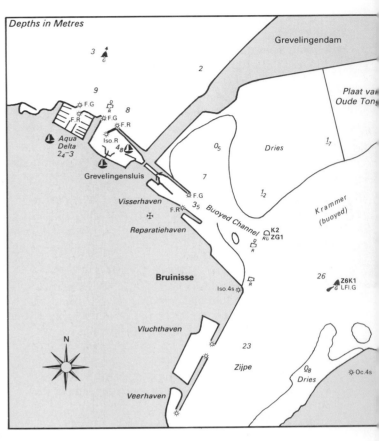

Bruinisse and Grevelingensluice

parallel with Brouwersdam bound withies/G buoys are on dam side and unbound withies/R buoys on the E side of channel. The buoyage is unlit, and the only Lts are at harbour entrances except for 3 Lt Bns between Bruinisse and Brouwershaven. RW buoys mark forks in channels and ends of spits. Many islands have pontoons at which to lie but use the echo sounder (also see small-craft charts).

⚓ BRUINISSE

Jachthaven WSV Bru, 4·8m depth, S of exit from lock. Toilets, showers, 1t crane.

HrMr ☎ (01113) 1506.

Depart between F.R&G entrance Lts N side of harbour then dogleg round R unlit buoy *GG2* N of entrance and S into Jachthaven Aquadelta.

Jachthaven Aquadelta, 2·4–3m depth, entrance between F.R&G Lts. Toilets, showers, laundrette. HrMr ☎ (01113) 1485. 16t crane at Rowi Watersport B.V. ☎ (01113) 2195.

Follow the *G* channel buoys NW.

11·6km/6·3M

GEUL VAN BOMMENEDE

Lt Bn RG *G22/GB1*. 8m depth in this channel. *GB* series buoys S of Stampersplaat (small harbour on island 1·5–2·5m depth) and S of Dwars in den Weg (a pontoon on this island). 8m depth in channel.

Bruinisse, Aqua Delta marina

BROUWERSHAVEN

R unlit buoy *GB20* marks end of spit where the approach channel to Brouwershaven doubles back SE between G and R posts (topmarks, unlit). F.RWG sector Lt on S bank initial approach and Ldg Lts 142° for last part of channel. Channel 2·5m depth min.

4·8km/2·6M

⚓ Open *keersluis* entrance to harbour, 2m on sill, up to 2·2m in harbours. Nieuwe Jachthaven boxes to port of entrance. If over 12m LOA moor to head posts. Oude Haven at end of Havenkanaal has a visitors' pontoon. Both harbours have toilets and showers. HrMr (*keersluis*) ☎ (01119) 1330/1364. 9t crane at Jachtwerf Kesteloo ☎ (01119) 1252.

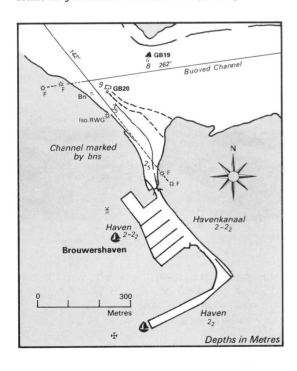

Brouwershaven

Continue N following *GB* channel buoys (9m depth min).

2·0km/1·1M

⚓ DEN OSSE

Entrance to yacht haven of WV Den Osse, F.R&G entrance Lts, 3·8–6m depth. Toilets, showers, 25t crane. HrMr ☎ (01119) 1457. Take care to clear shoal to W of entrance when leaving.

3·5km/1·9M

⚓ SCHARENDIJKE

Entrance to Scharendijke Jachthaven between F.R&G entrance Lts. Main pontoons through second entrance to port. Toilets, showers. Municipal HrMrs ☎ (01117) 1264/1214. 20t boat-lift at Jachtwerf De Grevelingen ☎ (01117) 1490.

⚓ Haven Middelplaat is 1·6km (0·9M) to the N behind dam, and has pontoons, refuse facilities, 3m depth min.

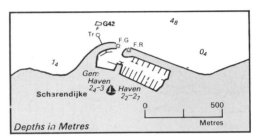

Scharendijke

Scharendijke municipal yacht haven and entrance

GEUL VAN OSSEHOEK

Depart Scharendijke heading ENE to E side Kabbelaarsbank. Steep side marked by bound withies E side, and unbound withies N side. Double back at R unlit buoy *GO4* along Geul van Ossehoek, *GO* series buoys. 5m depth in channel.

5·0km/2·7M

⚓ Haven Kabbelaarsbank (depth 3–5m). Entrance F.R&G Lts. Moorings and refuse disposal dam side.

1·6km/0·9M

⚓ Haven Springersdiep (depth 3–8m). Entrance F.R&G Lts. Moorings and refuse disposal dam side.

SPRINGERSDIEP (buoys series *SP*)
Keep clear to W of Hompelvoet's offlying shoal (marked by withies). Channel 3m near edges.

5·2km/2·8M

⚓ **OUDDORP HAVEN** (entrance)
F.R&G Lts. WV Goeree. Depth 1·4m E arm, 2·3m W arm. Toilets, showers, 10t crane. HrMr ☎ (01878) 1583.

Ouddorp haven

Ouddorp haven

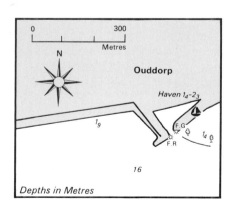

Ouddorp

SPRINGERSDIEP (buoys series *SP*)
Keep clear of wide shoals each side (marked by withies). Channel 3m near edges. Keep clear to N of withy-marked shoal N of Vlieger channel to R *SP2* and G *SP1* buoys.

6·9km/3·7M
R *SP2* and G *SP1*.

HALS CHANNEL (buoys series *H*)
Wide shoals each side.

7·6km/4·1M
To G unlit buoy *H1*.

GEUL VAN HERKINGEN (buoys series *GH*)
Very wide shelf on N side of channel marked by withies. To head of Herkingen entrance channel.

3·0km/1·6M
Herkingen entrance channel. R and G unlit posts at the head.

HERKINGEN
Herkingen Geul, channel marked by port and stbd withies, 2·5m depth min.

1·1km/0·6M

⚓ F.R&G Lts entrance to Herkingen Jachthaven. Port into marina, 2·1–2·5m depth. Yacht haven of WV Herkingen, toilets, showers. 17t crane at L.v.d. Velde ☎ (01876) 256. HrMr ☎ (01876) 623.

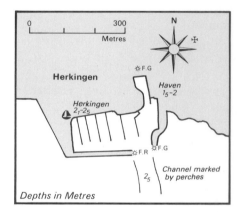

Herkingen

Herkingen, yacht haven of WV Herkingen

Return along entrance channel and SE round E side of Mosselbank, marked by withies and *GH* (Geul van Herkingen) and *SJ* (Bocht van St Jacob) buoys then course to Bruinisse.

4·8km/2·6M

⚓ **BRUINISSE**
Jachthaven Aqua Delta. See above.

5. The Northern Delta
Haringvliet and Rotterdamse Waterweg

Route 5
Hellevoetsluis to Dordrecht via the Spui

Commentary

This is a passage rather than a scenic route between two interesting towns with ample moorings and facilities. Hellevoetsluis was the seventeenth and 18th-century ferry harbour to which the Harwich packets plied, and from which William III sailed to take the British throne in 1688. It is now a yachting complex with a large village, some interesting houses, a windmill, a small lighthouse, and a historic naval dry-dock (1804) built and operated with the help of a steam engine and pump and in use until 1930. There is also a fire service museum with some very early fire-fighting equipment in the 18th-century naval quarters.

Dordrecht is the oldest city in Zuid-Holland at one of the world's busiest river junctions with a fascinating waterfront, the 17th-century Groothoofd-spoort gate at the junction of three rivers, a Gothic Grote Kerk, many beautifully gabled streets like the Wijnstraat, and two museums, the Dordrecht and the Van Gijn which pay tribute to the city's painters (Bols, Van Hoogstraten, Cuyp, Maes) and its island history as centre of the early polder experiments. As in Amsterdam many of the beautiful gabled buildings are leaning slightly on their marshy foundations. This is a wide canal route through open country with occasional factory developments, and a few convenient, unspectacular mooring places en route. The winding Spui with its rushes is like the Broads and wind direction often allows sailing throughout this route.

Distances 45km/24M

Bridges 4 opening, of which 1 the Dordrecht railway/road bridge.

Locks None

Tides, heights and soundings
On the Dutch small-craft charts soundings are to OLW (agreed low river level) throughout. In the Haringvliet OLW = NAP, so this gives a safety margin since normally levels are maintained at NAP +·25m to +·50m. In the Hollands Diep range is NAP +·45m to +·65m, and in the northern tidal tributaries (MLW to MHW): Spui NAP +0·1 to +0·6m, Oude Maas near Dordrecht +0·1 to +1·0m. Heights are to MHW.

Streams can run fast, particularly along the Oude Maas, so it pays to work them. Passage duration for a normal yacht is around 5 hours, 13M along the Haringvliet and Spui where the ebb is north (with), and 11M along the Oude Maas where the ebb is west (against). In both rivers the ebb starts at approximately HW Hoek +4½ hours. It pays to take the last 3 hours of ebb along the Spui, and the first 2 of flood along the Oude Maas, starting at Hellevoetsluis at about 2½ hours before HW Hoek. The reverse journey is easy to plan with the Stroomatlas. However, you cannot count on an immutable schedule since streams in the N-S trending Spui are erratic and dependent also on the Haringvliet sluicing programme, and when there is a heavy discharge from the Rhine there is sometimes no northerly ebb at all in the Spui.

Minimum depths en route
1·8m parts of Hellevoetsluis Groote Dok, 1m parts of Blinckvliet Haven, 0·6m parts of Nieuw Beijerland, 1·2m parts of Oud Beijerland, 1·8m parts of Heerjansdam, 0·9m in parts of Puttershoek, 1·8m parts of Wijnhaven Dordrecht.

Charts
Dutch small-craft charts *1807* and *1809*, together with *Stroomatlas e*.

Route description

HELLEVOETSLUIS Heliushaven entrance
Heliushaven (depth 3–5m)
3 ⚓ F.R&G entrance Lts. 3 yacht harbours on W side all with toilets, showers. In southerlies the outside pontoons can be very uncomfortable. WV Helius, laundrette, 10t crane ☎ (01881) 1703, WV Haringvliet ☎ (01883) 14039, WV Hellevoetsluis, 2·5t crane ☎ (01883) 15868.

Het Groote Dok
De Haaven (depth 3·8–4·8m), entrance to Het Groote Dok (depth 1·8–4·3m). Marked only by LtHo Iso.RWG.10s (sectored) on W pier, and pilings angled inwards.
⚓ Southerly-exposed mooring along municipal quay (summer toilets, showers).
⛵ **Swing bridge** (ht 1·2–2m) to Groote Dok.
2 ⚓ At Groote Dok are WV Hellevoetsluis ☎ (01883) 14640, and Jachthaven Arie de Boom, toilets, showers, 25t boat-lift ☎ (01883) 12166.

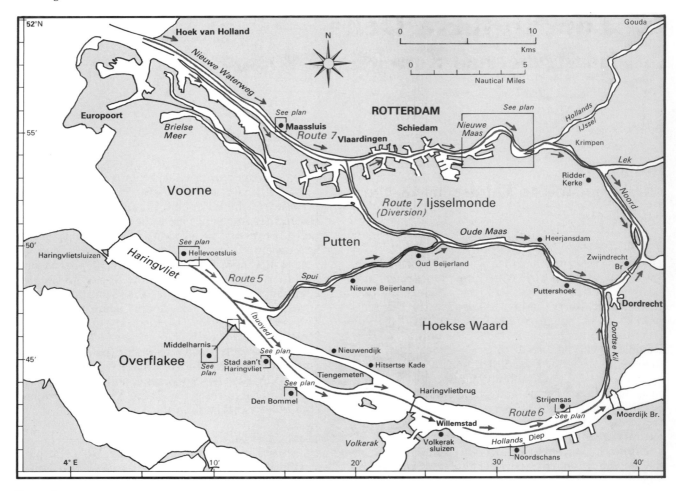

Route plan

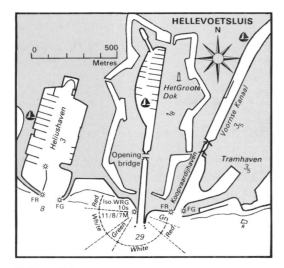

Hellevoetsluis

Bridge service hours m-f *1/10-1/4* 0800, 1000, 1130, 1300, 1500, 1630; *1/4-1/10* 0800, 0900, 1000, 1100[1], 1130, 1300, 1400[1], 1500, 1600[1], 1630, 1800[1], 1930 (not Apr and May), 2030 (not Apr and May). sa/su/h[2] *1/10-1/4* 1000, 1300, 1630; *1/4-1/10* 0800, 0900[1], 1000, 1100[1], 1130, 1300, 1400[1], 1500, 1600[1], 1630, 1800, 1930[1], 2030[1].

1. Not in April
2. No service on Xmas Day or New Year's Day.

Hellevoetsluis. Mooring pontoons in the Koopvaardijhaven approach to the Voornse canal locks

Koopvaardijhaven (5m depth)
Entrance to Voornse Kanaal (3–4m depth). F.R&G entrance Lts.

⚓ Southerly exposed. Municipal moorings W side, summer toilets and showers.

《 ⛵ **Lock and opening bridge** into canal. Tramhaven to the E is forbidden for yachts, but Jachtwerf Devo has a 10t crane, ☎ (01883) 12605.

Hellevoetsluis. Het Groote Dok (previously Industriehaven) looking W

2⚓ In Kanaal door Voorne: W side 500m N of lock is WV Haringvliet ☎ (01883) 12924; E side N of lock is WV Waterman ☎ (01883) 14257.
Lock and bridge service hours m-f *1/10-1/4* 0815, 1015, 1145, 1315, 1515, 1645, *1/4-1/10* 0815, 0900, 1000, 1100[1], 1130, 1315, 1400[1], 1500, 1600[1], 1630, 1830[1], 1930 (not Apr and May), 2030 (not Apr and May); sa/su/h[2] *1/10-1/4* 1015, 1315, 1645; *1/4-1/10* 0815, 0900[1], 1000, 1100[1], 1130, 1315, 1400[1], 1500, 1600, 1630, 1830, 1930[1], 2030[1].
1. Not in April
2. No service on Xmas Day or New Year's Day.

Precinct shopping centre 1·6km N of the lock, E side of the canal with a bridge across.

HARINGVLIET
HV series buoys some lit, withies round 2m contour of central shoals. Minimum depth in channel 3·7m. Keep clear Slijkplaat. Hoornse Hoofden point with Oc.RWG.5s sector Lt can be passed close to.

BENINGEN CHANNEL
BN series buoys some lit (R to port).

SPUI RIVER
SP series buoys, unlit. (R to stbd). Daylight route for strangers. Winding, increasingly tidal, keep clear of shallows on bends. Minimum depth 3m, but often deeper, up to 15m. N-going ebb can exceed 2kn.

12·2km/6·6M
⚓ Zuidland (town is over 3km away), WV Blinckvliet on N bank. Depth 1–2·2m, toilets, showers, 8t boat-lift, ☎ (01881) 1991.

5·0km/2·7M
NIEUWE BEIJERLAND
MHW NAP +0·85m, MLW NAP +0·15m.
H WV Nieuwe Beijerland in W basin. Depth 1·7–2·1m. E Haven moorings depth 0·6–1·5m. Close to town. HrMr ☎ (01817) 1517.

6·1km/3·3M
OUDE BEIJERLAND
MHW NAP +0·70m, MLW NAP −0·20m.
⚓ WV Het Spui, S bank, depth 1·2–1·7m. Toilets, showers, 5t crane, ☎ (01860) 14879. Close to town. Municipal HrMr ☎ (01860) 14122.

1·7km/0·9M
⚓ OUDE MAAS river junction
E following *O* series buoys, (R to port) some lit, Lt beacons on banks. Heavy barge traffic. Shallow bends well marked. Tidal, ebb over 2kn.

8·5km/4·6M
HEERJANSDAM
MHW NAP +0·95 to +1·05m, MLW NAP −0·17 to −0·49m
⚓ Jachthaven Oude Maas, N bank, depth 1·8 to 3·6m, toilets, showers, 30t boat-lift, ☎ (01857) 2445. On a N bend with sector Ldg Lts down each straight. Town 1½ km.

3·1km/1·7M
PUTTERSHOEK
MHW NAP +0·85m, MLW NAP +0·05m.
⚓ Puttershoek Haven, small open dock S bank. Depth 0·9–1·7m, very shallow. Iso.G.4s Lt on W pier. Close to town.
⚓ Lorregat. WV De Waterlelie. Depth 1·2–2m. Shallow. Close to town.

Continue past junction with Dortse Kil

DORDRECHT
MHW NAP +0·9m, MLW 0·1m.
HrMr Binnenkalkhaven 47, ☎ (078) 134211, (available 0800-1230, 1330-1700).

8·7km/4·7M
⚓ Railway bridge (ht 5·6–6·3m closed, 44–45·5m open) next to road bridge. VHF Ch 22, manned 15 minutes before and to end of opening. VHF Ch 71, *Post Dordrecht*, ☎ (078) 132421, other times.
Service periods Average 17 times per 24 hours, night and day, see booklet *Openingstijden spoorbruggen*. Waits of over 2 hours possible.

Dordrecht. Approaching the daunting road/rail bridge where long queues are frequent

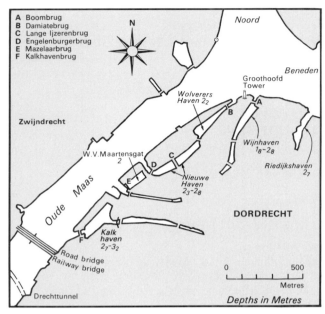

A Boombrug
B Damiatebrug
C Lange Ijzerenbrug
D Engelenburgerbrug
E Mazelaarbrug
F Kalkhavenbrug

Dordrecht

Leuvehaven/WV Maartensgat (depth 2m)

⚓ Stbd into the Leuvehaven and port through **Mazelaarsbrug** swing bridge (ht 0·70m). Bridgekeeper also runs Engelenburgerbrug, so you may have to press buzzer on the posts for attention. Quiet small harbour. 12m length max, toilets and showers. HrMr ☎ (078) 131053

Bridge service hours ☎ (078) 143209, *1/4-1/11* m-sa 0900-1200, 1400-1900; su/h 0900-1200, 1500-2000; *1/11-1/4* m-f 0900-1000, 1500-1800; sa/su/h closed. Opens for 10 minutes on the hr and half hr.

Nieuwe Haven/Jachthaven van de Koninklijk Dordtse Roei- en Zeil- V (depth 2·3–2·8m)

2 ⚓ **Engelenburgerbrug** and **Lange IJzerenbrug** (ht 2·06m). Toilets, showers, ☎ (078) 133905.
Bridge service hours See Mazelaarsbrug above.

Wolwevershaven (depth 2·2m)

⚓ **Damiatebrug** (drawbridge, ht 1·60m) to a commercial dock also catering for large sailing vessels.
Bridge service hours See Boombrug below.

The double bridge over the Oude Maas at Dordrecht. The traffic bridge is a double bascule, and the railway is a lift bridge

⚓ **Road bridge** (ht 10·6–11m closed) service is usually coincident with railway bridge but only during these periods:

Service periods m-sa *1/4-1/10* 0600-2200; *1/10-1/4* 0600-2000; su/h *16/4-16/10* 0712-0937, 1825-2105; *16/10-16/4* closed.

When railway bridge only is raised height under nearest part of road bridge is 10·7m MHW.

The harbours below are all on E bank in consecutive order S to N and in the town of Dordrecht.

Kalkhaven (depth 2·7–3·2m)

⚓ **Swing bridge** (ht 0·5m/1·3m MLW) to commercial harbour which is not recommended (see HrMr above if you wish to try).
Bridge service hours m-f 0800-1200, 1300-1700; sa 0800-1130, 1330-1800; su/h closed.

Dordrecht. Hotel Bellevue is a conspicuous waterfront landmark on the promontory between Wolwevershaven and Wijnhaven

Hotel Bellevue and Groothoofdspoort gate on promontory between Wolwevershaven and Wijnhaven.

Wijnhaven (depth 1·8–2·8m)
⌐ **Boombrug** (ht 1·7m MHW).
4 ⚓ Wijnhaven WVs: Drechtstad, Het Wantij, Tuuredrecht and Kraanvogel.
Bridge service hours ☎ (078) 144242. *1/4–1/11* m-sa 0900-1200, 1400-1900; su/h 0900-1200, 1500-2000; *1/11–1/4* m-f 0800-1200, 1300-1800; sa 0800-1200, 1300-1700; su/h closed. Opens for 10 minutes on the hr and half hr.

Riedijkshaven (depth 2·7m)
⚓ Riedijkshaven, S bank junction of Wantij. Temporary moorings by arrangement with HrMr, ☎ (078) 134211. Commercial.
Laundrette, 'Joke', Spuiplein 1, ☎ (078) 141243. There are many lifting facilities, see ANWB *Almanak*, but the heaviest facilities tend to be 2–4km away in the Wantij river: e.g. Jachthaven v. d. Heuvel-de Graaf, 1st yacht haven S bank, 40t boat-lift, ☎ (078) 136911/132319; Jachthaven Westergoot, N bank, 25t crane, ☎ (078) 160780.

Dordrecht. Wijnhaven for smaller vessels

Dordrecht. Entrance to Wolwevershaven where the larger pleasure craft tend to congregate

Route 6
Hellevoetsluis to Dordrecht via the Hollands Diep

Commentary (See also Route 5)
Although slightly longer to Dordrecht than Route 5 there is more room for sailing, there are more places to stop with better facilities, and there is the additional bonus of picturesque Willemstad en route. Middelharnis is the old municipal centre of Overflakee, and has a lovely 17th-century town hall. Overflakee is no longer an island being completely joined to its NW neighbour Goeree, and southwestwards via the Volkeraksluizen to the mainland.

Distances 50km/27M
Bridges 4 opening, of which 1 is the Dordrecht railway/road bridge.
Locks None
Tides, heights and soundings (see also Route 5)
Streams are weak and insignificant in the Haringvliet/Hollands Diep. In the Dordtse Kil they become more significant northward and the ebb off Dordrecht can run at 2·5kn or more in exceptional conditions. The ebb northward starts about 6 hours before HW Hoek van Holland and the flood about half an hour after HW Hoek. However, you cannot count on an immutable schedule since streams in the N-S trending Dordtse Kil, as in the Spui, are erratic and dependent also on the Haringvliet sluicing programme. When there is a heavy discharge from the Rhine sometimes no northerly ebb occurs.
Minimum depths en route
Generally over 3m throughout but all of the harbours with the exceptions of Hellevoetsluis, Middelharnis and Dordrecht are shallow and in parts as little as: Stad aan't Haringvliet 1·2m, Den Bommel 1·6m, De Hitsert 1·6m, Willemstad 1·5m, Noordschans 1·8m, Strijensas 1·4m.
Charts
See Route 5.

Route description

HELLEVOETSLUIS
Heliushaven entrance. See Route 5 for chart and detail.

HARINGVLIET
HV series buoys some lit, withies around 2m contour of central shoals. Channel minimum depth 4·7m. Keep clear Slijkplaat and shoal NE of Middelharnis entrance.

6·9km/3·7M
MIDDELHARNIS Buitenhaven entrance
F.WRG sector Lt on N pier and F.R on S.
⚓ Buitenhaven and Tramhaven (minimum depth 5m). Municipal moorings, temporary stop. HrMr ☎ (01870) 2068.

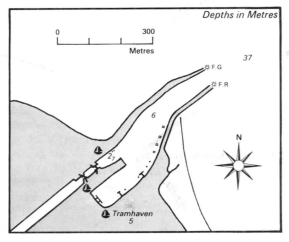

Middelharnis entrance

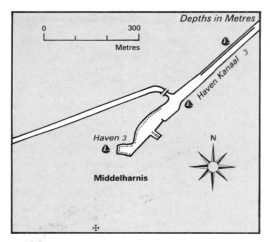

Middelharnis

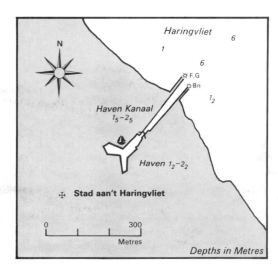

Stad aan't Haringvliet

HARINGVLIET

HV series buoys continuing S side of Tiengemeten island. Minimum depth 5·5m.

3·4km/1·8M
DEN BOMMEL entrance
F.G Lt W pier, unlit RW beacon on E pier which is usually awash. HrMr ☎ (01871) 2224.

⚓ WV Het Bommelse Gors, toilets and showers. Depth 1·6–2m.

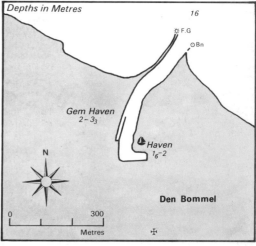

Den Bommel

HARINGVLIET

HV series buoys continuing S side of Tiengemeten island. Keep clear of withy-marked edges of Ventjagersplaat to the S, and Tiengemeten with spit and shoal patches to N. Channel minimum depth 4·9m.

NIEUWENDIJK AND HITSERTSE KADE

⚓ N of Tiengemeten island on the bank there are yacht moorings at Nieuwendijk (1·4–2·2m). Opposite the eastern end of the island is a yacht harbour, Jachthaven WV De Hitsert (depth 1·4–2·2m), at Hitsertse Kade, toilets and showers, HrMr ☎ (01866) 2605/1328.

≪ ⌐ **Lock and opening bridge** into Havenkanaal (depth 3m). VHF Ch 12.
Service hours m-sa 0700-2000 (on the hr, and in summer 0700-2100); su/h 0800, 1000, 1700, 2000 (2100 instead of 2000 in summer); *1/10-1/5* 1000, 1700.
It is 2·2km (1·2M) to the Haven (depth 3m) in centre of town.
⚓ End of canal, W side, municipal moorings, HrMr ☎ (01870) 2068, temporary stop. On Havenkanaal is JSF Jachtservice. Both have toilets and showers. JSF Jachtservice has 20t crane, ☎ (01870) 3458. Fa de Groot has 25t crane. Laundrette at Mastenbroek, Achterweg.

HARINGVLIET

HV series buoys towards S side of Tiengemeten island. Minimum depth 4m.

5·5km/3·0M
STAD AAN'T HARINGVLIET entrance
F.G Lt W pier, unlit R beacon E pier. Flood lock stays open. Keep clear of obstructions E side of lock approach.

⚓ Moorings in W basin (depth 1·2–2·2m).

8·3km/4·5M

HARINGVLIETBRUG

VHF Ch 13, ☎ (01862) 1865

145m pylons with F.R Lts at either end on W side. Pillars numbered 1 to 10 from S to N. Pillars 2, 3, 5, 8, 9 have ht gauges on their W sides. Pillars 3, 4, 6, 9, 10 have ht gauges on their E sides.

Opening bridge at N end of bridge. Clearance between pillars 5 and 6 is NAP +14m. MHW = NAP +0·7m and MLW = NAP +0·5m giving a range of actual clearance of 13·3m to 13·7m, but the small-craft chart lists 12·4m minimum safe clearance. If your height is marginal use the scales on the pillars and if in any doubt go through opening bridge.

Service hours 1/4-1/11 daily 0900, 1000, 1100, 1200, 1400, 1500, 1600, 1800[1], 1900[1]. *1/11-1/4* m-f (on special request) 0900, 1000, 1100, 1200, 1400, 1500, 1600; sa/su/h closed.
1. Except on m-th during periods *1/4-1/6, 1/9-1/11*.

HOLLANDS DIEP

HD series of buoys, some lit, giving wide berth to the Volkeraksluizen entrance to S. Channel minimum depth 5·4m.

3·7km/2·0M

WILLEMSTAD Voorhaven entrance. See Route 3, chart and detail.

HOLLANDS DIEP

Continuing *HD* series of buoys. Keep clear isolated shoals (withied). Channel minimum depth 6m.

5·7km/3·1M

⚓ NOORDSCHANS entrance

Direct across 1·5m shallows to entrance. Unlit beacon, R triangle topmark, on W wall which will be awash or flooded at high water levels. Iso.WRG.4s sector entrance Lt at root of W wall. To port into Jachthaven Noordschans (depth 1·8–2·4m), toilets and showers, 30t boat-lift, ☎ (01682) 2944/3550. ½hr walk to village.

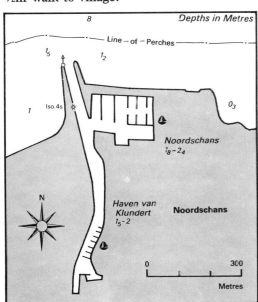

Noordschans

HOLLANDS DIEP

Continuing *HD* series of buoys. Channel minimum depth 6m. Keep N of Sassenplaat, Zuid Hollands Diep prohibited to pleasure craft.

5·2km/2·8M

⚓ STRIJENSAS entrance

F.R Lt at end of partly submerged W stone pier. Unlit Bn with R inverted triangle topmark on E, also partly submerged, pier. Channel (depth 1·6m) marked by unlit beacons each side. Oc.RW.5s sector Lt root of W pier. Westhaven (depth 1·8m). Oostelijke haven (depth 1·4–1·8m). Jachthaven Strijensas ☎ (01854) 2182, toilets, showers, 14t boat-lift. Village close by.

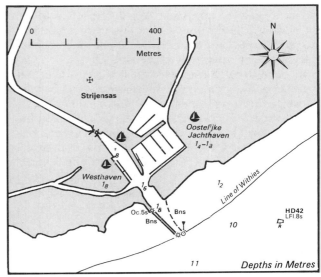

Strijensas

⚓ MOERDIJK

ESE from Strijensas on opposite bank is a large open harbour, moorings on walls at S end by arrangement with HrMr ☎ (01683) 2834/2302. 10 minutes from village.

HOLLANDS DIEP

Continuing *HD* series of buoys. Channel minimum depth 6m.

2·0km/1·1M

⚓ DORDTSE KIL

Tidal, see above for tides. Entrance between RG spherical Lt buoy *D7/HD48* and Iso.RWG.8s sector Lt. N along increasingly industrial canal, keep well to stbd. Stream can be fast. No anchoring or mooring. Minimum depth 8m, steep sided.

9·3km/5·0M

⚓ OUDE MAAS junction. Stbd joining Route 5.

DORDRECHT railway and road bridge.
See Route 5 for bridge and facilities in Dordrecht.

Route 7
Hoek van Holland to Dordrecht via Rotterdam.

Commentary

This is a passage rather than a scenic route. There are typically 10 to 15m depths in the main channel and 4 to 10m beyond Rotterdam, with a generally steep-edged channel, but in keeping near the edges beware of possible underwater boulders. It has the world's heaviest sea-going and barge traffic. A reliable engine is essential and it is not advisable to put up sail given the erratic wind conditions caused by the traffic and the varied shore installations and built-up areas. A radar reflector is also essential.

Care should be taken to keep to the letter of the International Collision Regulations; large numbers of tugs, barges and launches leave and depart from the many side channels, often at a high speed and from behind blind corners, whilst there is constant overtaking by large ships. If necessary to cross the channel do so as quickly as possible at a right-angled aspect. A 55-channel VHF radio is advisable and you should check into the Hoek waterways traffic control system to be passed down river from section to section and for permission to enter major harbours (see Chapter 3).

En route, Maassluis is a pleasant residential town with an old fishing harbour and its Churchisland, in the midst of an industrial region. Vlaardingen was once a major fishing harbour and has a picturesque fish market, a fishing museum and yet another town hall from the Dutch Golden Age, the 16th century. In case you have the taste Schiedam is a major centre for distilling *genever*. Rotterdam is a major regional shopping centre, substantially rebuilt since the War, and with a pleasant park and boulevards near the Veerhaven. Any visit must include the Euromast. A lift rotates externally up the 590ft mast and as well as offering a breathtaking view there is also a restaurant at the top.

Distance 50m/27M

Bridges 5 opening

Locks None

Tides, heights and soundings
Tidal throughout. See Chapter 3. Soundings to OLW (agreed low river level), heights to MHW (mean high water). Tidal streams can run up to 4kn, particularly on the ebb and nearer the entrance, so it is advisable to work them. If you wish to do the whole trip in a single set then starting at Berg Haven about 2 hours before HW Hoek gives about 5½ hours of flood before the ebb turns against at the turn-off down the Noord, 22M away and 5M from Dordrecht. If you cannot average 5kn you may need to push the tide for a short period either at beginning or end depending on when you start. On the return journey starting at Dordrecht 5 hours after HW Hoek again gives 5½ hours of ebb to Berg Haven. In this direction it definitely pays to start

earlier than this and push the much weaker streams at the beginning if necessary. Very similar timing applies in both directions if you wish to use the more rural Oude Maas and avoid the passage past Rotterdam.

Minimum depths en route
Deep water throughout. Spuihaven (Schiedam) with 2m in parts, and Jachthaven WV Hoogvliet (0·8m) near Spijkenisserbrug on the detour to the Spui are the shallowest harbours.

Charts
Dutch small-craft chart *1809* and *Stroomatlas e*.

Route description

BERG HAVEN, HOEK VAN HOLLAND
See Chapter 3 for these and for port radio and traffic control system to Rotterdam.

NIEUWE WATERWEG
Lt beacons and buoys.

10·7km/5·8M
MAASSLUIS Buitenhaven entrance
MHW 2·0m, MLW 0·4m.
HrMr by railway bridge, VHF Ch 80, ☎ (01899) 12852.

Customs
Via HrMr or VHF Ch 80, m-f 0800-1645, or ☎ (010) 4761666.

Entry signals
F.R&G Lts entrance to Buitenhaven (minimum depth 3·8m). F.R under the G if entrance partly blocked. All R Lts means entrance prohibited.

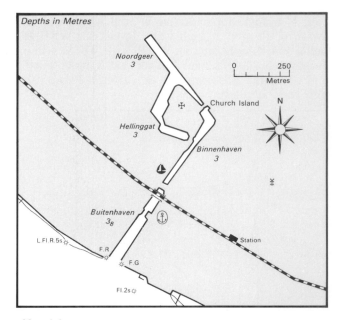

Maassluis

≪ 2 ⚓ Continue through usually open **Keersluis** to **railway bridge** (ht 1·2m) and **road bridge** (bascule, ht 1·1m) into Binnenhaven (minimum depth 3m).
⚓ Mooring by quaysides Binnen- and Buitenhavens.
Bridge service hours m-f 0545-0700, 0900-1630, 1800-2100; sa 0645-0700, 0830-1300; su/h closed. 10 minutes before hr and ½hr depending on trains.

5·7km/3·1M
⚓ OUDE MAAS to stbd beyond Petroleumhaven.

DETOUR TO JOIN THE SPUI AND ROUTE 5
Distance from Oude Maas junction (above) to Spui junction is 10·9km/5·9M

⚓ **Botlekbrug** (opening railway bridge ht 5·7–6·1m, NAP +8m). Lift bridge, height gauges on each side. VHF Ch 18. Serviced all times depending on trains.

⚓ N side of Spijkenisserbrug E bank. Jachthaven WV Hoogvliet Depth 0·8m. HrMr ☎ (010) 416-7032.

⚓ **Spijkenisserbrug** (opening road bridge, ht 10·9m, NAP +12·5m; possible for many yachts). Lift bridge, height gauges. VHF Ch 18.
Bridge service hours m-f 0000-0645, 0715-0800, 0830-1630, 1700-1730, 1800-2400; sa/su/h no fixed times.
Special traffic signals (Botlekbrug the same): Single R or G obvious. R&G = no entry, being prepared. R&R = no entry, no service. Y = pass under bridge, two-way traffic. Y&Y = pass under bridge, no opposing traffic. RWR (Spijkenisserbrug only) = no traffic under this span.

CONTINUATION ROUTE 7

NIEUWE MAAS
Continuation of Nieuwe Waterweg. Lit beacons.

2·1km/1·1M
VLAARDINGEN Buitenhaven entrance
MHW 2·0m, MLW 0·4m.
HrMr ☎ (010) 4340044. Prinses Julianabrug ☎ (010) 4342370.
Customs m-f 0800-1645 ☎ (010) 4357333, other times (010) 4761666.
F.R&G entrance Lts at km 1010·8. Buitenhaven (minimum depth 3·2m) is uncomfortable. Continue through Keersluis (closed when river level is NAP +1·10m).
Railway bridge (ht 0·7m), and **Prinses Julianabrug** (ht 0·8m) to Oude Haven (minimum depth 2·7m).
⚓ E quay, WV Vlaardingen ☎ (010) 4346786/434-9535/4742332. 7·5t crane at PVV De Kulk, ☎ (010) 4709223.

5·4km/2·9M
⚓ SCHIEDAM. Entrance to Spuihaven.
N bank at km 1007·3. F.R Lt on W entrance wall only, at km 1007·2. Yacht haven of WV Nieuwe

Waterweg and Jachtclub Schiedam, toilets and showers. Depth 2–3m. Laundrette 750m. Yards and lifting facilities in Schiedam (ent at km 1006·5).
Customs Merwehaven, km 1006, Marconistraat 105, ☎ (010) 4761666

5·7km/3·2M
⚓ ROTTERDAM. Entrance to Veerhaven.
MHW NAP +1·20m, MLW NAP −0·45m.
Haven Coordinatie Centre (see Chapter 3) VHF Ch 11, 14 ☎ (010) 4251400/4251410
Customs ☎ 4765144 (weekdays, working hours), 4761666 (other times).
Veerhaven. N bank at km 1001·5 between Westerkade and Willemskade; moored tugs, ships or barges sometimes make it difficult to spot. No entrance Lts. Pontoon marina of Kon. R and ZV (Royal Rowing and Sailing Club) De Maas, toilets and showers. ☎ (010) 4137681 (moorings), 4138514 (club). Chandlery facilities in the city. 10t slipway, Jachtwerf De Hudson, Vroesenkade 160, ☎ (010) 4662051

1·5km/0·8M
2 ⚓ Stbd side of river. **Koninginnebrug** (bascule ht 2·5m) and **railway lift bridge** (ht 7·2m), on port side of the river fixed clearance is 8m. VHF Ch 18.
Service hours once per hour or per two hours depending on trains, Sundays only 4 to 5 times whole day. See *Openingstijden spoorbruggen.*

4·4km/2·4M
⚓ **Brienenoordbrug** (ht fixed part 23·8m NAP +25·04m). For opening span at N end 2 hours advance notice, ☎ (010) 4142685/4143911, VHF Ch 20. Not during peak hours 0700-0845, 1600-1800.

0·8km/0·5M
⚓ WV IJsselmonde, S bank, toilets and showers, depth 1–2m, opposite the mouth of Hollandse IJssel. 1½t crane, 15t slipway, ☎ (010) 4828333.

Rotterdam's Euromast from across the Coolhaven

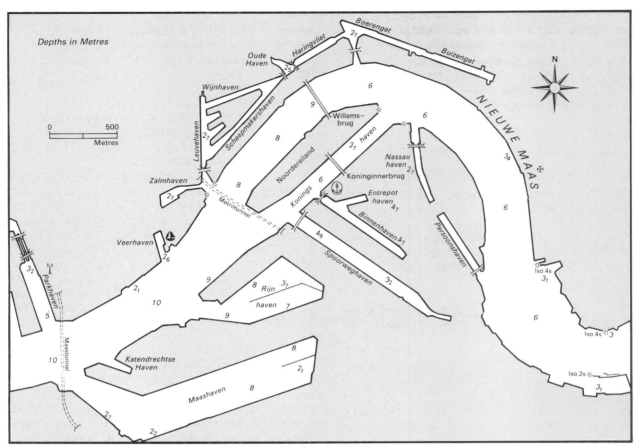

Rotterdam and the Nieuwe Maas bend

1·9km/1·0M

⚓ Bakkerskil entrance to buoyed channel (G to stbd, R to port entering) N bank. Port along channel then port at *BK6* R buoy (minimum depth 1·9m) into Sliksloot and stbd into WV De Hollandse IJssel toilets and showers. MHW NAP +1·0 to 1·25m. MLW NAP −0·35m.

3·0km/1·6M

⚓ **NOORD**. Stbd. Lt beacons. Minimum depth 3·6m, mainly over 5m.

1·7km/0·9M

⚓ Jachthaven WV St Joris, Ridderkerk. W bank. Iso.G.4s Lt on N corner of entrance, yacht haven on S side. Toilets and showers, 10t slipway. ☎ (01804) 23357. MHW NAP +0·97 to 1·22m. MLW NAP −0·30 to −0·38m.

2·3km/1·3M

⚓ **ALBLASSERDAM**. Entrance to Alblas river.
MHW NAP +1·10M. MLW NAP −0·04m
E bank unmarked entrance to Alblas river. Through opening bridge, at all times. Immediately beyond on N side Jachthavens WV Alblasserwaerdt (showers) ☎ (01859) 18381/17427, and WV Alblasserdam. Depth 1·5–2m.

🚗 **Road bridge** (bascule ht fixed span 11·8m, NAP +12·94m, possible for many yachts, particularly at LW). **Opening bridge** E side (ht 6·4m):
Service hours m-sa 0600-2200 (to 2000 only *1/10-1/4*); m-f *1/6-1/10* closed 0700-0845, 1600-1730; su/h *16/4-16/10* 0830-1100, 1800-2000, *16/10-16/4* closed.

0·9km/0·5M

⚓ To port round E side of Sophiapolder.

3·6km/2·0M

⚓ **DORDRECHT**
Wijnhaven entrance on Dordrecht Island.

See Route 5 for Dordrecht and its facilities.

Dordrecht. Water front over the Oude Maas

6. Zuid-Holland – lakes and canals

Route 8
Rotterdam to Amsterdam via Schiphol

Commentary

This is a route which needs time, with 37 opening bridges, including one problem railway bridge at Gouda, and the night convoy through Amsterdam's Nieuwemeersluis and 14 opening bridges including a railway bridge at each end. But there is much to see meandering through mainly non-industrial and typical early Dutch canal and polder scenery. There are lakes, windmills, and interesting old towns and villages, and the final part of the route is past Schiphol Airport on the 19th-century Ringvaart van de Haarlemmermeerpolder (not quite as difficult to pronounce as that unmentionable Welsh town!).

Kagerplassen. Yacht haven at Buitenkaag

The IJssel is typical of the unending interest along this route, passing waterside towns, shops, a ferry, houses, gardens and private docks. Gouda has a beautiful spacious market square with a 15th-century town hall, a 1668 cheese weigh-house (*waag*), and a long commercial history: cloth trading, pipe-making, pottery, bricks, candles, and cheese. Visit the Municipal Museum in the 17th-century Catharina Gasthuis, and do try the *stroopwafels* (syrup waffles) of the area.

Alphen aan de Rijn is a leafy town with plenty of open spaces and a famous tropical aviary and park.

Mooring and sailing facilities are excellent on the lakes, the Braassemermeer, Westeinder Plas, and on the Nieuwe Meer near Amsterdam with restaurants, yacht clubs and interesting residential areas near the shores and entrance channels.

Oude Wetering looking towards Braassemermeer

Distance 80km/43M
Bridges 37 opening, 1 of which has 25m fixed clearance, and including a major rail/motorway bridge, and a major rail/motorway/lock complex.
Locks 3
Tides, heights and soundings
Non-tidal except for 24km/13M tidal stretch from Rotterdam along the Nieuwe Maas and IJssel to Julianasluis, Gouda. In this stretch heights are given to MHW and soundings to MLW, and these range from: Rotterdam MHW NAP +1·0m, MLW NAP −0·5m; Gouda MHW NAP +1·3m, MLW NAP −0·6m.

In the non-tidal areas heights and soundings are given to canal level (*kanaalpeil KP*), weir level (*stuwpeil SP*) or polder level (*polderpeil PP*).

On the short tidal stretch at Rotterdam the flood starts about half an hour before HW Hoek and the ebb at Gouda at 3 hours after HW Hoek, just about long enough to take the distance on one tide although the stream, particularly up the IJssel, is weak, 3km/1·6kn maximum unless there are exceptional river-flood conditions.

Minimum depths en route
2·4m on the Ringvaart, but often less than 2m in many of the small yacht harbours.
Charts
ANWB *J*, *H* and *I*. Stroomatlas *e*.

Route description

ROTTERDAM Veerhaven entrance
See Route 7 for details of facilities.

NIEUWE MAAS
Take the river eastwards.

1·5km/0·8M
2 ⌂ Stbd side of river. **Koninginnebrug** (bascule ht 2·5m) and **railway lift bridge** (ht 7·2m). On the port side of the river fixed clearance is 8m. VHF Ch 18.
Service hours once per hour or per two hours, depending on trains; Sundays only 4 to 5 times whole day. See *Openingstijden spoorbruggen*.

4·4km/2·4M
⌂ **Brienenoordbrug** (ht fixed part 23·8m NAP +25·04m). For opening span at N end 2 hours advance notice, ☎ (010) 4142685/4143911, VHF Ch 20. Not during peak hours 0700-0845, 1600-1800 nor sa/su.

⚓ WV IJsselmonde, S bank, toilets and showers, depth 1–2m, opposite the mouth of Hollandse IJssel. 15t crane ☎ (010) 4828333.

1·1km/0·6M
⌐ **HOLLANDSE IJSSEL** to port. Minimum depth 3m.

2·0km/1·1M
« ⌂ **Krimpen aan de IJssel storm flood barrier.** MHW NAP+1·2m. MLW NAP−0·27m
Algera bascule bridge (ht 7·5m MHW) and **lock**, N side.
Service hours m-f 0600-0700, 0845-1645, 1830-2000; sa 0600-2000; su/h *16/4-16/10* 0700-0900, 1700-1900, *16/10-16/4* closed.

3·0km/1·6M
CAPELLE AAN DEN IJSSEL
⚓ W bank. Jachthaven 't Zandrak (depth 1·75m), ☎ (010) 4503444, toilets, showers, 3·5t crane, 30t boat-lift, laundrette near cafeteria 'Kapiteiskamer'.

11·5km/6·2M
GOUDA
⌐ To port and 400m to:
« 2 ⌂ **Julianasluis lock** and 2 **drawbridges** (ht 1·7m, 3·2m). VHF Ch 18.
Service hours m-f 24 hours; sa 0000-2200; su/h *16/4-16/10* 0600-2400, *16/10-16/4* 0800-1600, 2200-2400.

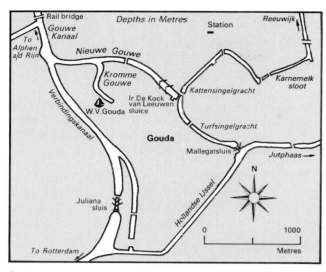

Gouda

GOUWE KANAAL
13·5kph/7·3kn max, 9kph/4·9kn in Boskoop built-up area and Gouda town canals. Minimum depth 3·1m.

NIEUWE GOUWE AND KROMME GOUWE
Stbd after 1·5km into Nieuwe Gouwe and stbd again after 500m yacht harbour into Kromme Gouwe. WV Gouda, toilets, showers, ☎ (01820) 20610. Laundrettes: Lent, Karnemelksloot 84; Wassen en stomen, Graaf Florisweg 155.

If you are prepared to go through an opening bridge, a lock and other opening bridges you can lie in this picturesque town's Turfsingelgracht or Kattensingelgracht.

2·7km/1·5M
⌒ **Railway swing bridge** (ht 4·3m). Opens for a few minutes once per hour so long waits are possible. Particularly short working day Sundays (1145-1550, *16/4-16/10*) see ANWB *Openingstijden spoorbruggen*.

1·1km/0·6M
⌒ **Coencoopbrug** (bascule, ht 4·3m). VHF Ch 18.
Service hours m 0450-2400; t-th 24 hours; f 0000-2200; sa 0600-1800; su/h *1/6-1/9* 1000-1800, *1/9-1/6* closed.

Coencoopbrug

2·2km/1·2M
WADDINXVEEN
⌒ **Waddinxveen lift bridge** (ht 2·5m). VHF Ch 18.
Service hours as above for Coencoopbrug except: m 0500-2400.

3·4km/1·8M
BOSKOOP
⌒ **Boskoop lift bridge** (ht 2·5m). VHF Ch 18.
Service hours as above for Coencoopbrug except: m 0530-2400.

OTWEGWETERING
⌒ ⚓ 1·2km N of bridge on W bank turn to port into Otwegwetering through opening drawbridge (ht 1·4m) to WV De Gouwe.
Bridge service hours m-f 0730-0815, 0945-1130, 1330-1500, 1600-1800; sa/su/h via arrangement with yacht haven.

5·5km/3·0M
⌒ **Gouwsluis railway swing bridge** (ht 1·5m). VHF Ch 18.
Service hours Usually left open for two 18-minute periods per hour, but see ANWB *Openingstijden spoorbruggen*.

0·3km/0·2M
⌒ **Gouwsluis lift bridge** (ht 4·4m). VHF Ch 18.
Service hours as above for Coencoopbrug except: m 0600-2400.

Passing through the railway swing bridge looking towards the lift bridge at Gouwsluis

OUDE RIJN
⌐ To port is Oude Rijn. 9kph/4·9kn max. Depth 2·8m.

ALPHEN AAN DE RIJN
3 ⌒ **Drawbridge** (ht 1·6m, 1·95m fixed part). VHF Ch 18. **Kon. Julianabrug** (bascule bridge, ht 4·4m) **Alb. Schweitzerbrug** (bascule bridge, ht 5·5m).
Service hours as above for Coencoopbrug except: m 0600-2400.

A simple Dutch church at Alphen aan de Rijn

Albert Schweitzer bascule bridge at Alphen aan de Rijn

⚓ For 2-hour periods only, on E bank near town centre where signposted. For commercial vessels and large yachts on the E bank between Juliana- and Albert Schweitzer bridges. Laundrette, Listerlaan 46. 12t crane, Jachtwerf Daniel, ☎ (01720) 22219. 50t boat-lift, Scheepswerf Kempers, ☎ (01720) 31301.

HEIMANSWETERING
➤ To stbd is Heimanswetering. 13·5kph/7·3kn max. Depth 3·1m. **WOUDWETERING** continuation also.

3·8km/2·1M
🌉 **'s-Molenaarsbrug** (bascule bridge, ht 4·4m) VHF Ch 18.
Service hours as above for Coencoopbrug except: m 0600-2400.

2·6km/1·4M
WOUBRUGGE
🌉 **Woubrugge bascule bridge** (ht 2·5m, 2·75m fixed part), VHF Ch 18.
Service hours as above for Coencoopbrug except m 0600-2400.

⚓ Several boatyards each bank of Woudwetering, from S to N:
S of Woubrugge: Gebr. v. d. Laan, W side 12t crane, ☎ (01729) 8113/8177. Jachtwerf Molenaar, W side, S of the Woubrugge. 3½t crane ☎ (01729) 8105.

N of Woubrugge: Jachtwerf Hollandia, W side, toilets, washing facilities, 5t crane, ☎ (01729) 8130/8297. Woubrugse Jachtwerf (both banks), toilets, showers, 16t crane, ☎ (01729) 8120.

Yacht haven on the W side of Woudwetering N of Woubrugge

BRAASSEMERMEER
13·5kph/7·3kn max, 16kph/8·6kn outside the channel. Generally 2m depth, and 3·5m in channel. Buoyed channel (R on west side).

2·0km/1·1M
➤ Paddegat entrance to lake. Fl.R.8s Lt on western point.

⚓ **W bank Oude Wetering**: Jachthaven W.S.V. Braassemermeer. Watersportcentrum Braassemermeer, 3t crane ☎ (01713) 4002. Jachthaven De Brasem, toilets, showers, 2t crane ☎ (01713) 2664. 80t boat-lift at De Bock en Meijer B.V. ☎ (01713) 2208.

⚓ **E bank Rijnsaterwoude**: Jachthaven Meerzicht, toilets, showers, ☎ (01721) 8204.

3·0km/1·6M
➤ ⚓ Entrance to Oude Wetering. Fl.R.8s Lt on W point. Moorings each side.

RINGVAART VAN DE HAARLEMMERMEER-POLDER. 9kph/4·9kn max. Depth 2·3m.

1·2km/0·6M
➤ **Weteringbrug** and stbd along the Ringvaart

2·1km/1·1M

⌕ Leimuiderbrug bascule bridge (ht 2·56m)
Service hours m 0500-2400; t-th 24 hours; f 0000-2200; sa *16/4-16/10* 0600-2000, *16/10-16/4* 0600-1900; su/h *16/4-16/10* 0800-1300, 1400-2000, *16/10-16/4* closed.

WESTEINDER PLAS
16kph/8·6kn max, 9kph/4·9kn after sunset, and in the Ringvaart channel. Minimum depth 2·2m over most of Grote Poel, 1·6–2m over most of Kleine Poel, and 2·4m in Ringvaart channel at N edge.

2·5km/1·3M

Wijde Gat entrance, keep to channel along bank.

⚓ N shore Westeinder Plas there are at least 16 yacht harbours in and around the Kleine Poel (see plan), mostly with showers and toilets. Various lifting facilities, including 50t crane at Eshuis Marine on the Ringvaart near Aalsmeerderbrug, ☎ (02977) 40666.
SW end Grote Poel: Jachthaven Princessepaviljoen, toilets, showers, 10t crane.
E bank/Kalslagen: Jachthaven De Westeinder.
E bank/Kudelstaart: Jachthaven Kempers, toilets, showers, 1t crane, ☎ (02977) 24790.
Laundrette at Jachthaven 't Drijfhuis, Recreatiepark Aalsmeer.

Sunset over the Ringvaart near Westeinder Plas

RINGVAART VAN DE HAARLEMMERMEER-POLDER

4·6km/2·5M

⌕ Aalsmeer bascule bridge (ht 2·5m).
Service hours as above for Leimuiderbrug.

Vessels over 23m air draught require 2 weeks advance permission from Schiphol flight control to continue as far as Nieuwe Meer, since Schiphol flight path crosses the canal in this stretch. This is obtained via Provincial Waterstaat Noord-Holland, ☎ (023) 174242.

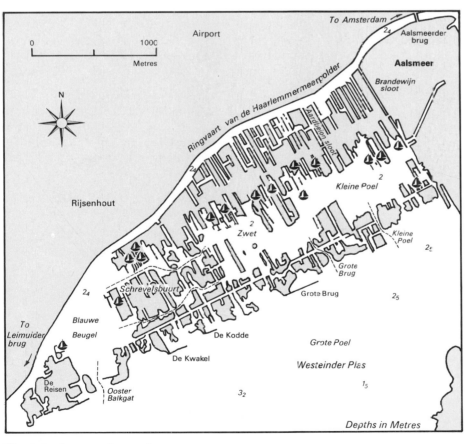

Westeinderplassen northern end

5·3km/2·9M

Bosrandbrug (ht 1·46m, 1·73–1·88m fixed part)
Service hours as above for Leimuiderbrug except sa *16/4-16/10* 0600-2200; su/h *1/4-6/4* and *16/10-1/11* 0800-1200, 1400-1700, *16/4-16/10* 0800-1300, 1400-2200, *1/11-1/4* closed.

Bosrandbrug on the Ringvaart near Schiphol

0·8km/0·4M

Schiphol drawbridge (ht 3·45m)
Service hours m 0500-0730, 0830-1630, 1800-2400; t-th 0000-0730, 0830-1630, 1800-2400; f 0000-0730, 0830-1630, 1800-2200; sa *16/4-16/10* 0600-2200, *16/10-16/4* 0600-1900; su/h *16/4-16/10* 0800-1300, 1400-2100, *16/10-16/4* closed.

Entrance to Rieker Plas from Ringvaart

0·2km/0·1M

Schiphol bascule bridge (ht 6·5m, 7·5m fixed part)
Service hours m-f 0500-0630, 1230-1330, 2000-2100; sa *16/4-16/10* 0700-0800, 1230-1330, 1900-2000, *16/10-16/4* 0700-0800, 1230-1330, 1800-1900; su/h *16/4-16/10* 0800-1030, 1830-2100 (on hr and ½hr), *16/10-16/4* closed.

RIEKER PLAS/NIEUWE MEER
7·5kph/4kn max. Depth 2–3·6m generally, but shallower in places so stay close to the buoys.

1·6km/0·9M

Entrance. Lt R buoy to stbd. F.Y Lt to port. 3 other R Lt buoys along S side of lake.

Behind Rieker Plas entrance Lt: Jachthaven Driessen, toilets, showers, laundrette, 25t boat-lift, 1·5t crane, ☎ (020) 151508.

N side Rieker Plas: WV Onklaar Anker, 2·6m, toilets, showers.

S side Nieuwe Meer S to N: Watersport B.V. WV De Schinkel ☎ (020) 445713 (and several other yacht havens and boatyards on the IJsloot creek). WV De Koenen, toilets, showers.

Jachthaven Het Bosch, toilets, showers, 5t crane, ☎ (020) 449696. WV Amsterdam, toilets, washing facilities, 10t crane.

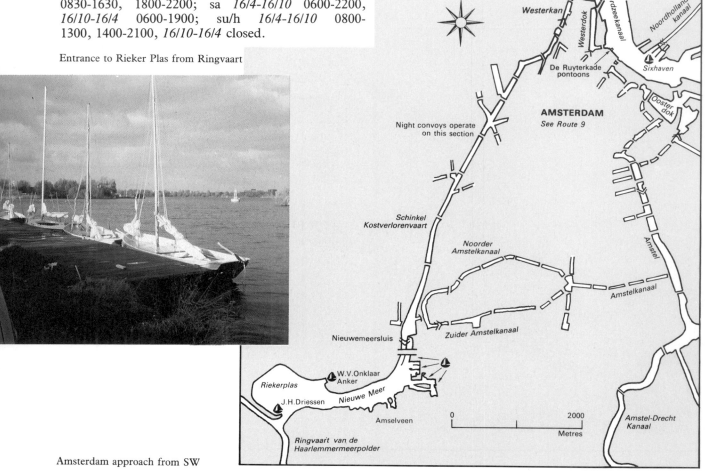

Amsterdam approach from SW

2·7km/1·5M

AMSTERDAM

« 3 ◢. **Nieuwemeersluis**, and **14 opening bridges,** including a railway bridge at each end (ht 5m) and 12 road bridges ht 2·4–3·66m).

Service hours Because of the heavy railway traffic night convoys are arranged for vessels over 5m air draught. At Nieuwemeersluis vessels must gather at 2300 and those travelling S gather at the Singelgracht at the other end at 0200. For instructions contact Nieuwemeersluis or Westerkeersluis on VHF Ch 22, or HrMr for the inland waterways, James Wattstraat 84, ☎ (020) 5683683/225113.

Service hours road bridges m-f 0000-0700, 0900-1600, 2000-2400; sa/su/h 0900-1700.

6·8km/3·7M

⌐ **NOORDZEEKANAAL** to starboard
See Route 13 for details of rest of route to Amsterdam.

1·8km/1·0M

⚓ **AMSTERDAM SIXHAVEN**

Amsterdam. Harbour office building, with pontoon marina off De Ruyterkade

Buitenkaag on the Kagerplassen

Route 9
Rotterdam to Amsterdam via Haarlem and the Noordzeekanaal

Commentary

See also Route 8. This route is 12M longer than Route 8, with roughly similar numbers of locks and opening bridges, but has more places to visit and avoids the night convoy of Amsterdam, entering the city along the Noordzeekanaal. The Sassenheim road and motorway bridge has limited opening times particularly at weekends so take care to look up the timetable; the same applies to the Spaarndam motorway bridge.

The Keukenhof Gardens at Lisse are en route if you are lucky enough to be cruising during the tulip season. On this stretch of the Ringvaart it is interesting to look east down a four metre bank onto the Haarlemmermeerpolder whilst to the west the pasture land is level with the canal. The Cruquius Museum, the old steam-pumping station of the Haarlemmermeerpolder, is on the approach to Heemstede.

Haarlem, built on a network of canals off the river Spaarne with serrated moated ramparts on its northern side, is another city with a charter dating from the 13th century and a wealth of old buildings. These include the famous almshouses one of which houses the Frans Hals museum, the Grote Kerk with Frans Hals tomb and a magnificent organ once played by Mozart, the Vleeshal and Vishal (guildhalls) with their painting exhibitions, and the ancient Teijlers museum. After an exhilarating sail on the Noorder Buiten Spaarne or the Mooie Nel it is also well worth lying in the yacht harbour of the attractive village of Spaarndam with its painted gabled houses before going through the lock and heading for the Noordzeekanaal.

Finally if you are fit and have a good bicycle you must visit the national park De Kennemer Duinen. It is the wooded dune park between Haarlem, IJmuiden and the sea, nearest to the Spaarne at Haarlem.

Distance 102km/55M

Bridges 38 opening bridges; including 9 through Haarlem which can if necessary be opened in succession, 2 rail and 1 motorway bridge.

Locks 2

Tides, heights and soundings
See Route 8.

Minimum depths en route
2·3m in the Ringvaart, but often less than 2m in some yacht harbours, for example 1·2m in the Mooie Nel .

Charts
ANWB *J*, *H*, and *G*. *Stroomatlas e*.

Route description

ROTTERDAM Veerhaven entrance
See Route 7 for details of facilities in Rotterdam.

See Route 8 for details of route from Rotterdam to Ringvaart van de Haarlem mermeerpolder.

RINGVAART VAN DE HAARLEMMERMEER-POLDER. 9kph/4·9kn max. Depth 2·3m.

51·3km/27·7M
⚓ **Weteringbrug** and to port through **Weteringbrug bascule bridge** (ht 2·6m).
Service hours m-f 0600-2200; sa *16/4-1/6* 0700-2000, *1/6-1/9* 0700-2100, *1/9-16/10* 0700-2000, *16/10-16/4* 0700-1700; su/h *16/4-16/10* 0900-1300, 1400-2000, *16/10-16/4* closed.

1·6km/0·9M
⛵ **Meerbrug** (0·85m swing bridge)
Service hours as above for Weteringbrug except: su/h *1/6-1/9* 0800-1300, 1400-2100 (other su/h as Weteringbrug).

BUITENKAAG
VVV pontoon on the N bank of Ringvaart near ferry.

DETOUR TO THE KAGERPLASSEN
Several entrances to lakes on S side of Ringvaart opposite Buitenkaag/Huigsloot bank. 13·5kph/7·3kn maximum speed in lakes. Depths range from less than 1m to 10m, so the ANWB chart is essential. There are no bridges en route to the moorings listed below:

⚓ Harbours at Rijpwetering
On eastern offshoot of lakes, best approached from either the Ringvaart, via the Ade (2·4m depth), or via the Kagerplassen through the Kever (1·5m depth) and the Diepenhoek (2·5m) into the Koppoel (1·6m depth), 6kph/3·2kn max.

⚓ Moorings at: town quay, Jachthaven De Koppoel/V.J. Jonkman (1·6m depth), Jachthaven P. van Haestregt (7t crane), Jachtwerf G.J. Zoetemelk (4t crane).

⚓ Sassenheim
200m along Sassenheimervaart (2·5m depth) off the Dieperpoel at N end of lakes; Jachthaven Jonkman, depth 1·5m, showers, ½t crane, ☎ (02522) 11583.

⚓ Kaag Island area at N end of lakes
Jachthaven Kaagdorp on S side Ringvaart before ferry, 2m depth. Jachthavens Schuilenburg, 't Kompas, Twee Wilgen, Jachthaven Eymershof (showers and toilets, 1t crane, ☎ (02524) 5157), J. van Asselt (1·5t crane, ☎ (02524) 4233). Also Möllers, 3t crane, ☎ (02524) 4494, and V.d. Wansem Service, 1t crane.

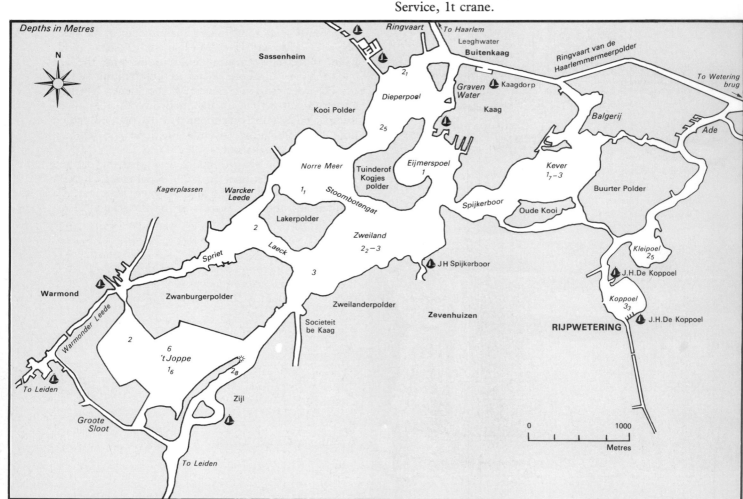

Kagerplassen

⚓ Zevenhuizen

S shore, at entrance of Zevenhuizervaart, depth 1·4m. Jachthaven Spijkerboor, toilets, showers, 4t crane, ☎ (01712) 8869. 4t crane at Jachthaven De Horizon.

Kaag Societeit

S shore, is a private club with limited mooring availability.

Warmond

SW end of lakes. 7·2kph/3·9kn max Warmonder Leede. Municipal HrMr, ☎ (01711) 11192).

⚓ Moorings municipal 445 quay NE of bridge, and round Leede and 't Joppe sides of Koudenhoorn where there are toilets and showers.

⚓ **N end of town**: Jachthaven Gebr. Visch, toilets, washing facilities, 3t crane, ☎ (01711) 10300. Jachthaven 't Fort, toilets, showers, 2t crane, ☎ (01711) 19205. Jachthaven Cieco, toilets, showers. **Groote Sloot**: Jachtbouw Aad Juffermans, toilets, 20t boat-lift, ☎ (01711) 10548.

⚓ **S end of town**: Jachthaven Houweling K.P.M., toilets, showers, 25t crane, ☎ (01711) 10226. Jachthaven Lockhorst, toilets, 8t crane, ☎ (01711) 10378. Jachthaven KWV De Kaag, W Haven, toilets, showers, 2·5t crane, ☎ (01711) 10035. Several other boatyards.

RINGVAART VAN DE HAARLEMMERMEER-POLDER Continue along Ringvaart.

4·9km/2·6M

2 ⮧ **Sassenheim rail and road bascule bridges** (ht 4·4/5·13m opening parts, 4·7/4·95m fixed parts). No mooring between.

Service hours (joint) m-f 0605-0715, 1220-1320, 1840-1930; sa 1010-1100, 1410-1430, 1850-1900; su/h *16/4-16/10* 1710-1930, *16/10-16/4* closed.

4·2km/2·3M

⮧ **Lisserbrug** (drawbridge ht 1m)

Service hours m-f 0700-0800, 0900-1700, 1800-2100; sa *16/4-16/10* 0900-1700, *16/10-16/4* 0900-1400; su/h *16/4-16/10* 1000-1200, 1630-1830, *16/10-16/4* closed.

Lisserbrug

4·2km/2·3M

⮧ **Hillegommerbrug** (drawbridge ht 1m)

Service hours as above for Lisserbrug except: m-f 0700-2100; su/h *16/4-16/10* 0930-1130, 1700-1900, *16/10-16/4* closed.

3·7km/2·0M

⮧ **Bennebroekerbrug** (bascule ht 1·05m)

Service hours as above for Lisserbrug except: m-f 0700-2100; su/h *16/4-16/10* 0900-1100, 1730-1930, *16/10-16/4* closed.

⚓ WV Van Merlenhaven (toilets and showers) in the Sportpark is approached along an inlet from the N bank 1km before the next bridge, but I found only 1m of water in the entrance in 1987.

3·2km/1·7M

⮧ **Cruquiusbrug** (drawbridge ht 2·7m)

Service hours m-f 0700-2200; sa *16/4-16/10* 0800-1700, *16/10-16/4* 0800-1600; su/h *16/4-16/10* 0830-1030, 1800-2030, *16/10-16/4* closed.

Cruquius Polder Museum is on the S bank immediately after the bridge, and there are shored-up banks on each side of the bridge, but pick your place and beware of grounding.

0·2km/0·1M

🢆 **ZUIDER BUITEN SPAARNE** to port 6kph/3·2kn max. Depth 2·5m.

HEEMSTEDE and HAARLEM

⚓ Small yacht harbour without facilities, possible free space, 1·3m depth, inside entrance and on N side Haven Kanaal which leaves E bank Spaarne just before first bridge.

9 ⮧ Haarlem HrMr ☎ (023) 274556. VHF Ch 18 Havendienst. Harbour office N bank N of Prinsenbrug. Opening bridges in succession from S to N:

Schouwbroekerbrug (drawbridge ht 4·3m), **Buitenrustbrug** (double drawbridge ht 2·15m), **Langebrug** (drawbridge ht 2·2m), **Melkbrug** (swing bridge ht 2–2·1m), **Gravestenenbrug** (double drawbridge ht 2·55–3·55m), **Catharijnebrug** (swing bridge ht 2·4m), **railway bridge** (bascule ht 4·5m), **Prinsenbrug** (bascule ht 2·85m), **Waarderbrug** (drawbridge ht 1·9m).

Haarlem railway bridge and beyond Prinsenbrug

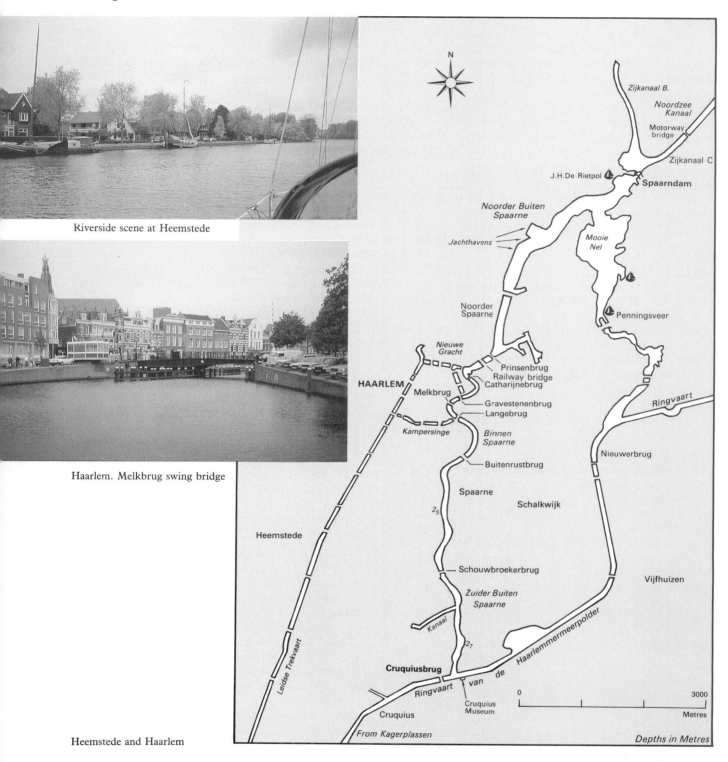

Riverside scene at Heemstede

Haarlem. Melkbrug swing bridge

Heemstede and Haarlem

Road bridge service hours m-f 0840-1600, 1740-2100, vessels passing Prinsenbrug S or Buitenrustbrug N before 2100 hours allowed through all bridges. sa *16/10-16/4* 0900-1400, *16/4-1/6* and *1/9-16/10* 0900-1700, *1/6-1/9* 0900-1830. Vessels passing Waarderbrug or Schouwbroekerbrug before 1400, 1700, 1830 on above respective dates allowed through all bridges. su/h *16/4-1/6* and *1/9-16/10* from Waarderbrug 1800, from Schouwbroekerbrug 1700, 1900; *1/6-1/9* from Waarderbrug 1745, 1900, from Schouwbroekerbrug 1700, 1900.

Railway bridge service hours These are coordinated by the Haarlem HrMr and on weekdays in season vary from 1 to 3 times per hour, so the route through all 9 bridges is governed by the times arranged for this bridge. Make sure you inform the HrMr which bridges you do intend to go through; you may not need the railway bridge .

⚓ In Haarlem, K.R. and Z.V. Het Spaarne (W bank Zuider Buiten Spaarne), E bank between Gravenstenen and Melkbrug, and various other stretches S of the railway bridge with the agreement of HrMr.

Spaarndam. Looking back to the town from N of the lock. Note wreck in right foreground, this is a dangerous shallow, keep to the main channel or the E bank

Haarlem. Langebrug drawbridge. We had half an hour to wait here, and from then on the 7 bridges northward opened in succession

7·4km/4·0M
NOORDER BUITEN SPAARNE
At Waarderbrug, 16kph/8·6kn max. Depth 3·5m.
⚓ **E shore from S to N**: Haarlemse Jachtclub, showers. Jachtwerf De Drijver, showers, toilets, 1t crane, 10t boat-lift ☎ (023) 379204. Jachtwerf Wetterwille, 1t crane.

MOOIE NEL
Entrance W of island, keeping about 25m off the Haarlem side. Lake generally 1–10m depth sometimes less than 1m, so take care. Jachthaven Haarlemse Z.V. E side of lake, only 1·4m depth, keep to middle of entrance channel, showers. S end near Penningsveer only 1·2m depth. Jachthavens Watervrienden, A. Peetoom (toilets, showers, 10t crane. 30t boat-lift), Assema, and L.J. Poolman.

SPAARNDAM
⚓ Jachthaven De Rietpol, N corner of Noorder Buiten Spaarne, at visitors' boxes through narrow entrance (with a houseboat to stbd) immediately to the S of the sheds and offices on the peninsula. Toilets, showers, 40t crane, ☎ (023) 371470.

Jachthaven de Rietpol at Spaarndam

ZIJKANAAL C
15kph/8·1kn max. Depth 3·5m.

2·9km/1·6M
≪ ⚓ **Grote Sluis lock** (exposed when entering in SW winds) and **drawbridge** (ht 2·35m). Shallows to port beyond lock.
Service hours (bruggeld payment) m-f 0600-2200; sa 0600-2000; su/h *16/4-16/10* 0730-1000, 1700-2100, *16/10-16/4* 0900-1000, 1600-1700.

1·0km/0·5M
⚓ **Motorway bridge** (bascule ht 6·9m), not opened in high winds and poor visibility.
Service hours m-f 0545-0700, 1200-1300, 2000-2100; sa 0700-0800, 1200-1300, 1645-1715; su/h *1/4-16/10* 0800-0900, 1730-1740, 2040-2050, *16/10-1/4* 0900-1000, 1600-1700.

⚓ WV IJmond, N bank, toilets, showers, 20t crane, ☎ (023) 375003.

2·0km/1·1M
⚓ **Drawbridge** to Buitenhuizen (ht 3·8m)
Service hours m-f 0500-2300; sa 0500-2100; su/h *1/4-16/10* 0700-0750, 0910-1030, 1700-1715, 1800-1815, 2010-2020, 2100-2115, *16/10-1/4* 0830-1030, 1530-1730.

0·2km/0·1M
⚓ **NOORDZEEKANAAL** to starboard
See Route 13 for the rest of this route to Amsterdam.

14·7km/7·9M
⚓ **AMSTERDAM SIXHAVEN**

7. The Great Rivers and the Biesbosch

Route 10
Rotterdam to Lobith via the Lek and Neder-Rijn

Commentary

This is the best route for travelling eastwards since the three major sluices with their neighbouring locks at Hagestein, Amerongen and Driel control and reduce the downstream current. You need a VHF radio to contact the sluices as well as a powerful and reliable engine as there is heavy barge traffic from all over Europe on these wide rivers, and the weirs are sometimes partially or fully open and the downstream current is stronger. You also need to be sure of your mast height – anything much above 12m and you cannot negotiate the fixed bridges. Another caution, beware of the many cross-river ferries of several varieties, e.g. near Pannerden, one which hangs from moorings upstream and crosses the river in an arc.

There is no adequate mooring at Tolkamer/Lobith on the West German border unless your height is less than 9m, in which case the nearby Watersportcentrum de Bijland with a fixed bridge over its entrance is an excellent yacht harbour. The best plan is to double back after Arnhem into the Waal (Route 11) making Nijmegen your next stop. In short, those with motor-cruisers heading for West Germany can afford to smile smugly at this point.

The rivers are marked mainly with lit and painted metal beacons, red on the northern banks and green on the southern; on the Lek and Waal most are occulting, and on the western rivers flashing. On the ends of the spits at major river junctions there are usually white lights isophase or flashing, and at some near-right-angled junctions there are port and starboard-hand (entering) F.R&G lights.

The scenery on all of the Great Rivers is varied; industrial and residential building, spires of old towns, long stretches of open countryside with pasture land, market gardens and fruit orchards often obscured by the dykes, many ferries, and graceful sweeping road and railway bridge-spans of many differing shapes on reach after reach. It has always been a frontier area and often a battleground in Europe and there is a string of fascinating ancient fortress towns along the Lek and Waal most of which have convenient if small yacht harbours.

At Vianen you can take a long walk from WV de Peiler to this delightful small fortified town with its ancient town hall, 14th-century church and broad shopping street running down from the town gate (Lekpoort). From ZV de Lek on the other side of the river you can visit the carefully preserved canal town of Vreeswijk to the south of the new town of Nieuwegein. Culemborg is yet another fortified

town with canal, town hall, Grote Kerk and museum. Wijk bij Duurstede has a castle, a windmill and a variety of ancient buildings. Rhenen has parts of a town wall and a windmill.

Arnhem, municipal centre of Gelderland, was of course badly damaged during the war but has been extensively restored, some old buildings being completely rebuilt. From the Malburgse Haven it is not too far to walk to John Frost bridge renamed after the commander of the airborne battalion which held it for a few heroic days in 1944, and there is a memorial in the nearby Airborneplein sunken garden. At Oosterbeek to the west is the Airborne Monument, a British war cemetery, and a museum in the original command post of the operation.

Distance 133km/72M

Bridges/maximum clearance 3 opening. 8 fixed, minimum clearance weir datum +12·5m. Can be more in certain river conditions. A maximum air draught of 12¼m is comfortable, although you should always consult the height scales before going through.

Locks 3 with occasional alternative direct passages through their sluice/weir gates alongside the normal locks. Hagestein, Amerongen and Driel sluices control the flow of water down the upper Lek and Neder-Rijn, but above all also divert the necessary amount of water along the IJssel further east which flows northwards and in turn tops up the IJsselmeer to the correct levels. The sluice gates are usually lifted when the river is above average levels (Lobith water level (*waterstand*) is broadcast on Dutch radio), but summer water levels are the lowest and usually you will use the locks alongside. If you do have to use the sluices the clearance varies according to the water level of Lobith.

Hagestein (at MHW) 13·2m[1]
Amerongen (when Lobith water level is NAP +12m) 12·9m[1]
Driel (when Lobith water level is NAP +12m) 12·1m[2]

1. Opened when Lobith water level exceeds NAP +11·4m
2. Opened when Lobith water level exceeds NAP +10m

But you need not worry about these calculations. In some cases the channels to the gates are buoyed, and all are well lit and traffic-signposted with standard signs and lights (See Chapter 2 page 17 under *Shipping regulations*) indicating which spans/gates are available. There are mooring places above and

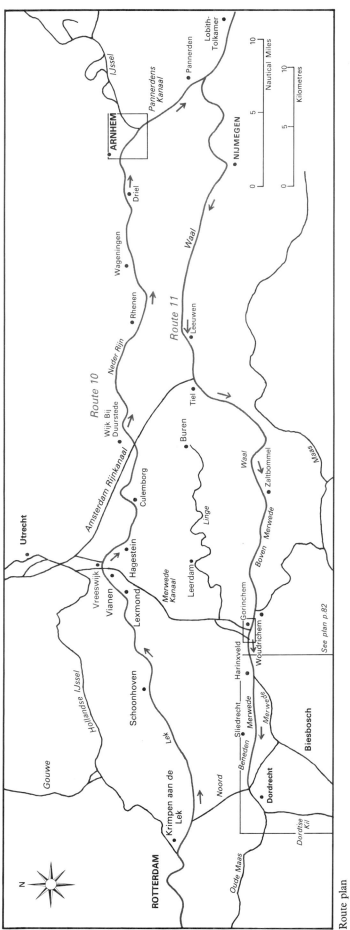

Route plan

Beneden Merwede. Riverside houses on the N bank, which is not all industrial

Hagestein lock and barrage

below each complex, and you should contact Hagestein on VHF Ch 18 and Amerongen and Driel each on Ch 20 for full instructions, giving your air draught if necessary.

Tides, heights and soundings
The route is tidal for 29km/16M upstream as far as Schoonhoven at which point the flood tidal stream becomes weaker than the downstream current. For another 23km/12M to Hagestein the Lek has a downstream current mainly influenced by the outflow from Hagestein. The remaining 81km/44M are sluice-controlled with varying rates of downstream current which also affects the non-canalised section of river below. For example at Wijk bij Duurstede on the canalised section the current varies markedly:

Sluices fully open 4–5kph (2·2–2·7kn)
Sluices partially open 3–4kph (1·6–2·2kn)
Sluices closed 0·5–1kph (0·3–0·5kn)

Off Rotterdam the flood and ebb streams average 1½kn so on the non-canalised section it helps to start off by using the flood, which starts at Rotterdam about 1 hour before HW Hoek possibly starting an hour or so earlier to give plenty of time to reach Hagestein.

The ANWB chart and the route description below gives bridge heights to MHW and soundings to MLW as far as Hagestein. Above this point heights and soundings are to weir level, *stuwpeil*, which also gives a minimum safe height clearance. The route description below also gives the MHW and MLW NAP differences for the tidal part to show the additional potential range available under the bridges.

Minimum depths en route
Passage route over 3m depth, but some of the small yacht harbours are as little as 1 to 1·5m.

Charts
ANWB charts *J*, *K* and *L*. Stroomatlas *e* gives stream directions for first 9 miles. *Getijtafels voor Nederland* give approximate times of HW and LW on the Great Rivers up to Hagestein (Lek) and Herwijnen (Waal).

Entrance to Sliedrecht haven and WV Sliedrecht

Route description

ROTTERDAM Veerhaven entrance
See Route 7 for details of facilities.

NIEUWE MAAS
Take the river eastwards.

1·5km/0·8M
2 🛥 Stbd side of river. **Koninginnebrug** (bascule ht 2·5m) and **railway lift bridge** (ht 7·2m). On the port side of the river fixed clearance is 8m. VHF Ch 18.
Service hours Once or twice per hour or per two hours depending on trains, Sundays only 4 to 5 times whole day. See *Openingstijden spoorwegbruggen*.

4·4km/2·4M
🛥 **Brienenoordbrug** (ht fixed part 23·8m NAP +25·04m). For opening span at N end 2 hours advance notice, ☎ (010) 4142685/4143911, VHF Ch 20. Not during peak hours 0700-0845, 1600-1800.

0·8km/0·4M
⚓ WV IJsselmonde, S bank, toilets and showers, depth 1–2m, (0·5) Opposite the mouth of Hollandse IJssel. 1·5t crane ☎ (010) 4828333.

1·9km/1·0M
⚓ Bakkerskil entrance to buoyed channel (G to stbd, R to port entering) N bank. Port along channel then port at *BK6* R buoy (minimum depth 1·8m) into Sliksloot and stbd into WV De Hollandse IJssel, depth 1·65-4·15m, toilets, showers. MHW NAP +1·0 to 1·25m, MLW NAP −0·35m.

⚓ RIVER LEK
Stbd to follow the river.

4·1km/2·2M
⚓ Krimpen aan de Lek. Depth 1·3m. N bank. Jachthavens WV 'Smit-Kinderdijk' ('t Balkengat), toilets, showers, ☎ (01807) 15562, and WV De Lek.

7·8km/4·2M
⚓ Streefkerk. S bank. Jachthaven Streefkerk B.V., depth 1·5m, toilets, showers, ☎ (01848) 1828/1873.

9·0km/4·9M
⚓ Schoonhoven. N bank. WV De Zilvervloot through a usually open *keersluis*. Vessels to 1·2m draught. Further E is WV 't Wilgerak, depth 2·5m, toilets, showers.

15·1km/8·2M
⚓ Lexmond. S bank. WV Lexmond. Depth 1·5m. 6t crane, ☎ (03474) 1896.

⚓ VIANEN
S bank. WV De Peiler, depth 2·6m, toilets, showers, ☎ (03473) 76356. 15t boat-lift, Le Comte-Holland B.V. ☎ (03473) 71904.

4·6km/2·5M
🚉 **Vianensebrug** (ht 13·3m MHW)
MHW NAP+1·4m, MLW NAP+0·4m.

VREESWIJK/NIEUWEGEIN-ZUID
⚓ N bank. Jachthaven ZV 'De Lek', depth 1·65m, toilets, showers, HrMr ☎ (03402) 62970.

⚓ If you are prepared to go through the **Koningin-nensluis** there are moorings on the W side of the canal. You may also be able to moor in the Buiten-haven S of the Beatrixsluisen if the lock-keeper agrees.

Vreeswijk

2·8km/1·5M
🚉 **Hagesteinsebrug** (ht 13·8m MHW), MHW NAP+1·4m, MLW NAP+0·4m.

1·8km/1·0M
« **Hagestein lock and weir**. VHF Ch 18.
☎ (03472) 1544 See *Locks* page 73 for instructions to lock through.

Lekbrug. The fixed bridge on the Lek W of Hagestein weir

5·0km/2·7M
CULEMBORG
🚉 **Culemborg railway bridge** (ht 12·9m)
⚓ Jachthaven of WV de Helling close E on S bank. Showers, toilets, laundrette, HrMr ☎ (03450) 16493.

6·4km/3·5M
⚓ S bank. Jachthaven Beusichem. Depth 1·5m. Toilets, showers, laundrette, 7t crane, ☎ (03453) 2530.

4·2km/2·3M
NEDER-RIJN
🚤 Cross Amsterdam-Rijn Kanaal into Neder-Rijn. There are R&G entrance Lts on each side, and in advance on the stbd bank a Fl.Y Lt indicates a ship is about to cross.

1·6km/0·9M
WIJK BIJ DUURSTEDE
⚓ N bank in an old meander of the river with a 'dead end'. Jachthaven WV Rijn en Lek, toilets, showers, HrMr ☎ (03435) 73049.

2·0km/1·1M
EILAND VAN MAURIK
⚓ S bank. Depth 2m-4m. 'Dead' river arm. Jachthaven Watersportcentrum De Loswal, toilets, showers, ☎ (03449) 1572. Jachthaven Eiland van Maurik (in an arm at the eastern end), toilets, showers, laundrette, ☎ (03449) 1502/1232.

1·8km/1·0M
AMERONGEN WEIR
« **Amerongen lock and weir**. VHF Ch 20. See *Locks* page 73 for instructions to lock through.

12·0km/6·5M
RHENEN
⚓ S bank. Jachthaven WV Midden Betuwe, depth 2m or greater, toilets, showers, ☎ (08886) 2772.

0·7km/0·4M
🚉 **Rhenen road bridge** (ht 13·5m)

6·0km/3·2M
WAGENINGEN
⚓ N bank. Jachthaven R.Z. and M.V. Vada. Depth 2·5m, toilets, showers, 10t crane. HrMr ☎ (08370) 15986/14557.

8·8km/4·8M
🚉 **Heteren road bridge** (ht 13·5m)

2·8km/1·5M
DRIEL WEIR
« **Driel lock and weir**. VHF Ch 20. See *Locks* page 73 for instructions to lock through.

3·5km/1·9M
🚉 **Oosterbeek railway bridge** (ht 12·5m)

4·0km/2·2M
ARNHEM
🌉 **Roermondspleinbrug** (ht 13·74–15·78m)

1·0km/0·5M
🌉 **John Frostbrug** (ht 12·6m)

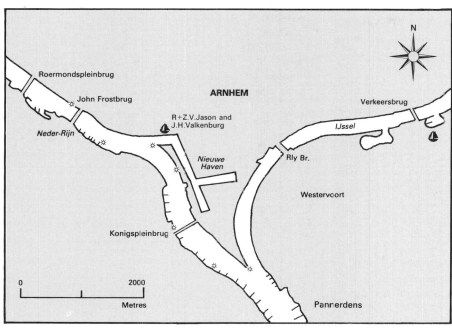

Arnhem

Arnhem. Malburgse Haven on the Neder-Rijn, and the pontoons of ZV Jason and WV Valkenburg

1·6km/0·9M
⚓N bank E of town. Malburgse Haven/Nieuwe Haven. Depth 4·7m. HrMr ☎ (085) 421916/232805, (08812) 1850. R. and Z.V. Jason, toilets, showers, 1t crane, ☎ (085) 615207. Jachthaven Valkenburg, toilets, showers, ☎ (085) 615200. 16t crane, Gebr. van Workum, ☎ (085) 216035.

1·6km/0·9M
🌉 **Koningspleinbrug** (ht 13·9m)

PANNERDENS KANAAL/BIJLANDS KANAAL/BOVEN RIJN

16·2km/8·7M
TOLKAMER/LOBITH
⚓ Customs pontoon for temporary stop.
Vluchthaven is full of commercial shipping and is only advisable as a last resort. Watersportcentrum de Bijland has fixed bridge ht 9m above MR (summer river level) at the entrance, manager's ☎ (08365) 1596/1635/1686/1924. Wibo B.V. 80t crane.

Tolkamer. Customs clearance pontoons for yachts

Route 11
The big rivers – Lobith to Dordrecht via the Waal

Commentary

Read carefully the commentary for Route 10 as well. On this return route westward there are no locks or opening bridges to delay a vessel of up to 12m height, and the downstream current makes the journey fast. If you are prepared to have bridges opened then the trip is feasible with an air draught of up to 13½m.

The scenery is similar to Route 10 but with a little more industrial sprawl along the banks of the Boven and Beneden Merwedes at the end. It has an ample share of old frontier fortress towns with some, often limited, mooring facilities, although most are close to the towns.

Nijmegen dates from Roman times and is associated with the Emperors Charlemagne and Frederick Barbarossa, and with many sieges including its capture in 1944 prior to the Arnhem battle. The river bank rises steeply to the Valkhof, the site of the early stronghold. Like Arnhem, Nijmegen has had to be rebuilt, but there are many places of interest, including remains of the 15th-century town walls, a weigh-house (*waag*), a cloth market, the Belvedere Tower restaurant with views over the river, old houses on the Waalkade, an 11th-century chapel and several museums.

Tiel, market centre for a fruit-growing area, is another 12th-century fortress town also rebuilt as a result of the war. It still has its town wall remains, a Grote Kerk, a rebuilt 17th-century *waterpoort* (gate) and the inevitable museum.

Zaltbommel, like Tiel is an old Hanseatic League town, which survived the war better with most of its historic circular defence works in place. It also has a town hall, weigh-house, Grote Kerk, *waterpoort* and market place.

Gorinchem's fortifications and moats are mainly 16th-century, and there is a town gate (*dalempoort*) and an interesting church, all not far from WV Merwede.

Further west the banks become much more industrial and at Sliedrecht the yacht harbour is reached via an entrance next to a factory building and through a clutter of rusty barges and coasters. Most impressive is the final approach to Dordrecht (see Route 5) with its Groothoofdspoort and Bellevue Hotel on the promontory.

Distance 115km/62M

Bridges/maximum clearance 6 fixed. 3 opening. Maximum clearance of fixed bridges MR (average summer river level) +14·2m so a maximum air draught of 14m is comfortable. The fixed parts of the opening bridges also have a high maximum clearance of MHW +12·2m. A maximum air draught of 12m is comfortable for the latter, but you should always consult the height scales before going through.

Locks None

Tides, heights and soundings

The route is tidal for only 8km/4M downstream from Sliedrecht above which point upstream the flood tidal stream becomes weaker than the downstream current. Off Dordrecht the flood averages 1¼kn and the ebb 1¾kn so leaving with about two hours of flood helps. In the remaining non-canalised rivers Waal and Boven Merwede the downstream current can vary from 3kph/1·6kn to 7kph/3·8kn, but is mainly in the 3·5kph/1·9kn to 5·5kph/3kn range. Travelling downstream therefore is no problem (unless you wish to stop!). A 9kph/4·9kn water speed and an average current of say 3kph gives a speed over the ground of 12kph/6·5kn, so the maximum nonstop time for the whole trip to Dordrecht is under 10 hours. In these conditions it requires a lot of willpower to moor up and rubberneck en route.

On ANWB chart *K* heights are to MHW and soundings to MLW, and on chart *L* on this route both are given to MR, average river level in the six months from May to October inclusive, which is 12 to 20cm less than NR, normal river level, the average for the year as a whole, so always consult the height scales.

Minimum depths en route

At MR (mean summer level) depths on the Waal are over 4m and in the yacht havens mentioned below minimum 1·5m and often 2m or more.

Charts

ANWB charts *K* and *L*. *Stroomatlas e* gives stream directions off Dordrecht. The *Getijtafels* gives approximate times of HW and LW for places up to Herwijnen (Waal).

Route description

TOLKAMER/LOBITH (West Germany on opposite bank). *See Route 10 for details of facilities.*

Westward taking the stbd fork along the Waal river.

NIJMEGEN

Traffic office, VHF Ch 68, ☎ (08897) 74555. Harbour office VHF Ch 12. HrMr ☎ (080) 292696.

19·7km/10·6M

⌖ **Nijmegen road bridge** (ht 16m MR).

⚓ Vluchthaven, depth 4·5m, parallel with the S bank and close downstream of bridge, protected from the current behind a breakwater lined with poles with triangular topmarks, and approached round its western (usually under water) end round a river beacon and close by a RW pole marking the end. New pontoons were scheduled for May 1988. Maximum stay 48 hours. Watch out for river traffic and the current when entering.

Nijmegen railway bridge

1·1km/0·6M

⚓ **Railway bridge** (ht 14·1m MR)

⚓ Waalhaven is a commercial harbour on the S bank close W of bridge. It is usually crammed with large barges, and is only a last resort mooring after contact with the HrMr.

9·0km/4·9M

⚓ **Ewijk road bridge** (15·2m MR)

16·6km/9·0M

BENEDEN LEEUWEN

⚓ S bank, pleasant natural harbour, on S bank, doglegging S and E. Fa. Woudenberg and Zn, toilets, showers, 40t boat-lift, ☎ (08879) 1257. 7t crane, Scheepsrep. Bedr. De Gerlien, ☎ (08879) 2957.

1·1km/0·6M

⚓ **Prins Willem Alexanderbrug** (ht 14·24m MR)

4·2km/2·3M

TIEL

⚓ N bank. Tiel haven, depth 5m. HrMr ☎ (03440) 12971. WV De Waal, toilets, washing facilities, ☎ (03440) 14834.

12·0km/6·5M

➷ Sint Andries Kanaal, continue around bend along Waal. MHW NAP +3·47, MLW NAP +3·34.

8·0km/4·3M

ZALTBOMMEL

2 ⚓ **Zaltbommel railway and road bridges** close together. North side W-going traffic span (ht 15·25–15·5m MHW). S side E-going traffic span (ht 14·95–15·45m MHW). MHW NAP +2·0m, MLW NAP +1·6m.

1·2km/0·6M

⚓ S bank. Zaltbommel Haven (depth 4·0m). Large yachts at quay, smaller at ZV De Golfbreker, S side of haven.

BOVEN MERWEDE

Waal becomes Boven Merwede above Gorinchem. At Herwijnen MHW NAP +1·4m, MLW NAP +1·0m.

18·2km/9·8M

WOUDRICHEM

➷ ⚓ S bank, 1st entrance on W bank of mouth of the Afgedamde Maas. Yacht haven of WV Woudrichem, depth 1·5m, toilets, showers.

3·0km/1·6M

GORINCHEM (GORKUM)

⚓ N bank 1st Voorhaven (Vluchthaven). W of the two Voorhavens. Entrance between F.R&G Lts. Depth 3·2m. WV De Merwede at SE corner, toilets, showers, 6t crane, ☎ (01830) 31697. Along the Linge to the north, well beyond the lock, Jachtwerf Gebr. van Pelt has a 20t crane, ☎ (01830) 25275. If you are prepared to go through the **Grote Merwedesluis** (VHF Ch 18, ☎ (01830) 22865) at the head of the 1st Voorhaven you may find room at the Gorinchemse R & ZV on the peninsula between the Merwede Kanaal and Steenenhoek Kanaal. Pontoons, toilets, showers and laundrette in the Lingehaven through the 2nd Voorhaven and N of the yacht lock, ☎ (01830) 33744.
MHW +1·11m, MLW +0·76m.

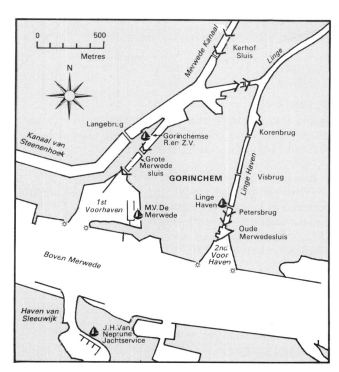

Gorinchem

Gorinchem. The bridge over the Boven Merwede. There is an opening part at the right-hand end

Gorinchem. The yacht haven of WV Merwede in the 1st *voorhaven*

SLEEUWIJK

⚓ S bank. Oude Veerhaven. Jachthaven Van Neptune Jachtservice, depth 3m, toilets, showers, ☎ (01833) 1747.

1·8km/1·0M

🌉 **Gorinchem road bridge** (ht 12·5m MHW, fixed part at S side) opening part N end:
Service hours m-f 0600-2130, sa 0800-1800, su/h closed. By arrangement with lock-keeper Gorinchem ☎ (01830) 33308 or VHF Ch 18.

4·2km/2·3M

BENEDEN MERWEDE

🔀 Beneden Merwede to stbd.

1·0km/0·5M

HARDINXVELD

MHW NAP +0·78 to 1·33m, MLW NAP +0·65 to 0·40m dependent on river outflow.
⚓ N Bank. Boven Hardinxveld, entrance Fl.R Lt on E pier, Gemeentehaven, E end, depth 4·5m, yard and lifting facilities nearby, ☎ (01846) 14904.

8·0km/4·3M
SLIEDRECHT

MHW NAP +0·84m, MLW NAP +0·20m.
⚓ N bank, R&G entrance Lts into Gemeentehaven depth 3·6m. Municipal HrMr ☎ (01840) 19099/ 14176. At E end of haven is WV Sliedrecht, toilets, showers, 10t crane, ☎ (01840) 20073.

Baanhoek railway bridge height scale N bank approach (2km/1·1M E).

Sliedrecht on the Beneden Merwede. Yacht entering the somewhat cluttered municipal haven

1·1km/0·6M
🌉 **Baanhoek railway bridge** (ht 12·16m MHW fixed part, S opening part 10·4m)
Service hours daily 0815-0825, 1337-1357[1], 1607-1627, 1746-1757, 1937-1957, 2007-2027[2]. Permission 3 hours minimum in advance from Dordrecht Rijkshavendienst ☎ (078) 132421.
1. Except sa/su/h.
2. Only from *16/4-16/10*.

Baanhoek railway bridge height scale S bank approach (1·5km/0·8M W).

Baanhoek railway bridge over the Beneden Merwede to Dordrecht. Note the scale on the centre pillar indicating 12·5m clearance

Papendrecht road bridge

2·5km/1·3M
PAPENDRECHT
MHW NAP +0·90m, MLW NAP +0·10m.
Papendrecht road bridge (ht 12·5m MHW fixed
S half, 10·5m MHW N end opening part), ☎ (078)
151564.
Service hours 16/4-16/10 0600-2200, *16/10-16/4*
0600-2000.

1·6km/0·9M
⚓ N bank. WV Papendrecht, depth 3m, max length
10m, 9t crane ☎ (078) 155756/159476. Office hours
1900-1930.

1·1km/0·6M
DORDRECHT Wijnhaven
See Route 5 for facilities in Dordrecht.

Approaching Dordrecht from the E near Papendrecht

Route 12
A tour of the Biesbosch

Commentary (See also Chapter 1)
This short route should be lingered over, taking care
not to go aground (when the tiny tidal range could
be all important), anchoring in tree-hung channels
and getting out the fishing rod, observing the wildlife, and visiting the museum near the Spieringsluis.
You will also need to ring *Post Dordrecht* well in advance to arrange a specific time for one of their men
to go down and wind up (manually, including him-
self as well as the span) the Wantij railway bridge.
If you do anchor in the channels you are allowed a
maximum of three days in a single place and must
then move at least 500m away.

There are many other places to visit on branch
channels not examined below: for example the Mer-
welanden Recreation Area visitors' centre in the
Sliedrechtse Biesbosch on a spur channel north-
eastward off the Wantij, or the single non-protected
channel of the Dordrechtse Biesbosch off the Hollands Diep, or the myriad shallow channels of the
Brabantse Biesbosch between the Steurgat and the
Gat van den Kleinen Hil. Finally en route you can
have a shower and a restaurant meal at the huge
Drimmelen yacht harbour on the Amer, or replenish
stores in the small town of Werkendam on the
Nieuwe Merwede which is about 1½km from its
yacht harbour.

An alternative route, for higher vessels, to that
listed below misses out the Sliedrechtse Biesbosch
with its railway lift bridge (ht 12·2m) and continues
from Dordrecht eastwards along the Beneden Merwede and then port into the Nieuwe Merwede and
across to Werkendam's Biesboschsluis direct into
the Brabantse Biesbosch, 14·6km from Dordrecht.
There are railway and road bridges on this route,
but with opening sections (see Route 11).

Note that the third potential route from Dordrecht southwards along the Dordtse Kil and then E
into the Hollands Diep under the Moerdijk road
and railway bridges and entering the Biesbosch from
the SW corner is only feasible for motor vessels and
very small sailing cruisers, since the clearance under
the latter bridges is only 9·78m.

Note also that the route below excludes many
possible detours into Biesbosch channels between
the Steurgat and the Noordergat, and particularly
the wide Gat van Kampen, as well as the Dordrechtse Biesbosch's one available channel, Maartensgat.

Distance 57km/31M

Bridges/maximum clearance 8 opening, including a
railway bridge requiring notice and with a maximum
height lifted of 12·2m, so maximum air draught is
about 12m.
Locks 3

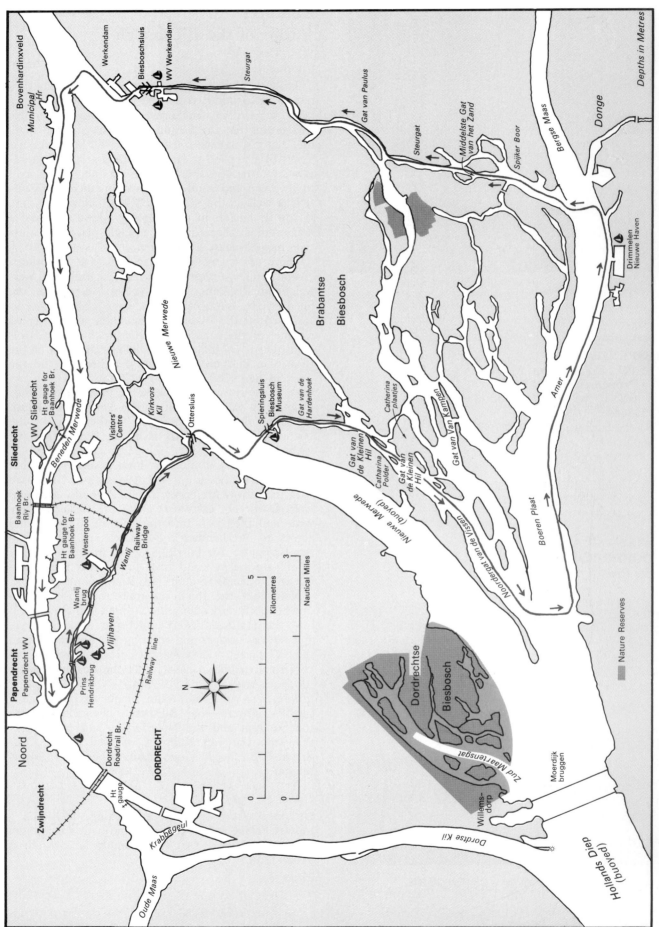

Tour of the Biesbosch

Tides, heights and soundings
On ANWB chart *N* heights are to MHW and soundings to MLW giving a small excess safety factor for each since the tidal range is small: 0·7m in the Wantij and 0·2m in the Brabantse Biesbosch, so grounding is definitely to be avoided! You may also be able to just scrape under the Wantij railway lift bridge with 12·5m air draught, if you can persuade them to lift it on time near low water. Tidal streams in both places are negligible, but there is usually a weak downstream current in both the Nieuwe Merwede and the Amer on each side of the Brabantse Biesbosch varying with the Haringvliet and upper river sluicing programmes. See Route 11 for description of streams in the Beneden Merwede.

Minimum depths en route
The route is for shallow-draught vessels only, say 1·37m/4·5ft at very maximum if you wish to make more than a peripheral visit. In the main channels you can only reckon on a minimum of 1·5m depth, and in the subsidiaries there is often 1m or less.

Charts
ANWB charts *K* and *N*.

Route description

DORDRECHT Wijnhaven
See Route 5 for details of facilities in Dordrecht.

Eastward then stbd into the entrance of Wantij.

WANTIJ
9kph/4·9kn max. Minimum depth 2·0m MLW. Air draught 12m max. The Wantij passes the SW side of Sliedrechtse Biesbosch, a historic and picturesque part of the Biesbosch between the Beneden and Nieuwe Merwedes.

1·3km/0·7M
◢**Prins Hendrikbrug** (ht 3·63m MHW), ☎ (078) 133673.
Service hours 16/4-16/10 m-sa 0900-1200, 1400-1900, su/h 0900-1200, 1500-2000; *16/10-16/4* m-sa 0800-1200, 1300-1700, su/h closed.
Note Closed at peak times 0815-0830, 1315-1330, 1615-1645, 1715-1730.

Wantij. Prins Hendrikbrug where Dutch industry gives way to the Sliedrechtse Biesbosch scenery

2 ⚓ S bank. 1st entrance to stbd is Jachthaven Heuvel-de-Graaf, toilets, showers, 3t crane, 40t boat-lift, ☎ (078) 136911/132319. 2nd entrance to stbd is WV De Biesbosch. Each harbour depth 2·5m MLW.

2 ⚓ S bank. Vlijhaven. 1·2km along the shallow, 1·2m depth, Vlij channel doglegging S and W to WV Drechtstad and WV Kievit, depth 1·5m.

1·4km/0·8M
◢**Wantijbrug** (ht 5·5m MHW)
Service hours 16/4-16/10 m-sa 0900-1200, 1400-1700 (f to 1900), su/h 0900-1100, 1600-2000; *16/10-16/4* m-sa 0900-1200[1], 1300-1700[1], su/h closed.

1. On 8-hour arrangement by ☎ (078) 164454.

⚓ N bank. 1·3m-deep channel to Jachthaven Westergoot (depth 3·5m), toilets, showers, 25t crane, ☎ (078) 160780.

2·2km/1·2M
◢**Railway bridge and Wantijfietsbrug** (cycles) (ht closed 4·3m MHW, ht opened 12·2m MHW).
MHW NAP +0·77m, MLW NAP +0·10m.
Bridge service hours 16/6-16/9 m-f 0812-0822, 0912-1622[1], sa 0812-0822, 1212-1222, 1612-1622; *16/9-16/6* m-f 0812-0822, 1012-1622[1], sa 0812-0822, 1212-1222, 1612-1622; su/h *16/4-16/10* 0812-0822, 1212-1222, 1612-1622, 2012-2022, *16/10-16/4* closed.

1. 2 hours notice required NS/Verkeerspost ☎ (078) 142367. At all other times 3 hours notice Verkeerspost Dordrecht, ☎ (078) 132421, or VHF Ch 71 or 22 (also controlling Dordrecht railway bridge).

Wantij. The railway lift bridge

2·4km/1·3M

OTTERSLUIS

MHW NAP +0·8m, MLW NAP +0·1m

≪ Port and stbd dogleg to **Ottersluis** (sill depth NAP −2·2m) with moorings on each side.
Service hours 1/4-15/5 and *1/9-1/11* daily 0800-1300, 1400-1700 (f/sa/su/h to 2100); *15/5-1/9* daily 0800-1300, 1400-2100. *1/11-1/4* m-sa 0800-1200, 1300-1700, su/h closed. Not operated if 2m or more fall of water.

NIEUWE MERWEDE

MHW NAP +0·67m, MLW NAP +0·46m. Depth 4m. Stbd and along Nieuwe Merwede crossing at right angles to Spieringsluis.

2·0km/1·1M

SPIERINGSLUIS

≪ ⌐ **Lock and drawbridge** MHW NAP +0·55m, MLW +0·46m (Biesbosch side of lock).
☎ (01835) 1631. Sill depth 3·7m (MLW).
Service hours See Ottersluis above.
Lock is not operated if Biesbosch water level is NAP −0·3m or lower. To visit the Biesbosch museum S of the bridge yacht moorings, the quay on the N bank is useful for a temporary mooring. Jachthaven Spieringsluis on the S bank, very shallow, ☎ (01835) 1633.

Spieringsluis drawbridge. The dark building under the trees is the fascinating Biesbosch Museum

BRABANTSE BIESBOSCH

9kph/4·9kn max, but 6kph/3·2kn max in the narrow and shallower channels. Constant use of depth sounder and hand-bearing compass in conjunction with chart is essential, and beware of clumps of reeds on the edges of shallows.

GAT VAN DE HARDENHOEK

Minimum depth 2·5m in middle fairway, but only 1·3m if you accidentally enter the channel west of the reeds near Catharina Polder bank. Follow 3·8m-deep channel W of Catharinaplaatjes, taking care not to enter the stbd fork into the 1m-deep Gat van de Kleinen Hil.

NOORDERGAT VAN DER VISSEN

Minimum depth 3·9m but 1m and less unmarked shallows to N and S. Sound round unmarked N side of the Boeren Plaat, keeping away from 0·6m shoal on the stbd side of the channel. Back bearings on the moorings and wooded area, and, when sighted, front bearings on the beacons with triangular topmarks on each side of the gap into the Amer are useful.

Spieringsluis with its drawbridge opening. W entrance to the Brabantse Biesbosch

Noordergat. Tricky SW entrance to the Brabantse Biesbosch from the Amer

8·2km/4·4M
⚓ AMER
16kph/8·6kn max. Minimum depth 3m close inshore. Cross river and follow S bank eastwards to Drimmelen.

8·8km/4·8M
DRIMMELEN Nieuwe Haven
F.R&G entrance lights, new yacht haven. Old harbour to E is commercial. Nieuwe Haven depth 2·5m, toilets, showers, restaurants, WVs De Amer ☎ (01626) 2788, De Biesbosch ☎ (01626) 2264, Drimmelen ☎ (01626) 3309, coordination ☎ (01626) 3166. 25t boat-lift, Snoek Botenberging, ☎ (01626) 2478.

Drimmelen marina entrance

Drimmelen. A huge marina with all facilities on the S side of the Amer opposite the Brabantse Biesbosch

Continue eastwards crossing the river at right angles to Brabantse Biesbosch.

1·9km/1·0M
⚓ BRABANTSE BIESBOSCH
Spijkerboor entrance. 9kph/4·9kn max in main channels, but 6kph/3·2kn max in the remaining branch channels.

SPIJKER BOOR
Minimum depth 3m.

1·6km/0·9M
⚓ MIDDELSTE GAT VAN HET ZAND to port.
Depth 2·5m.

1·5km/0·8M
⚓ STEURGAT/NAUW VAN PAULUS to port.
Depth 4·3m.

1·9km/1·0M
⚓ GAT VAN PAULUS to port. Depth 2·8m.
Keep to E bank and beware of spit and reeds in mid-channel entering the northern Steurgat.

STEURGAT
Depth 3·6m.

WERKENDAM
⚓ WV Werkendam E bank below bridge, depth 2·9m, toilets, showers, 10t crane, ☎ (01835) 1698. Haven De Steur, W bank opposite, depth 1·5m, showers and crane ☎ (01835) 1812.

5·9km/3·2M
« ⛵ **Biesboschsluis and drawbridge** (ht 4·5m MHW). VHF Ch 13 *Biesboschsluis.* ☎ (01835) 1587. Steurgat side of lock MHW NAP +0·35m, MLW NAP +0·15m. Merwede side of lock MHW NAP +0·9m, MLW NAP +0·6m. There is little accommodation for yachts in Biesboschhaven to the N of the lock.
Service hours 1/4-1/11 m-f 0600-1300, 1400-2100; *1/4-15/5* and *1/9-1/11* sa/su/h 0800-1300, 1400-2100; *15/5-1/9* sa/su/h 0700-1300, 1400-2100; *1/11-1/4* m-f 0600-1200, 1300-2000, sa 0800-1200, 1300-1900, su/h closed.

Depart between F.R&G entrance Lts and R&G buoys. Also Fl.G.10s Lt on S outer pier, and Ldg Lts into this entrance. To port following E bank and then to port at right angles across river to Beneden Merwede.

2·0km/1·1M
⚓ BENEDEN MERWEDE
Kop van de Oude Wiel spit. Fl.10s Lt.

For rest of route westward to DORDRECHT see Route 11.

15·3km/8·3M
⚓ DORDRECHT Wijnhaven
For details of facilities in Dordrecht see Route 5.

Dordrecht. Kalkhaven is completely commercial, so keep out!

III. THE NORTH

8. Approaches to Noord-Holland and the Frisian Islands

Charts Admiralty *112, 122, 124, 191, 1405, 1408, 2182A, 2322, 2593, 3509, 3510, 3761*
Imray *C25*
Dutch small-craft *1801, 1811, 1812*
Dutch nautical *1014, 1035, 1037, 1350, 1352, 1353, 1450, 1454, 1456, 1458, 1460, 1543, 1546, 1555*

Tidal atlases Admiralty *North Sea – southern portion*
North Sea – eastern portion
Dutch *Stroomatlassen j, k, l, m, n*

Tidal streams

Holland coast Maasmond to Noorderhaaks
(based on HW Hoek van Holland and HW Dover)

Position	*Start times*			
	H.VAN HOLLAND		DOVER	
	North	*South*	*North*	*South*
Off Maasmond ent.	−0200	+0430	+0105	−0450
3M W of IJmuiden	−0120	−0430	+0145	−0420
Off IJmuiden ent.[1]	−0210	−0350	+0055	−0530
W of Noorderhaaks Is	−0030	+0545	+0235	−0340

Note
1. For IJmuiden Buitenhaven, which has circular tidal streams which set towards and away from each of the northern entrance pierheads, see Dutch *Stroomatlas j*.

Frisian coast and zeegats
(based on HW Helgoland and HW Dover)

Position	*Start times*			
	HELGOLAND		DOVER	
Offshore	*NE*	*SW*	*NE*	*SW*
W of Noorderhaaks Is	+0245	−0330	+0235	−0340
Off outer grounds of Eems				
Estuary (1kn max)	−0600	+0020	+0605	HW

Zeegats	*Flood*	*Ebb*	*Flood*	*Ebb*
Zeegat van Texel (Texel/mainland)				
Schulpengat (1·5kn average)				
(Flood NE)	+0325	−0330	+0305	−0350
Molengat (1·3kn average)				
(Flood SE)	+0425	−0145	+0405	−0205
Eierlandsche Gat (Texel/Vlieland)				
Engelschmangat[1]				
(2·5kn max)	+0300	−0300	+0240	−0320
Zeegat van Terschelling (Vlieland/Terschelling)				
Zuider Stortemelk				
(2·5kn max)	+0325	−0230	+0305	−0250
Noordgat[2](max 1·3kn)				
(Flood SW)	−0500	HW	−0520	−0020
Vliesloot				
(2·5kn max)	+0315	−0215	+0305	−0235
Schuitengat				
(2kn max)	+0410	−0215	+0350	−0235
Zeegat van Ameland (Terschelling/Ameland)				
Westgat				
(2kn max)	+0425	−0150	+0405	−0210
Friesche Zeegat				
N end Zoutkamperlaag				
(2·5kn max)	+0410	−0215	+0350	−0235
Monden van de Eems[3] (Eems entrance)				
Huibertgat, Westereems and Rifgat				
(1·5kn max)	+0530	−0030	+0510	−0050

Notes
1. Engelschmangat is unmarked, changing and only of use in emergency.
2. Thomas Smit Gat is no longer marked
3. Streams tend first to cross the outer grounds at the turn before setting directly into the Eems river channels.

Tidal differences and ranges

Place	*HW*	*Springs/Neaps*
	(time)	*(range in metres)*
N and S Holland (based on HW Dover)		
Scheveningen	+0340	1·9/1·4
IJmuiden	+0420	1·8/1·3
Den Helder	−0340	1·5/1·1
Harlingen	−0131	2·0/1·6
Frisian Islands and Waddenzee (based on HW Harlingen)		
Harlingen	HW	2·0/1·6
Den Helder	−0209	1·5/1·1
Den Oever	−0112	1·7/1·3
Kornwerderzand	−0017	1·9/1·4
Vlieland	−0056	2·1/1·5
West Terschelling	−0022	2·1/1·4
Nes	+0034	2·5/1·8
Schiermonnikoog	+0038	2·6/1·8
Lauwersoog	+0027	2·6/1·9
Delfzijl	+0215	3·2/2·6

Major lights

Name of light	Characteristics	Position	Structure
Scheveningen Ldg Lts			
156°, Front	Iso.4s17m14M (6M day)	52°05'·8N 4°15'·7E	Grey metal mast
Rear	Iso.4s21m14M (6M day)		Grey metal mast
Scheveningen	Fl(2)10s48m29M	52°06'·3N 4°16'·2E	Brown metal tower, 014°-vis-244°
Noordwijk aan Zee	Oc(3)20s32m18M	52°14'·9N 4°26'·1E	Wh square stone tower
IJmuiden Ldg Lts			
100·5°, Front	F.WR.30m16/13M	52°27'·8N 4°34'·5E	Dark R round metal tower, RC 050°-W-122°-R-145°-W-160°
by day	F.4M		090·5°-vis-110·5°
Rear	Fl.5s52m29M		Dark R round metal tower, 019°-vis-199°
by day	F.4M		090·5°-vis-110·5°
Egmond aan Zee	Iso.WR.10s36m18/14M	52°37'·3N 4°37'·6E	Wh round stone tower, 010°-W-175°-R-188°
Texel LtV	Fl(3+1)20s16m26M Horn(3)30s	52°47'·1N 4°06'·6E	R hull, Wh band, RC, Racon. RW buoy, Oc.10s, Racon, during maintenance
Huisduinen	F.WR.27m14/11M	52°57'·2N 4°43'·3E	Square stone tower 070°-W-113°-R-158°-W-208°
Kijkduin	Fl(4)20s56m30M	52°57'·4N 4°43'·6E	Brown metal tower, rear Ldg Lt 253·5° with Den Helder Marinehaven Willemsoord, Harssens Island, W breakwater head
Schulpengat Ldg Lts			
026·5° Front	Iso.4s18M (9M day)	53°00'·9N 4°44'·5E	Metal pedestal, 024·5°-vis-028·5°
Rear, Den Hoorn	Oc.8s18M (9M day)		Church spire, 024·5°-vis-028·5°
Schilbolsnol	F.WRG.27m15-11M	53°00'·6N 4°45'·8E	Green tower, 338°-W-002°-G-035° 035°-W-038° Ldg for Schulpengat 038°-R-051°-W-068·5°
Den Helder Wierhoofdhaven ferry Ldg Lts 207°			
Front	Iso.2s10m14M (5M day)	52°57'·8N 4°46'·8E	Grey mast, 199°-vis-215°
Rear	Iso.2s14m14M (5M day)		Grey mast, 199°-vis-215°
Den Helder	Ldg Lts 191°		
Front	Oc.G.5s16m14M (6M day)	52°57'·4N 4°47'·2E	B ▲ on building, 161°-vis-221°
Rear	Oc.G.5s25m14M (6M day)		B ▼ on B framework tower, 161°-vis-247°
Eierland (Texel)	Fl(2)10s52m29M	53°11'·0N 4°51'·4E	R round masonry tower
Vlieland	Iso.4s53m20M	53°17'·8N 5°03'·6E	Brown round metal tower, RC
Terschelling, Brandaris tower	Fl.5s55m29M	53°21'·7N 5°12'·9E	Y square stone tower
W Terschelling Rear Ldg Lt 053°	Iso.5s14m19M	53°22'·0N 5°14'·7E	Grey metal mast, 045°-vis-061°
Ameland (W end)	Fl(3)15s57m30M	53°27'·0N 5°37'·6E	Brown round metal tower, Wh bands, RC
Schiermonnikoog (W end)	Fl(4)20s43m28M	53°29'·2N 6°09'·0E	Round stone tower, dark R seaward, grey landward
	F.WR.28m15/12M		210°-W-221°-R-230°
Borkum Grosser	Fl(2)12s63m24M	53°35'·4N 6°39'·8E	Brown round brick tower
Borkum Kleiner	F.32m30M Fl.3s Q(4)10s	53°34'·8N 6°40'·1E	R tower Wh bands
Fischerbalje	Oc(2)WRG.16s15m16-11M	53°33'·2N 6°43'·0E	Wh round tower, R top and lantern, on tripod on 3 B piles. 256°-R-313°-G-014°-W-081·1°-R-108·9°-W-113·2°-R-119·8°-W-125°. Ldg sector to Westereems 125°-R-140°
Campen	F.62m30M Fl.5s Fl(4)15s	53°24'·4N 7°01'·0E	R metal framework tower, 2 galleries, Wh central column, G cupola. 125·7°-Fl-127°-F-127·8°-Fl(4)15s-128·3°

Radiobeacons

Name	Freq. (kHz)	Ident.	Range (miles)	Seq.	Position
Marine radiobeacons					
IJmuiden Group	294·2				
IJmuiden		YM	20	1,4	52°27'·8N 4°34'·6E
Hoek van Holland		HH	20	2,5	51°58'·9N 4°06'·8E
Eierland Lt (fog only)		ER	20	3,6	53°11'·0N 4°51'·4E
Vlieland Group	308				
Vlieland LtHo		VL	70	1	53°17'·8N 5°03'·6E
Deutsche Bucht LtF		DB	50	4	54°10'·7N 7°26'·1E
Texel LtV		HK	50	5	52°47'·1N 4°06'·6E
Elbe LtF		EL	10	6	54°00'·0N 8°06'·6E
Ameland Group	298·8				
Ameland LtHo (fog only)		AD	20	1,3,5	53°27'·0N 5°37'·6E
Borkum Little LtHo		BE	20	2,4,6	53°34'·8N 6°40'·1E
Aero beacons					
Valkenburg/ Scheveningen	364	GV	25	H24	52°05'·7N 4°15'·2E
Amsterdam/ Spijkerboor	381	SPY	75	H24	52°32'·5N 4°50'·5E
Den Helder	109·2	HDR		H24	52°54'·5N 4°46'·0E

Coast radio stations

Scheveningen Radio covers the whole of the Netherlands via nine separate VHF transmitting/receiving relay stations. You simply tune in to the appropriate channel of the nearest station and call *Scheveningen Radio*. The stations relevant to the routes in the northern part of the country covered in Section III of this book are listed here. Those for the southern area, Section II, are listed in Chapter 3 on page 23. Also listed below are the details for MF radiotelephony at Scheveningen.

Station	VHF Channel	Position
Scheveningen	Ch 16,26,83[1]	52°06'N 4°16'E
Wieringerwerf	Ch 16,27[1],87	52°55'N 5°04'E
Location L7	Ch 16,28[1],84	53°32'N 4°13'E
Terschelling	Ch 16,25[1],78	53°22'N 5°13'E
Nes	Ch 16,23[1]	53°24'N 6°04'E
Appingedam	Ch 16,27[1],24	53°18'N 6°52'E
Lelystad	Ch 16, 83[1],84	52°32'N 5°26'E

Station RT (MF)	Transmits (kHz)	Receives (kHz)	Freq[4] (kHz)	Traffic lists (times)	Storm warnings (times)	Weather messages (times)	Navigational warnings (times)
Scheveningen (PCG)(PCH)	1764[2],1862[5], **1890,1939,** 2182[2,5],**2600,** 2824[2],**3673**	2049[3] 2182[3] 2520[3]	1862[5]	odd H+05	On receipt	0340,0940, 1540,2140	0333,0733,1133, 1533,1933,2333
			1890	odd H+05	On receipt	0340,0940, 1540,2140	0333,0733,1133, 1533,1933,2333
			1939		On receipt		
			2600		On receipt		
			2824	0105,0305, 0505,2305		0340	0333,2333

Notes

1. VHF Channel for traffic lists at every H+05; storm warnings at every H+05, weather messages at 0605, 1205, 1805, 2305 (in Dutch). Broadcasts given 1hr earlier when DST is in force. Ch 16 and all working VHF channels (bold) have 24hr watch.
2. 24hr service.
3. 24hr watch. Use 2049 when 2182 is distress working. 2520 is calling frequency, alternative is 2182.
4. Frequency (kHz) on which traffic lists, storm warnings, weather messages and navigational warnings are given as listed (in English and Dutch).
5. 1862 located at Nes only 53°24'N 6°04'E. 2182 located at Scheveningen and Nes.

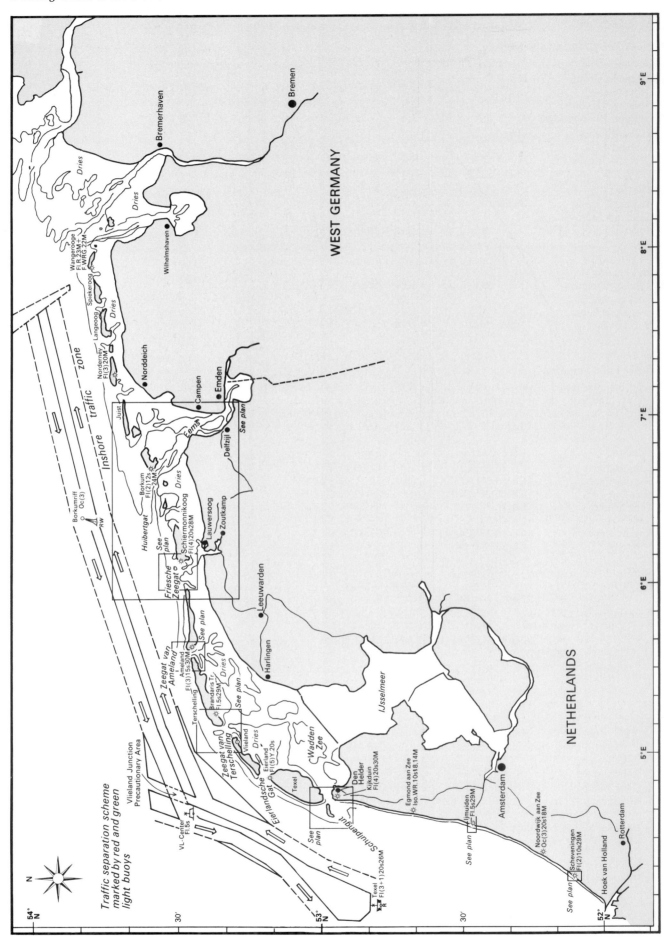

Major fixed daylight marks

Hoek van Holland to Schulpengat

Church towers of 's-Gravenzande, Monster and Ter Heijde S of Scheveningen

Kijkduin tower blocks

Radio masts (73m) close SW of Scheveningen

Scheveningen Lt (30m brown metal tower)

The Vredespaleis tower behind Scheveningen

Scheveningen pier N of the town and a water tower to its E

Katwijk aan Zee: 2 church towers, offshore platform 6M NW of Katwijk

Noordwijk aan Zee: Main Lt (25m Wh square tower)

Zandvoort: water tower, 2 churches and tall buildings

IJmuiden: Main Lt (43m dark R tower), 2 steelworks chimneys N of entrance (138m and 166m, R Lts), 3 chimneys further inland (157m, 155m, 115m, R Lts), radio masts further N (76m)

Wijk aan Zee: 2 churches

Egmond aan Zee: Main Lt (28m Wh round tower), church spire

Bergen aan Zee: houses on dunes

Petten: nuclear power station with 2 chimneys (45m, R Lts)

Zanddijk: Grote Kaap Lt (17m, Lt 31m, brown round tower)

Huisduinen Lt (18m square tower) and Kijkduin Lt (55m brown tower)

Den Helder: town hall midway between Kaap Hoofd and harbour entrance, a water tower inland behind it, and a church further E.

Schulpengat to Borkum

Texel: Schulpengat Ldg Lts can be seen by day, the rear being Den Hoorn church spire, Schilbolsnol Lt (21m G tower), Loodsmansduin (conspic dune WSW of Den Hoorn church), Den Burg mast (76m, R Lts), De Koog church and close NW a mast with rectangular framework on top on a dune, the Nol (conspic dune) just over 1M SW of Eierland LtHo (35m R round tower)

Vlieland dune coast with groins N half, Vlieland LtHo (17m brown round tower) on highest forested dune, Kaap Bol is N point of island.

Terschelling Noordvaarder (W end of island) is flat sand, Terschelling LtHo on Brandaris sq stone tower in W Terschelling, isolated building/lifeboat station 2·6M NE of W Terschelling, Midsland and Hoorn church spires over dunes, Noordkaap framework Bn near flat E end of island.

Ameland sand dune coast, Ameland LtHo (55m brown round tower, white bands), Hollom church tower, Blinkert (a white patch on dunes) just over 3M E of LtHo, Nes church tower, framework Bn with round topmark near flat E end of island, pyramidal framework of disused LtHo on Engelsmanplaat.

Schiermonnikoog flat W end with dunes eastward, Schiermonnikoog LtHo (43m R round tower) with signal mast and beach hotel close to, round water tower to the SE, Oosterburen small church tower, a triangular framework in middle of island, and on flat E end a Bn with a diamond above rectangular topmark.

Simonszand is a very low small island.

Rottumerplaat has a few dunes and a Bn at the E end.

Rottumeroog also has dunes with an iron framework Bn (Grote Kaap) on top.

Borkum, the first of the German islands, has two sets of dunes to its N (Ostland) and S (Westland) looking like

two islands from a distance but with Borkum village in between and a number of prominent objects clustered around, including (from S to N along the W end of the island): Kugelbake triangular Bn with spherical topmark, Borkum Kleiner LtHo (27m R tower Wh bands), Borkum Oude LtHo (disused), Borkum Grosser LtHo (60m brown round brick tower), Neue Bake framework Bn, Grosse Bake framework Bn, water tower due E of latter.

Terschelling. Approach along the Noordergat. Note the prominent Brandaris tower and the wooded N end of the island

Offshore approaches

The 170M of outer coastline from Hoek van Holland to Delfzijl inside the Eems entrance is inhospitable cruising country, emphasising the Netherlands' main cruising asset, its inland waterways. The N trending 65M from Hoek to Zeegat van Texel is a smooth sand-dune lined coast with two artificial harbours. The remaining 105M of NE and E trending coast round into the Eems is a string of low sand-dune edged islands, some of which are partly coniferous-wooded, with six sandbar-strewn *zeegats* and the Eems river entrance. Four of the *zeegats* and the river lead to harbours of refuge behind the islands and on the mainland, one of the *zeegats* is not effectively navigable, and another leads nowhere.

Weather

Although the offshore approaches are deep and navigable it is essential for the skipper of a small cruising vessel to listen to the shipping forecasts and choose his weather. The S coastal stretch tends to be raked by the prevailing SW winds as well as by N winds and although in season the N stretch is generally better protected, it is exposed to not infrequent N and NE winds which tend to occur early in season.

Although there are no offshore banks or boulders to create tide rips the steep coastline in strong lee-shore conditions with winds at an angle to the coast creates rolling, often breaking, seas which can be dangerous particularly in wind-over-tide conditions. Wind-funnel effects in harbour entrances and *zeegats* can also be dangerous, for example Hoek, Scheveningen and IJmuiden in NW through N to NE winds, the Schulpengat in SW to S, the nearby Molengat in N to NW, and in the northern *zeegats* NW through N to NE winds also create dangerous seas on their offshore bars. If conditions are bad, particularly on the S coast, a yacht can sometimes stand well offshore and wait for an improvement before running in. The TSS makes this difficult on the N coast but here fortunately protection is nearly always close at hand inside the islands via the nearest *zeegat* and should be sought at the earliest sign of potential lee-shore conditions.

With the reduction in smoke pollution in recent years fog has become much less frequent, tending to occur early in the season and more often on the northern islands' coasts. In fog anchoring is not usually feasible on the southern coast without running dangerously close inshore. Standing well off is again often advisable, making sure to keep well away from the approach channels to the harbours, and particularly from the IJmuiden-Geul. Along the coast from the Schulpengat and northwards it is often possible to carefully sound and anchor away from traffic inshore behind the banks and inside the *zeegats*.

Traffic separation schemes and precautionary areas

The northern coasts are obstructed by a major TSS stretching from Texel LtV to the precautionary area off the Jade and Weser estuaries with the 3M wide E-going lane closest to the coast. This must be avoided if at all possible by small vessels except in a crossing situation.

A major amendment was made to this in 1987 by the placing of a Lanby, *VL-Center* Fl.5s, 15M NW of Vlieland island where traffic either turns through a 43° angle round the 'corner' or passes directly across the turning traffic to leave or join the TSS. The diamond-shaped area where the N-going crosses the W-going lane has been designated a

Dutch yacht in rough weather

precautionary area with *VL-Center* buoy just off its SW corner. The whole length of the S edge of the TSS separating it from the inshore traffic area is marked by G Lt buoys, at 6–7½M intervals, and the *Borkumriff* buoy is located in the 2M wide central TSZ (traffic separation zone) 16M NW of the Eems estuary. The part of the inshore area near the 'Vlieland junction' is officially designated an ITZ (inshore traffic zone) which sailing vessels and vessels of less than 20m are positively required to use rather than the TSS.

Some 10 to 20M N of the E end of this mainly Dutch coastal TSS and joined to it by another precautionary area off the German Frisian coast lies a second almost parallel TSS stretching W from the Deutsche Bucht LtF and ending about 20M NW of the *Borkumriff* buoy.

Small vessels should if at all possible avoid crossing the TSSs, but above all are advised to keep out of the precautionary areas where ships may be turning and taking avoiding action of all kinds. Use the inshore area which varies from 5 to 12M in width from the island coasts. Much of this ITZ has over 10m and up to 20m depth and the 5m contour is often 1M or less offshore except near the sandbank-obstructed *zeegats*. From S of Texel to just N of the Hoek the offshore approach is completely unobstructed: no TSS, a steep-shelving coast, and the 5m contour usually less than 1M offshore.

Given the right weather, therefore, approach to the S part of the coast, and along the N coast from the E without touching the TSS is not difficult although yachts should give a reasonable clearance to the ends of the TSSs. Yachts crossing the North Sea from NE through N to W should keep well away from the precautionary area near Vlieland and cross the TSS at right angles to the traffic observing Rule 10. As well as or in the absence of Decca, location of the Deutsche Bucht, *Borkumriff* buoy and Texel LtV, and of the island lighthouses visually or by radiobeacon can be helpful in position-fixing, and having crossed the TSS yachts can then coast to their selected *zeegat* entrance.

Marks and lights

The essence of approach and coasting is to avoid getting too close to the flat and deceptive coastline particularly in onshore winds, so keep the hand-bearing compass at work. This is not difficult in one of the world's best marked areas. Onshore navigation marks are unmistakable and shapes of landmarks are often drawn on the Dutch small-craft charts. Towns, villages, factories, chimneys, water towers, beacons, lighthouses, outstanding sand dunes, church towers and spires rise like candles from the flat shore. The steelworks close N of IJmuiden is typical, as is Petten nuclear power station and the various high light-towers and beacons on the islands. There are no less than 12 major lights strung along the coast and into the Eems, averaging 15 miles apart with nominal ranges from 18 to 30M, and to the average small vessel, geographical ranges of 14 to 19M. There are also a number of offshore

platforms (e.g. the Rijn field near IJmuiden, and some outliers of the Helder field to the SW of Texel LtV) amply lit with F.R and Mo(U) Lts. There are also a large number of wellheads, marked by Y Lt buoys, particularly in the inshore area. Inshore as well are large numbers of cardinal Lt buoys, particularly near wrecks, and safe-water offing buoys at the approaches to the major *zeegat* channels which are also laterally marked and lit. There is rarely any necessity to navigate blind at night in this area even at some considerable distance offshore.

Radio aids

Whilst many more yachtsmen are now using Decca a useful string of three groups of radiobeacons and three aero beacons (listed above) covers this coast. These are particularly useful for navigation well offshore. Vlieland for instance has a 70M range and Amsterdam/Spijkerboor (aero) 75M. The two most useful triangularly disposed series of stations are Texel LtV (50M), Den Helder (aero) and IJmuiden (20M); and Vlieland (70), Ameland (20M) and Borkum (20M).

Scheveningen coast radio station with its network of VHF transmitters covers the whole area, and the German *Norddeich Radio* in the extreme E may occasionally be useful. *Scheveningen Radio* also feeds information into the NAVTEX system, can be contacted and provides medium wave weather forecasts in English. In addition the BBC shipping forecasts covering Thames, Humber and German Bight are particularly useful.

Rescue services   See also Appendix IV

VHF Ch 16 provides quick access to the rescue services. In addition to coastguard watch posts there are 7 offshore lifeboats based at Hoek van Holland, Scheveningen, IJmuiden, Den Helder, West Terschelling, Harlingen, and Lauwersoog, leaving the N coasts of the outer islands not quite as well covered. However, there are additional locations of the more mobile inshore lifeboats. On the S coast there are 6: Ter Heijde (N of Hoek), Katwijk aan Zee N of Scheveningen, Noordwijk aan Zee, Zandvoort, Wijk aan Zee N of IJmuiden, and Egmond aan Zee. On the N coast, 5: Eierland 8 cables SE of the LtHo, Vlieland harbour, the N coast of Terschelling 2·6M NW of W Terschelling, Hollum on Ameland, and Oosterburen on Schiermonnikoog. Many of the offshore lifeboat locations also have inshore lifeboats.

Tides and tidal streams

HW is progressively later moving N and E round the coast; at Noorderhaaks it is about 4 hours later than at Scheveningen, and at Delfzijl yet another 4½ hours later. Tidal range is small but also tends to increase in this direction, springs range being 1·9m at Scheveningen, 2·1m at W Terschelling, 2·7m at Borkum, and 3·2m at Delfzijl. Both features are useful for yachts cruising eastward along the islands following the successive HWs, especially for those cruising the watershed (*wantij*) passages behind the islands.

Streams tend to follow the coast, the flood being N and E with the ebb in the opposite direction. There is a 1 to 2-hour slack offshore turn on the N coast and a slightly more rapid change, over a shorter period on the S coast. Streams are weak, 1½ knots maximum mean springs on the N coast and 2 knots on the S coast and round the 'shoulder' of Texel and Vlieland; and at neaps a mean maximum of 1½ and 1 knot respectively.

Again the advantage is on N and E-going passages. The N/NE-going stream starts at the Hoek 7¾ hours before the S-going stream turns against off Noorderhaaks island 65M away, and at Noorderhaaks starts running N nearly 10 hours before it turns E off the Eems estuary 105M away. This provides only a marginal advantage for the average 4 to 5-knot sailing yacht which can make 30M at most in a single set. However bearing in mind the weak stream it can be some advantage for the 8-knot motor-cruiser which can make the 65M passage in a single set and a considerable proportion of the 105M passage. In the opposite direction of course it is a slower passage.

The turns of the flood and ebb streams in the *zeegats* tend to be relatively close to the turns of the coastal streams, in some cases a little earlier and turning just after LW and HW. Since many of the navigable channels tend to head W between the sandflats, on the earlier part of the ebb the streams tend to cross these sands northward settling into the channels as the tide falls. On passage N and E with the flood, departure from a *zeegat* is usually better at or before LW to avoid the inwards flood. Short coastal passages from one island to the next can often benefit from a continuing flood tide into the next *zeegat* if an early enough start is made. Similarly short passages in the opposite direction can often be timed to obtain an outgoing stream from one *zeegat* and an ingoing stream into the next.

SCHEVENINGEN

Tidal range
MHWS 2·2m, MLWS 0·4m, MHWN 1·8m, MLWN 0·3m.

Port radio (VHF)
Scheveningen Haven Ch 14
Radar Scheveningen 21
HrMr ☎ (070) 52 77 12/52 77 13

Entry signals
Contact on VHF to obtain instructions for entering harbour.
Shown from signal station: R over Wh Lt – entry prohibited; Wh over R Lt – departure prohibited; Fl.Y Lt – large vessel leaving or entering, shown seaward if vessel leaving and landward if vessel entering.
Shown from W corner of fish market: Q.R Lt – vessel inward bound in the outer harbour.

Customs
Kranenburgerweg 202. ☎ (070) 51 44 81. Opening times m-f 0700-0100 (following day), sa/su/h 0700-2245.

Entrance and facilities
29M range light, as well as leading lights (daylight intensity 6M, night 14M) into the outer entrance and a second set into the Voorhaven (4M day, 11M night). There are a number of outstanding landmarks (see *Major fixed daylight marks* above, page 77) and there are no offshore hazards.

The entrance faces N and is uncomfortable in northerlies. Streams run fast across the entrance at certain times, consult *Stroomatlas j.*

The entrance is a triple one, passing between 3 sets of port and starboard Lts on the encircling walls and into the Voorhaven, then hard to port into the fish dock (1st Haven, least depth 4·8m) and hard to starboard and along the short 'canal' into the 2nd Haven (least depth 2·8m), turning to starboard again for the large pontoon marina at the S end.

WV Marina Scheveningen, ☎ (070) 52 00 17/55 02 75, has showers, toilets, washing machines, and alongside is the Jachtclub Scheveningen, ☎ (070) 52 03 08, with a restaurant, as well as several others along the waterfront. There are all repair, lifting and chandlery facilities nearby including a 14t crane (Hoogenraad en Kuyt ☎ (070) 51 43 21). This is a lively seaside resort with a Victorian casino, recreation centre, beaches, and pier, as well as an interesting shopping street and historic fishing harbour. Den Haag, the Dutch seat of government and of the International Court of Justice is only a short distance away by tram along the delightful, tree-fringed Scheveningenweg. It has a plethora of museums, art galleries, royal palaces and historic buildings. The Hoek ferries, useful for meeting crew, are only a short taxi or train journey away from Den Haag.

IJMUIDEN

Tidal range
MHWS 2·1m, MLWS 0·4m, MHWN 1·7m, MLWN 0·3m

Port radio (VHF)
Traffic Centre 1 (beyond 5M off) Verkeersdienst IJmuiden Ch 12
Haven IJmuiden (locks to 5M off) Ch 9
Sluis IJmuiden (locks) Ch 9
Sluis IJmuiden (approaching locks inland) Ch 11
Ch 11 broadcasts every H+30 when visibility less than 1000m
HrMr (at locks) ☎ (02550) 6 42 23

Entry signals
VHF contact useful, no outer entry signals. Signal frame for the locks is well inside harbour on S side of Zuider Buitenkanaal. Yachts are usually directed to the two southern smallest locks (of the four), the Zuidersluis and the Kleinesluis with uncomfortable pilings for mooring, but with a loudspeaker system as well as traffic signals (see below) at each lock. 24-hour service (see below).

Tidal signals from the signal station; vertical R and G Lts refer to depths of water over 11m, and can be ignored. G over Wh Lt – rising tide; Wh over G Lt – falling tide.

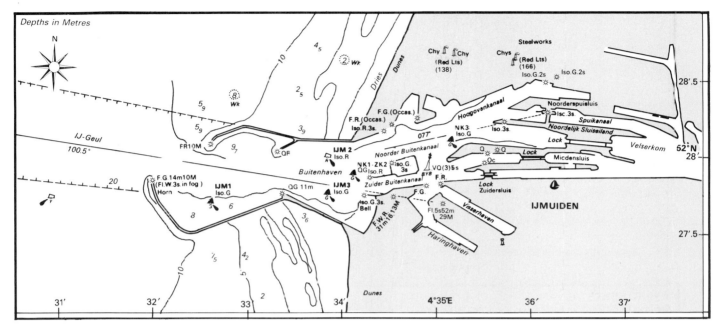

IJmuiden

Signal frame close S of signal station with a 3 by 3 square of 9 sets of lights for ingoing traffic. 6 are for the larger locks. The 3 right-hand sets apply to, from top to bottom, the Zuidersluis (there are none for the Kleinesluis), the Zuider Buitenkanaal, and fishing vessels and coastal craft.

Zuidersluis, Fl.G – lock being prepared; F.G – lock ready; Fl.R – outgoing traffic; F.R – lock out of use.

Zuider Buitenkanaal, Fl.R – outgoing traffic; F.R – traffic prohibited.

Fishing and coastal craft, F.R – entry prohibited except with permission.

For outgoing traffic the top left-hand set of 4 sets of signals applies to the Zuider Buitenkanaal, Fl.R – incoming traffic from sea; F.R – Zuider Buitenkanaal closed.

The Zuidersluis has a swing bridge. Lock entrances have traffic signals, G on each side – enter; R on each side – entry prohibited; RG horizontal on each side – wait, lock being prepared; and a G over G – make fast on this side of the lock.

All pleasure craft must use the Kleinesluis from *1/4-1/10*, m-f 0600-2400, tu-sa 24 hours, su/h 0000-2100. At other times they should consult the lock-keeper about use of the other locks.

Customs

On the N side of the outside entrance to the Zuidersluis, uncomfortable pilings to tie alongside. After customs clearance it is then necessary to clear Immigration, at either the office near the customs post or at an office on the road above the S bank close E of the locks.

Entrance and facilities

The 29M range light and the complex of chimneys as well as smoke rising from the steelworks N of the entrance are visible many miles out to sea. The IJmuiden-Geul approach area and channel has Y conical Lt buoys on its S side as well as a RW offing Lt buoy 5M from the entrance, so it is easy for yachts to cross the channel at right angles or when approaching the harbour to keep out of the channel until the entrance. There are also Ldg Lts with 4M daylight and 29/16M night range.

The entrance faces N and is uncomfortable in strong northerly winds. Tides also run fast across it, so consult *Stroomatlas j*. Like Scheveningen, the entrance is a triple one, between an outer set, an inner set, and the Zuider Buitenkanaal entrance set of port and starboard Lts. Between the second set of Lts and the canal there is a channel with a buoy on the S side and one on the N side off the end of the wall projecting from Forteiland. Then straight along the channel, past the fishing harbour entrance, to the locks.

The whole complex has over 4·5m depth. The only freely available moorings are on southern bank of the Noordzeekanaal at the approach to the locks, are uncomfortable from wash of passing vessels, and it is often necessary to lie alongside barges and other vessels.

The tidal Haringhaven and Vissershaven are extremely busy – this is the Netherlands' largest fishing port – but it is sometimes possible to tie alongside a fishing vessel or to the pontoons in the Haringhaven. If you succeed in achieving an acceptable mooring, places of interest are the huge fish market, the beaches and 'De Kennemer Duinen', the national sand dune park S of the town.

IJmuiden outer entrance

95

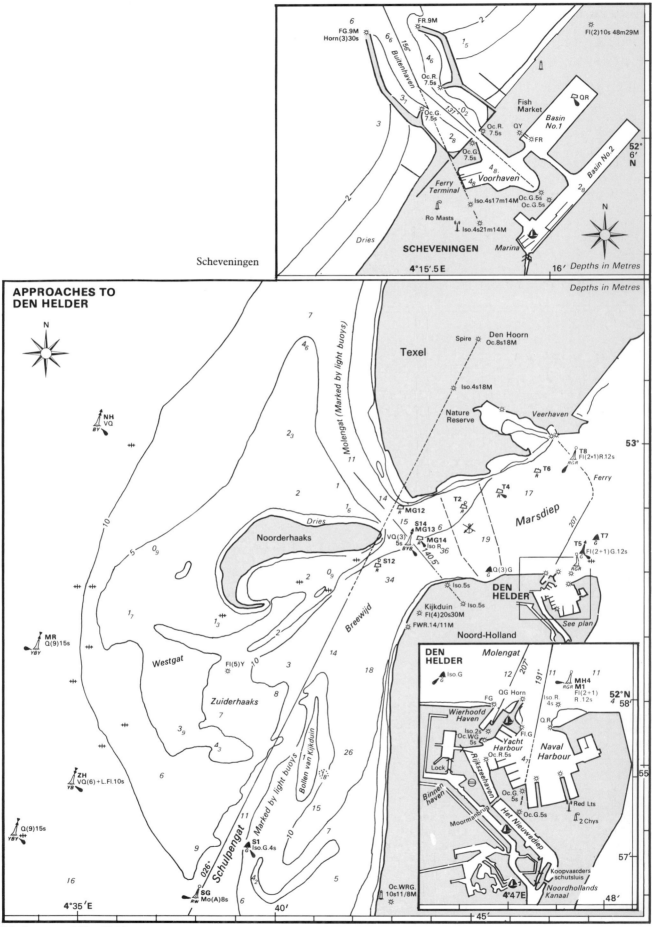

SCHEVENINGEN

6
FG.9M
Horn(3)30s

FR.9M

Fl(2)10s 48m29M

Oc.R.
7.5s

Oc.G.
7.5s

Buitenhaven

Fish
Market

QR

Basin
No.1

Oc.R.
7.5s   QY
FR

52°
6′
N

Oc.G.
7.5s

Basin No.2

N

Voorhaven

Ferry
Terminal

Iso.4s17m14M   Oc.G.5s
Oc.G.5s

Ro Masts

Iso.4s21m14M

Dries

Marina

4°15′.5E

16′ *Depths in Metres*

Scheveningen

**APPROACHES TO
DEN HELDER**

Depths in Metres

N

NH
VQ
BY

Texel

Spire

Den Hoorn
Oc.8s18M

Iso.4s18M

Nature
Reserve

Veerhaven

T8
Fl(2+1)R.12s
RGR

53°

Molengat (Marked by light buoys)

T6
R

Ferry

T4
R

Marsdiep

MG12
R

T2
R

17

S14
MG13
R

VQ(3)
5s
BYB

MG14
Iso R

19

207

T5
RGR

T7
G
Fl(2+1)G.12s

Dries

Noorderhaaks

S12
R

34

Q(3)G
G

**DEN
HELDER**

Iso.5s

Iso.5s

See plan

Breewijd

Kijkduin
Fl(4)20s30M
FWR.14/11M

MR
Q(9)15s
YBY

Noord-Holland

Westgat

Fl(5)Y

Zuiderhaaks

**DEN
HELDER**

Molengat

12   207°   191°   11   11

MH4
M1
Fl(2+1)
R.12s

Iso.G
G

RGR

Iso.R
4s

FG   QG Horn

*Wierhoofd
Haven*

Iso.2s
Oc.WG
5s

Fl.G

Q.R

*Naval
Harbour*

52°N

4   58′

*Yacht
Harbour*

Oc.R.5s

ZH
VQ(6)+L.Fl.10s
YB

Lock

15

Binnen
haven

Rijkszeehaven

Oc.G.
5s

Oc.G.5s

Red Lts

2 Chys

55

Q(9)15s
YBY

Moormanbrug

Het Nieuwediep

Marked by light buoys

Bollen van Kijkduin

26

S1
Iso.G.4s

Schulpengat

Koopvaarders
schutsluis

*Noordhollands
Kanaal*

57′

SG
Mo(A)8s
RW

026°

Oc.WRG.
10s11/8M

Oc.WRG.
10s11/8M

4°47E

48′

4°35′E

40′

45′

Schulpengat and Den Helder

The Schulpengat

Port radio (VHF)
Kustwacht Kijkduin Ch 12

Approach
South of the approach to the Schulpengat channel there is a 4·8m coastal spit, Pettemer Polder, lying off the Petten nuclear power station and marked by an unlit W card buoy. The power station is a square building with two 45m chimneys, R Lts. North of this the approach course starting at the *Verkenningston* offing buoy, *SG* Mo(A)8s, follows the narrow buoyed, lit (G to stbd) channel with leading lights (026·5°, daylight intensity) on Texel, rounding Kaap Hoofd and along the Marsdiep into Den Helder. There is also a cardinal Lt buoy off the end of Noorderhaaks opposite Kaap Hoofd at the junction with the Molengat channel.

DEN HELDER

Tidal range
MHWS 1·8m, MLWS 0·5m, MHWN 1·6m, MLWN 0·2m

Port radio (VHF)
Ch 14. HrMr ☎ (02230) 1 12 34
Moormanbrug Ch 18
Koopvaardersschutsluis Ch 22

Entry signals
Permission should be obtained on VHF for entry and departure.
From the signal station on the root of the west pier on Harssens island the following lights are shown when a naval vessel is entering or leaving.

Incoming traffic

R
W   no entry, stay beyond 200m of entrance
R
W   no entry, no traffic allowed within the harbour
R

Outgoing traffic

R
   W   no traffic allowed in Marinehaven
R
W   no traffic allowed in Nieuwe Diep N of Moorman-brug
R
W   W   no traffic allowed in Marinehaven and Nieuwe Diep N of Moormanbrug
R
W   no entry, no traffic allowed in Marinehaven and
R   Nieuwe Diep N of Moormanbrug

Customs
Clearance can be obtained in the yacht haven. Het Nieuwe Diep 23, ☎ (02230) 1 51 81 or 3 49 56.

Entrance and facilities
The harbour entrance has 2 sets of leading lights, for the Veerhaven and for the Marinehaven.

Tidal streams run fast across the entrance of Marinehaven Willemsoord (4·7 to 9m least depth), so once again use *Stroomatlas j*. Nearing the entrance keep a sharp lookout for ferries coming out of the Veerhaven and heading for 't Horntje on Texel. The main harbour entrance has two successive sets of port and starboard lights. The westernmost of the outer set of lights is on the wall projecting out from Harssens island (an island no longer), and the E one is a beacon *MH6* on the N corner of a dangerous drying patch extending N from the E wall. After passing between both sets of lights, the yacht harbour is to starboard in the first dock behind the island and signal station.

Den Helder. Vice Admiral Moormanbrug from the N side

Koninklijke Marine Jachtclub is part of the Dutch navy and usually a few berths can be found at the pontoons. There is a small clubhouse with showers and toilets.

Den Helder is the Netherlands' major naval port, used by merchant vessels only for shelter, repairs and provisions.

The town of Den Helder is a 15 to 30-minute walk W of the yacht harbour and has a good modern shopping precinct. The town has been associated with the Dutch navy since at least the 16th century.

To enter the Noordhollands Kanaal and the inner yacht harbours continue down the Nieuwe Diep along the W side of the harbour through Vice-Admiral Moormanbrug and Koopvaardersschutsluis.

For information on Den Helder's inland waterway area and facilities see Chapter 9, Route 14.

Eierlandsche Gat

Eierlandsche Gronden and Engelschmangat between Vlieland and Texel is unmarked in its approach channels, has no nearby harbour inside the islands, and is a complex area of shoals to be avoided by yachts without local familiarity, its most useful assets being the LtHo and the inshore lifeboat station to its SE.

Zeegat van Terschelling

Because of the screen of banks with drying patches and wrecks – Gronden van Stortemelk, Westergronden, Noordwestgronden, Noordergronden – approach must be along the buoyed channels which are frequently changing and the buoyage altered at short notice, requiring an up-to-date chart. As of late 1988 there are two marked channels from the W and NE, both with RW spherical offing Lt buoys. Zuider Stortemelk from the W is the deepest (5–14m) and stablest channel. Noordgat (3·2m minimum depth 1988) an extension of Boomkensdiep (5m) is to be avoided without local knowledge, particularly in strong lee-shore conditions, since depths are changing seasonally and the buoyage moved.

Thomas Smit Gat which also leads out of Boomkensdiep is no longer marked. However, from the NE it is not difficult to pass round the outer edge of the *gronden* to enter the Zuider Stortemelk using the cardinal Lt buoys round the outer edge of the banks and the two lighthouses for position-fixing. There is also a yellow beacon Fl(5)Y.2s 2½M N of Vlieland LtHo and N of the channel.

The inner part of this estuary is a very popular sailing area and the frequent ferries are the only major commercial traffic. Vliesloot channel leads out of the Zuider Stortemelk round the end of Vlieland in a dogleg marked by lateral beacons and buoys (some lit) to the tiny harbour of Oost Vlieland, on one of the prettiest of the Frisian islands. Alternatively the wide buoyed Vliestroom leads direct into the Waddenzee with several possible branching routes beyond, for example to Harlingen. Finally there are two laterally buoyed lit channels on the NE side of the Stortemelk leading to West Terschelling, one close round the sandbank edge of Noordvaarder on the island itself, and the Schuitengat (2·6m minimum depth in 1988) across Jacobs Ruggen from the SW.

But above all when choosing your approach channel have an eye for the wind direction and strength, for example the Zuider Stortemelk and Vliestroom entrance can be extremely uncomfortable in strong winds from W to NW.

Oost Vlieland, West Terschelling, and Harlingen. See Chapter 11, Route 18.

Zeegat van Ameland

There is a screen of banks, the Bornrif, across the whole of the wide gap between Terschelling and Ameland with one narrow channel, the Westgat, leading in from N of Terschelling. It is marked by unlit buoys, does not lead to any deep-water harbour, can produce dangerous seas in strong winds, and as an approach route is not recommended unless you have local knowledge. In reasonable conditions it can be a deep-water exit when cruising the *wadden* channels if for tidal reasons you need to make a detour outside the islands.

Friesche Zeegat

A maze of dangerous banks with wide drying areas and small islands fans N out of the wide gap between Ameland and Schiermonnikoog. Pinkegat and the other unmarked channels W of Het Rif island are in most circumstances unnavigable out to sea. Nearer to the Schiermonnikoog side is the only marked navigable channel, buoyed and lit, the Westgat, heading N between the two islands Het Rif and Engelsmanplaat to the W, and the Kuipersplaat drying bank to the E. A N cardinal (*WRG*) Lt buoy and a spherical RW offing (*VWG*) buoy mark the N approach to the lateral channel buoys which start at the 4·2m entrance bar, the Rif.

The main daylight marks from offshore are the disused LtHo on Engelsmanplaat, and the LtHo (also useful for night approach) and water tower on Schiermonnikoog. This passage is emphatically a fair-weather one since in strong winds seas break across all of the outer grounds. Once across the bar, depths increase from 5m to 16m in places in the Westgat and its extension the Zoutkamperlaag leading to the deep-water harbour of Lauwersoog, and the lock entrance to the Lauwersmeer with its canalised access to Friesland and Groningen. Commercial traffic in the area is limited mainly to fishing vessels and ferries, but the main channel is well buoyed and lit.

Gat van Schiermonnikoog leads off E from this channel S of the island of the same name and is narrow, at least 2m deep, and marked on its N side mainly by unlit R spar buoys although there is a RG offing Lt buoy and several Lt buoys and beacons near the head of the channel. A starboard and port-hand marked withied channel leads N out of the Gat and across the Siege bank to the small yacht harbour, refurbished in 1987, which has a sill and 1 to 1·6m of water when the sands dry out.

Schiermonnikoog, Lauwersoog and the Lauwersmeer. See Chapter 11/Route 18 and Chapter 12/Route 21.

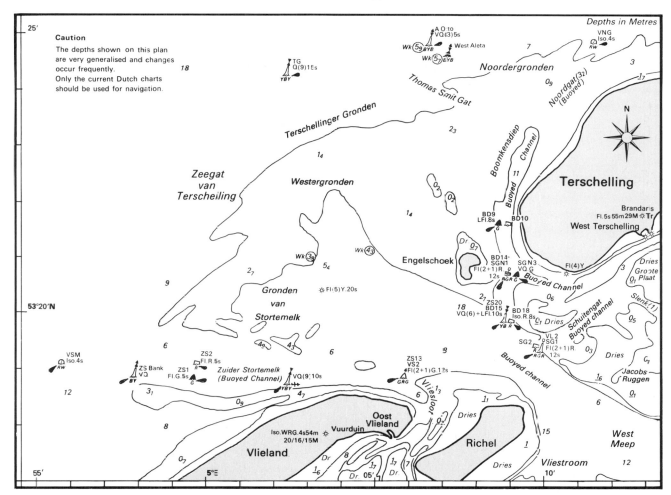

Zeegat van Terschelling

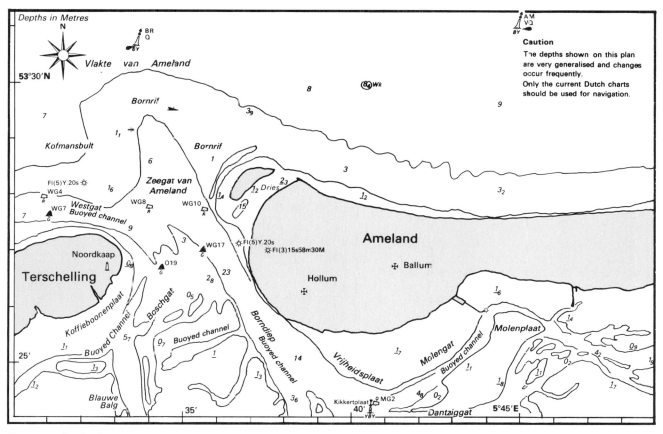

Zeegat van Ameland

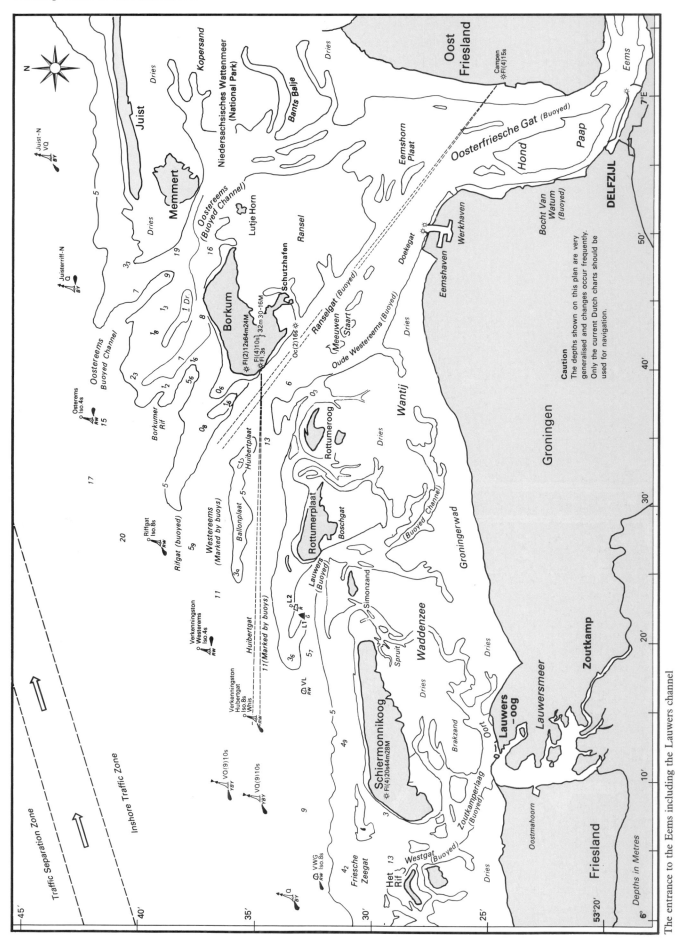

The entrance to the Eems including the Lauwers channel

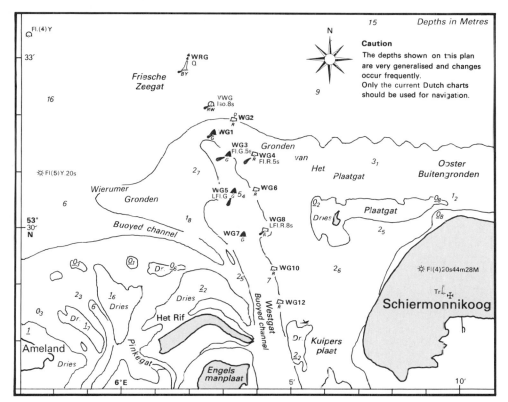

Friesche Zeegat

The Lauwers

Like the Friesche Zeegat a maze of drying banks and a small island, Simonszand, spreads between Schiermonnikoog and Rottumerplaat. There is only one marked channel E of Simonszand, the Lauwers leading to the Spruit and Boschgat channels. Use of the unmarked Eilanderbalg channel to the W of Simonszand is to be avoided in all circumstances. Like Zeegat van Ameland the Lauwers is narrow and heads in from the W under a wide screen of offshore banks, Gronden van der Lauwers, stretching W from the end of Rottumerplaat. Exactly the same advice applies as for Zeegat van Ameland: it is marked by unlit buoys, does not lead to any deepwater harbour, can produce dangerous seas in strong onshore winds, and as an approach route is not recommended unless you have local knowledge. In reasonable conditions it can be a deep-water exit when cruising the *wadden* channels if for tidal reasons you need to make a detour outside the islands.

The Eems

Port radio (VHF)

Borkum Radar Ch 18 or Havendienst Delfzijl Ch 14 are the nearest port radio stations if you need advice. Alternatively, Radio Die Ems (Ems Information Service) broadcasts every H+50 in German on Ch 15, 18, 20 and 21.

Entrance

Like most of the other *zeegats* offlying banks complicate navigation and the main channels head in from the west. The entrance is between the Borkumer Rif drying spit stretching NW from Borkum to the E and the islands of Rottumeroog and Rottumerplaat with their maze of offlying drying banks and shoals to the SW. The outer entrance is split into two channels by Ballonplaat and Huibertplaat (1m minimum depth).

The southern Huibertgat and the northern Westereems are both major, well buoyed, lit channels, with leading sector lights: Borkum Kleiner Lt for the Huibertgat, and Campen for the Ranselgat leading out of the E end of the Westereems. There is also a minor lit, buoyed deep-water channel, the Rifgat, crossing the far outer end of the Borkumer Rif and entering the Westereems channel.

The profuse buoyage as well as the many daylight marks and lights on the W end of Borkum close to the neck of the 1½M wide entrance proper make position-fixing easy in this area. Once into the Ranselgat there are two alternatives: to enter the well buoyed Fischerbalje off the N side and thus into Borkum's Schutzhafen where you must remember to clear West German customs; or to continue on down the river to Delfzijl or Emden.

Similar warnings apply to this as to other *zeegats* in rough weather. In strong winds from W to NW against an ebb the two channels, and often the Ranselgat, can be dangerous to yachts, whilst in strong onshore winds breakers can build up on the outer grounds of the Rifgat and Westereems.

Finally, these are major shipping channels to places such as Eemshaven, Delfzijl and Emden so care should be taken by yachts to keep out of the way of commercial shipping and obey the International Collision Regulations.

DELFZIJL *See Chapter 11/Route 18, and Chapter 12/Route 21.*

9. Noord-Holland and Amsterdam

Route 13
IJmuiden to Amsterdam via the Noordzeekanaal

Commentary

This is a route you will wish to put behind you quickly either after or before an exhausting North Sea passage. It is possible to sail in the country reaches near IJmuiden, motoring in the later industrial built-up reaches where the wind is more erratic. Traffic is lighter than on the Nieuwe Waterweg or Westerschelde but still requires great caution, particularly nearer to Amsterdam with its considerable barge, deep sea and ferry (there are many ferry crossings) traffic, in both directions and coming out of the many side docks and canals.

IJmuiden (see Chapter 7) is the Netherlands' largest fishing port and does not fully cater for yachts. If you can manage it however a visit to the wooded dunes and beaches of the national park to the south of the town, De Kennemer Duinen, is worthwhile.

Amsterdam in contrast has a number of scattered yachting facilities and its fleshpots are a good start to a Dutch cruise if you can stand the pace after a hard crossing! With more listed buildings than any other place in Europe, a surrounding spider web of early 17th-century canals embracing the medieval town, port and the Royal Palace on Dam Square, and its varied nightlife and open air cafés, it is well worth a protracted stop or a repeat visit en route homeward. The Rijksmuseum, the Vincent van Gogh Museum, the Royal Palace, the Nieuwe and Oude Kerks, the Netherlands' Centre for Old Crafts (cheese-making, etching, glass-blowing, etc.), Rembrandthuis, Anne Frank House, diamond-cutting factories, Heineken's brewery, the Stedelijk museum of modern art, a water-bus on the canals; the list of things to see and do should last for many visits.

There is also a bewildering choice for eating out: Argentinean, Indo-Chinese, Italian, Greek, and fish restaurants are just a few. Do not forget to try the *pannekoeken* and *poffertjes* available in most cafés, as well as *appelgebak* and *slagroom* with your coffee and *genever*. Both the Sixhaven and ZV Aeolus are easily accessible by ferry direct from the central station, and the De Ruyterkade yacht harbour is even closer.

Distance 24km/13M

Bridges and locks None

Tides, heights and soundings

Non tidal. Heights and soundings to KP (*kanaalpeil*, canal level).

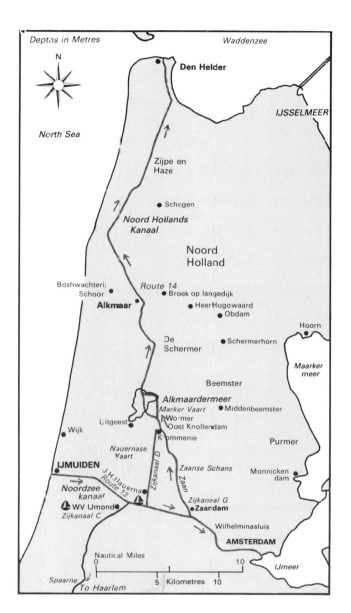

Route plan

Minimum depth en route

Generally 15m. The yacht harbours of course are much less: Nauerna 2m or a little less in places, Sixhaven in parts 1·8m, WV Aeolus 1·5m.

Charts

Admiralty *124*, Dutch sea chart *1543*, ANWB *G*

Route description

⚓ IJMUIDEN locks.
See Chapter 8 for details of facilities and entrance.

NOORDZEEKANAAL

9·8km/5·3M
⚓ ZIJKANAAL C, S bank, leads via 3 opening bridges and a lock to Spaarndam and the Mooie Nel. WV IJmond 1·4km/0·8M and through 1 opening bridge is a convenient resting-up place on a North Sea passage. *See Route 9, Chapter 6, for details of facilities.*

2·0km/1·1M
⚓ ZIJKANAAL D, N bank.

DETOUR ALONG NAUERNASE VAART to join Route 14 at West Knollendam. Distance 10·6km/5·7M. Jachthaven Nauerna is only 700m from the entrance, another convenient base for a North Sea passage.

ZIJKANAAL D, depth 2m. 15kph max.
⚓ Jachthaven Nauerna on W side. Club in a barge. Toilets, showers, 2·5t crane. ☎ (02987) 1722.

NAUERNASE VAART, Depth 2m, 7·5kph max.
⚓ ⚓ Lock and drawbridge (ht 2·70m) into Nauernase Vaart. ☎ (075) 163620/354488
Service hours 16/4-1/6 and *1/9-16/10* m-f 0900-1200, 1300-1800, f also 1800-2000, sa 0900-1200, 1400-1900, su/h 1000-1200, 1400-1900. *1/6-1/9* daily 0900-1200, 1300-1700, 1800-2000, (sa/su/h to 1900). *16/10-16/4* m-f 0900-1200, 1400-1800, sa 0900-1200 1st and last 2 Saturdays in period, contact lock-keeper other Saturdays.

⚓ Westzaan drawbridge (ht 2·49m). ☎ (02987) 1448.
Service hours m-f 0830-1630, sa/su/h closed.

KROMMENIE

2 **⚓ Krommenie railway bridge** (ht 0·75m) and drawbridge (ht 2·60m).
Drawbridge service hours See Westzaan bridge above.
Railway bridge service hours 15 to 30-minute waits for trains. See ANWB booklet *Openingstijden spoorwegbruggen.*

⚓ Vaartbrug, municipal drawbridge (ht 1·20m).
Service hours 16/4-1/6 and *1/9-16/10* m-f 0700-0900[1], 1000-1200, 1300-1630, 1800-2000 (f only), sa/su/h 1000-1200, 1400-1800. *1/6-1/9* m-f 0700-0900[1], 0930-1230, 1300-1630, 1800-2000, sa/su/h 0900-1200, 1400-1800. *16/10-16/4* m-f 0830-1630[1], sa 0900-1200 (only on first 2 and last 2 Saturdays in season).
1. By agreement with HrMr Zaandam. ☎ (075) 512888/552335, VHF Ch 20.

WEST KNOLLENDAM
Dogleg to starboard then to port into Markervaart, Route 14.

NOORDZEEKANAAL
Continue along Noordzeekanaal from Zijkanaal D.

6·2km/3·4M
⚓ ZIJKANAAL G, N bank, leads to Zaandam and the Noordhollands Kanaal. *See Route 14 for details of facilities.*

5·9km/3·2M
AMSTERDAM
De Ruyterkade yacht harbour and office.
Harbour information addresses
Gem. Havendienst voor de zeehavens Havengebouw (16), Amsterdam, VHF Ch 14, ☎ (020) 221-515.
Inland waterways Havengelddienst, James Wattstraat 84, Amsterdam ☎ (020) 5683683.
Routeing information Amstelsluis, ☎ (020) 225113. VHF Ch 22 for Nieuwemeersluis, Amstelschutsluis, Kortjewantbrug and Westerkeersluis.

Amsterdam. The municipal pontoon harbour off De Ruyterkade, although it has a baffle wall on the outside, is still uncomfortable from the wash of busy traffic

There are a large number of mooring places of which only a small selection of those near the centre are listed. Moving along the canal from W to E:
⚓ Het Realeneiland (toilets and showers) on the NW side of the Westerdok through the opening **Westerdoksbrug** (ht 2·65m). Jachthaven Hollandse Tuin in the Westerdok, toilets and showers, ☎ (020) 229962.
Bridge service hours m-f 0000-0700, 0900-1600, 1800-2400; sa/su/h closed. For opening outside of hours contact by VHF Ch 22 or ☎ (020) 241457.
De Ruyterkade to the W of the Centraal Station and in front of the harbour building. Pontoons on the river front but uncomfortable from the wash of passing ships.
WVDS Sixhaven 1021 HG, Amsterdam, ☎ (020) 315097 (evenings). On the N side of the river opposite the Centraal Station, to which there is a fre-

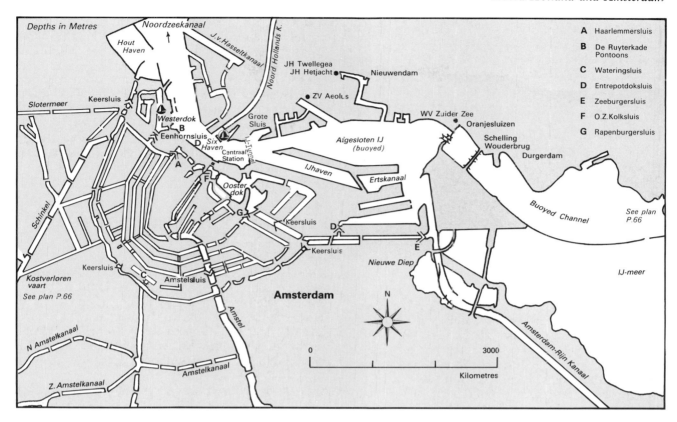

Depths in Metres

Hout Haven

Noordzeekanaal

J.v.Hasseltkanaal

Noord Hollands K.

JH Twellegea
JH Hetjacht
Nieuwendam

ZV Aeolus

WV Zuider Zee
Oranjesluizen

Schelling
Wouderbrug

Durgerdam

Afgesloten IJ (buoyed)

IJhaven

Ertskanaal

Buoyed Channel

See plan P.66

IJ-meer

Slotermeer

Keersluis

Westerdok
Eenhornsluis
Six Haven

Grote Sluis

IJ-Tunnel

Centraal Station

Ooster dok

Schinkel

Keersluis

Nieuwe Diep

Kostverloren vaart
See plan P.66

Keersluis

Amstelsluis

Amsterdam

N

Amstel

N Amstelkanaal

Amstelkanaal

Z. Amstelkanaal

0   3000

Kilometres

Amsterdam-Rijn Kanaal

A	Haarlemmersluis
B	De Ruyterkade Pontoons
C	Wateringsluis
D	Entrepotdoksluis
E	Zeeburgersluis
F	O.Z.Kolksluis
G	Rapenburgersluis

Amsterdam

quent nearby ferry service. A R buoy lies off its S corner and the entrance is a tree-overhung gap behind a baffle wall on its E side. Toilets, showers, bar and limited lifting facilities, ideally situated for the ferry and a short walk through the Centraal Station into city centre.

ZV Aeolus a small marina in the Johan van Hasseltkanaal-Oost, 1M E of the Sixhaven on the N bank with toilets and washing facilities.

Jachthaven Twellegea (3·5m depth) and Jachthaven Het Jacht on the N bank, ¾M up the zig-zag Zijkanaal K whose entrance is 6 cables W of the Oranjesluizen. Jachthaven Twellegea has 30t crane, toilets, showers, ☎ (020) 324877

Amsterdam. The Sixhaven's entrance is now protected from wash by a baffle

See Route 15 for continuation through Oranjesluizen to the IJsselmeer.

See Route 8 for approaches to Amsterdam via Schiphol and the Nieuwe Meer.

Route 14
Amsterdam to Den Helder via the Zaan and Noord-Hollands Kanaal

Commentary

From Alkmaar southwards this is a similar type of cruise to Routes 8 and 9, continuing through old Noord-Holland, with no navigational worries, winding canals, many bridges, a lake, two old towns and much to see on the canal banks. The canal keeps generally close to the North Sea coast, and in the south stretching eastwards are the 17th-century windmill-drained polders of Schermer, Beemster, Wormer and Purmer.

To the NW of Alkmaar and W of the canal are the wooded rolling dunes of the Boswachterij and Schoorl, and the North Holland Dune Reserve (Noordhollands Duinreservaat), well worth a cycle ride to its edges. The N stretch of the canal is bleaker, closer to and with less protection from North Sea winds, whilst the N9 main road to Den Helder follows the W side; but this is still infinitely better than being out at sea in rough weather.

Zaanse Schans windmills

The Zaanstad industrial complex along the river Zaan has an extremely varied waterfront from factories to churches. It is not difficult to negotiate the Wilhelminasluis and its two opening bridges (*bruggeld* must be paid), and the six succeeding bridges usually open promptly, particularly if, as is likely, you have become a member of a convoy.

In Zaandam you should see the Tsaar Pieterhuisje where Peter the Great lived during his 16th-century visit to study shipbuilding, the last restoration having been done in 1895 by the then Russian Tsar. In Koog aan de Zaan there is a windmill museum in an 18th-century house, and you must visit the Zaanse Schans windmill museum area (see Chapter 1) close to Jachthaven ZV De Onderlinge on De Poel to the S.

Near the Zaanse Schans there is a buoyed channel in the river with shoals first on the E side and further N on the W side; R buoys to stbd and G buoys to port going N. To the N of Zaandijk, Krommenie is a pleasant suburban area, the likes of which there are many along the whole length of this canal.

Alkmaar is yet another 13th-century Dutch city with an exceptional collection of preserved buildings, a town canal, narrow streets and market squares. Tie up alongside the Bierkade, or in July and August go into the Luttik Oudorp canal, wake up with the clock chimes, and visit the weigh-house (*waag*) housing the cheese museum and the VVV office. Built in the 14th century as a chapel, this was converted to the religion of commerce in the 17th century and looks like a cathedral. The cheese market is still held by the weigh-house on Friday mornings in summer with all the trimmings for the tourist to enjoy. Other places to visit are the 16th-century fish market, the 15th-century Grote Kerk, and the 15/16th-century town hall; again naming but a few.

Places of interest in the polders east of Alkmaar range from 3 to 12km E of the canal, so bicycles are useful. There are historic churches, windmills or museums at Broek op Langedijk, Heer Hugowaard, Obdam, Schermerhorn, Graft, De Rijp and Middenbeemster.

The polder land E of the canal and N of Alkmaar near Schagen is even earlier, the Burghorn Polder dates from 1461, and the Zijpe and Haze Polders behind the Frisian sea-dyke from 1552.

Den Helder has been the Dutch naval base for many centuries, as well as the ferry port for Texel. It is an open modern-style town with a nearby beach holiday area, a large precinct shopping centre and two museums: the Marine Museum which traces the Royal Dutch Navy from 1813 to date, and a lifeboat museum, the Dorus Rijkers.

Distance 76km/41M.

Bridges 26 opening bridges of which 8 are in Zaandam and 6 in Alkmaar, leaving 12 spread elsewhere. Includes 2 railway bridges.

Locks 2

Tides, heights and soundings
Non-tidal, except in Den Helder N of Koopvaardersschutsluis. Heights and soundings in the main waterway are based on standard summer reference levels, and on KP (canal level) in the Noordzeekanaal. In tidal Den Helder heights are to MHWS and LLWS (lowest low water springs).

Minimum depths en route
3m minimum over most of the waterway but less in side branches; e.g. 1·8m in De Poel at Zaanstad, 1·5m or less outside the channel across the Alkmaardermeer, 2·5m through Alkmaar and 1·5m in Alkmaar's Luttik Oudorp.

Charts
ANWB *G* and *F* are adequate. Useful additional sea charts for the Noordzeekanaal and Den Helder are Admiralty *124, 191*, Dutch small-craft chart *1811*, Dutch sea charts *1543, 1546*.

Route description

AMSTERDAM SIXHAVEN
See Route 13 for details of facilities in Amsterdam.
To stbd and W along the Noordzeekanaal.

NOORDZEEKANAAL
16·5kph/8·9kn max. Depth 15m.

6·3km/3·4M
To port into Zijkanaal G/Voorzaan.

ZIJKANAAL G/VOORZAAN
9kph/4·9kn max. Depth 9m entrance, 3m at locks.

ZAANDAM
HrMr West Kade 2, daily 6-21, ☎ (075) 512524, (only in emergency at other times ☎ (075) 323232).
Jachtwerf Th. Hoogmoed, Zijkanaal G, toilets, 15t boat-lift, ☎ (075) 169746.
Scheepswerf Porsius on Dirk Metselaarhaven, toilets, showers.
Dehler Jachtbouw B.V., E side of Voorzaan.
Passantenhaven, W side of Voorzaan alongside William Pontbrug.

There are a number of boatyards with lifting facilities.

Zaandam. Prins Willem Alexander bascule bridge

Zaan. W bank near Koog

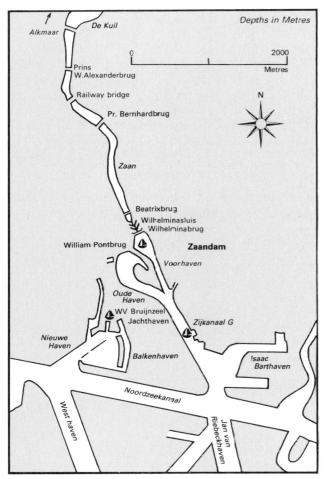

Zaandam

2·5km/1·3M

≪ 2 ⌒ Wilhelminasluis, and 2 bascule bridges, **Wilhelminabrug** (2·9m) and **Prinses Beatrixbrug** (ht 2·85m). *Sluisgeld* to pay. VHF Ch 20.
Bridge service hours m-f 0600-1700, 1715-1730, 1750-2145; sa 0730-1200, 1300-1800; su/h *16/4-16/10* 0800-1030, 1600-1900, *16/10-16/4* closed.

ZAAN
9kph/4·9kn max. Minimum depth 3m, but keep to buoyed channel between Julianabrug and Zaanbrug past the Zaanse Schans, G buoys to the W, and R to the E.

⌒ Prins Bernhardbrug (ht 2·25m)
Service hours m-f 0615-2100; sa *16/4-16/10* 0730-1200, 1300-1645, *16/10-16/4* 0730-1200, 1300-1630; su/h *16/4-16/10* 0815-1030, 1630-1900, *16/10-16/4* closed.

⌒ Railway swing bridge (ht 3m fixed part)
Service hours As for Prins Bernhardbrug, dependent on trains. Frequent openings except during rush hours.

⌒ Prins Willem-Alexanderbrug (bascule, (ht 2·85m fixed part)
Service hours See Prins Bernhardbrug.

⌒ Brug in de Coentunnelweg (ht 6·2m fixed part)
Service hours m-f 0615-0730, 0830-1200, 1300-1700, 1800-2100; sa *16/4-16/10* 0730-1200, 1300-1645, *16/10-16/4* 0730-1200, 1300-1630; su/h *16/4-16/10* 0830-0930, 1700-1900, *15/10-16/4* closed.

⚓ Jachthaven ZV De Onderlinge on De Poel, depth 1·8m, toilets, showers, and only 500m from the Zaanse Schans across the road to the N.

Approaching Julianabrug and the Zaanse Scans on the Zaan. Note the large vessel coming through. This is a busy commercial waterway

4·0km/2·2M
Julianabrug (ht 3·05m)
Service hours m-f 0615-2100; sa *16/4-16/10* 0730-1200, 1300-1715, *16/10-16/4* 0730-1200, 1300-1630; su/h *16/4-16/10* 0830-1000, 1600-1900, *16/10-16/4* closed.

Buoyed channel.

2·7km/1·5M
Zaanbrug (ht 2·33m)
Service hours m-f 0600-2100; sa *16/4-16/10* 0730-1200, 1300-1745, *16/10-16/4* 0730-1200, 1300-1630; su/h *16/4-16/10* 0830-1000, 1600-1900, *16/10-16/4* closed.

Yacht havens at W Knollendam

WEST KNOLLENDAM
3 yacht harbours on W side: Het Zwaantje, Jachthaven De Hennewerf, West Knollendam; all with toilets, showers. Jachthaven De Hennewerf has a 6t crane, ☎ (075) 285757.

TAPSLOOT
To port into this canal.

3·9km/2·1M
Beatrixbrug (ht 3·05m)
Service hours m-f 0615-2100. *16/4-16/10* sa 0730-1200, 1300-1900; su/h 0800-1200, 1500-1900. *16/10-16/4* sa 0730-1200, 1300-1630; su/h closed.

MARKERVAART
To stbd into this canal.

1·9km/1·0M
To port into entrance of Alkmaardermeer at Stierop.

ALKMAARDERMEER
12kph/6·5kn max. Depth 3m in channel, 1·8m outside channel.

0·9km/0·5M
1st R channel buoy. Follow channel between R and G buoys (G to port), some lit.

0·7km/0·4M
Iso.G.6s Bn to port. Channel turns N.

DETOUR TO UITGEEST
Turn to port round Bn. 2·3km/1·2M (4·6km/2·5M round trip) buoyed channel SW, 2·5m depth, outside channel 1m depth. 1·8m-deep channel at end to western yacht havens.
Jachthaven Zaadnoordijk, toilets, showers, 18t crane, ☎ (02513) 19008/12315.
Jachthaven Zwaansmeerpolder (WV Uitgeest) is E of the rest approached from channel across 1·5m depth area, toilets, showers, 10t crane, E.v. Breugel ☎ (02513) 13553.

Continue from Bn following channel across lake. Leave Iso.G.6s Bn near Nes Kalver Straat to port.

3·3km/1·8M
Jachthaven Laamens, 2m depth, toilets, showers, 1t crane, ☎ (02513) 12295, and Jachtwerf Gebr. Verduin 4·5t crane, ☎ (02513) 12970. Also Alkmaarse R. en Z.V. 5t crane, ☎ (02513) 13920.

0·1km/0.05M
Gat van de Meer entrance to Noordhollands Kanaal.

NOORDHOLLANDS KANAAL
10·5kph max. Depth 3·5–4·5m, but 2·5m through Alkmaar.

5·9km/3·2M
2 Leeghwaterbrug (bascule ht opening 4·45m, 4·71m fixed).
Service hours m-f 0500-1630, 1730-2300; sa 0700-1300, 1400-1900; su/h *1/6-1/10* 1000-1300, 1500-1800, *1/10-1/6* closed.

ALKMAAR
To port through Alkmaar (to stbd is Kraspolder Kanaal). HrMr ☎ (072) 117135/120533.

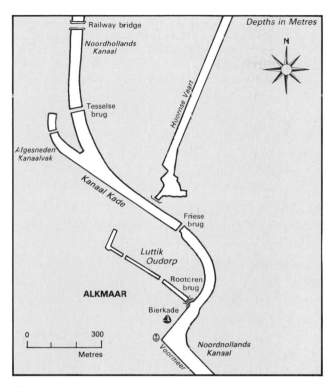

Alkmaar

Alkmaar. Make sure to ignore the left-hand branch at Kanaalkade and head right

⚓ Waiting place to port near harbour office on the Bierkade quay just after right-angled bend, for entrance to, also close N to port, Luttik Oudorp town branch canal (not on ANWB chart); depth 1·5m, and 3 opening bridges. Moorings. Toilets and showers at HrMr office. 40t crane at Nicolaas Witsen B.V., Kraspolderweg 4, ☎ (072) 112297. Laundrette Cor Vredenburg, Luttik Oudorp 60, ☎ (072) 112406.

Bridge service hours m-f 1000-1600; sa 1030-1230; su/h closed. *1/9-1/6* only by arrangement with HrMr.

⌁ **Friesebrug** (bascule, ht 3·84m)
Service hours m-f 0500-0745, 0845-1200, 1210-1220, 1236-1245, 1257-1610, 1710-2300; sa 0700-1300, 1400-1900; su/h *1/6-1/10* 1000-1300, 1500-1800, *1/10-1/6* closed.

⚓ To port 500m beyond is an other branch canal, the Afgesneden Kanaalvak, with moorings, toilets and showers, run by the bridgekeeper of the Tesselsebrug (see below). Contact on VHF Ch 20.

⌁ **Tesselsebrug** (ht 1·95m, fixed bridge 3m on each side)
Service hours See Friesebrug above.

⌁ **Railway drawbridge** (ht 2m opening bridge, 2·9m fixed bridge on W side)
Service hours Daily approximately twice per hour. See ANWB booklet *Openingstijden spoorwegbruggen.*

4·4km/2·4M
⌁ **Huiswaarderbrug** (ht 5·62m)
Service hours m-f 0500-2300; sa 0700-1300, 1400-1900; su/h *1/6-1/10* 0900-1300, 1400-1900, *1/10-1/6* closed.

1·6km/0·9M
⌁ **Koedijkervlotbrug**
Service hours m-f 0500-2300; sa 0700-1300, 1400-1900; su/h *1/6-1/10* 0900-1300, 1400-1900, *1/10-1/6* closed.

Alkmaar, a beautifully preserved medieval town

6·2km/3·3M
⚓ **Schoorldammerbrug**, drawbridge (ht 1·7m opening, 2·65m fixed)
Service hours See Koedijkervlotbrug above.

5·7km/3·1M
⚓ **Burgervlotbrug**
Service hours See Koedijkervlotbrug above.

Noordhollands Kanaal. Burgervlotbrug. The two spans slide across the water

4·0km/2·2M
⚓ **St Maartensvlotbrug**
Service hours See Koedijkervlotbrug above.

3·7km/2·0M
⚓ **Stolpen** (bascule ht 4·73m)
Service hours See Koedijkervlotbrug above.

2·9km/1·6M
⚓ **Vlotbrug te Het Zand**
Service hours See Koedijkervlotbrug above.

7·6km/4·1M
⚓ **Railway drawbridge** (ht 3·35m)
Service hours Daily, 8 minutes after the hour and half hour.

1·2km/0·6M
⚓ **De Kooy drawbridge** (ht 1·6–1·8m)
Service hours m-th 0500-1610, 1645-1655, 1715-2300; f 0500-1540, 1610-1615, 1645-2300; sa 0700-1300, 1400-1900; su/h *1/6-1/10* 0900-1300, 1400-1900, *1/10-1/6* closed.

DEN HELDER
HrMr (on Harssens Island on the N point of harbour), VHF Ch 14, ☎ (02230) 11234.
2 ⚓ 800m NW of lock along N side of Binnenhaven (leave lock to stbd, 4–5m depth) WSOV Breewijd (a naval yacht club) and WV Helder Willemsoord-Nieuwe Diep. Both have toilets and showers. WV-HWN has 500kg crane, ☎ (02230) 24422.

⚓ ⚓ Jachthaven Den Helder (3m depth) in the Industriehaven Westoever. Entrance to port 600m NW of lock (leave lock to stbd), through **Burg. Visserbrug**, an opening bridge (ht 3·58m). Toilets, showers, 35t crane, 15t boat-lift, ☎ (02230) 37444. Scheepswerf W. Visser & Zn 5t crane. Laundrettes Binnenhaven 12 and Jachthaven Den Helder.
Bridge service hours m-f 0500-2300; sa 0700-1300, 1400-1900; su/h *1/5-1/10* 0730-1230, 1430-2100, *1/10-1/5* closed. ☎ (02230) 25041/25042.

4·4km/2·4M
« ⚓ **Koopvaardersschutsluis and opening bridge** (ht 3·1m)
Service hours All times. VHF Ch 22.

⚓ Port along **NIEUWE DIEP** (5–7m depth LLWS)

⚓ **Vice-Admiral Moormanbrug** (ht 2·7m above MHWS)
Service hours All times. VHF Ch 18.

⚓ Stbd into Marinehaven Willemsoord (Oc.R.5s Lt to stbd).

2·0km/1·1M
⚓ Stbd. Jachthaven Koninklijk Marine

See Chapter 8 for details of facilities and offshore approach and entrance to Den Helder.

10. The IJsselmeer

Route plan

Route 15
Amsterdam to Den Helder via west shore of the IJsselmeer

Commentary

This is an easy route, providing the weather is moderate, but a number of warnings must be given.

Strong onshore winds, particularly if you are embayed in one of the corners of the lake and its dams, and winds well offshore with a long fetch can create a nasty chop in these shallow waters. There are motor lifeboats at Enkhuizen, Hindeloopen, Lemmer and Urk, i.e. a preponderance in the northern IJsselmeer, but there are other inshore life-saving stations at, for example, Marken and the Hollandse Brug in the south. Fishing stakes are another IJsselmeer danger, with nets slung between; some, but not all, of the fishing areas are marked on the chart, so keep a weather eye open. Finally take care in the Oranjesluizen, where barge traffic is heavy, and particularly at weekends when local yachts are also out in force.

Night sailing is quite feasible as there are good lights at all the prominent places and leading lights into many of the harbours.

All the harbours on this route have illustrious pasts from the Zuiderzee's golden age between the 17th century and the completion of both the Noord-Hollands Kanaal in 1824 and then the Afsluitdijk in 1932 when tourism took over in a very big way. All are worth visiting, have good yachting facilities, and it is frustrating to have missed out even a single town.

There is nowhere better than the Gouwzee towns for seeing local costume. In Marken, an island until the dam was built in 1957, many people unselfconsciously wear it most of the time, and traditional Marken fishermen's houses with meticulously preserved traditional contents are open for visiting.

Monnickendam, although now surrounded by teeming yacht harbours, retains a quiet old-world charm within its narrow streets. There are eel-smokeries around the harbour, a restaurant in the weigh-house, and the Speeltoren archaeological museum.

Volendam is a pleasant open harbour, only a short distance from Edam which is a canal town that was a flourishing shipbuilding town before it became a cheese-making centre in the 16th century. Edam has a magnificent church, an 18th-century town hall, a museum in a 16th-century house with a floating cellar, and many beautiful canalside buildings.

Hoorn was a major trading town of the East India Company and a herring fishery port. It also has many preserved buildings including a weigh-house, the Gunpowder Tower, and the 1632 council house for the seven towns of Noord-Holland now housing the Westfries Museum.

Enkhuizen was also an East India Company port. An essential visit on any IJsselmeer tour is the huge Zuiderzee Museum, consisting of an outdoor village section and an indoor section in the Peperhuis (headquarters of the East India Company). The Oude Haven quarter with its Drommedaris water gate towering over the yacht moorings is also attractive, and the municipal museum in the weigh-house, the Wapen Museum, the town hall and the churches are worth seeing.

Medemblik is a small very old and beautiful town, with a harbour fringed by trees, a 13th-century castle, Kasteel Radboud (open to visitors), and picturesque gabled town houses and cottages. It is also an international dinghy racing venue.

Den Oever has an artificial fishing harbour and lock complex through the western end of the Afsluitdijk, but its old village is one of the four on the ex-island of Wieringen, the others being Oosterland, Hypolytushoef, and Westerland, with many old house and churches. Wieringen was joined to the mainland by a dyke isolating the Amstelmeer in 1924, and finally the draining of the Wieringermeer-

polder in 1930 connected the south coast of the island to Medemblik far to the south. In 1945 the retreating German army blew a gap in the dyke south of Den Oever flooding most of the polder again, but this was easily repaired in 1946. The small lake created and the nearby Dijkgats Bos (wood) are now a nature reserve; yet another cycle trip!

Once through the dam the navigator has to redouble his vigilance in the Waddenzee channels where the streams run fast and the edges dry out, but fortunately the area is extremely well buoyed.
For Den Helder see Route 14 page 105 and Chapter 8 page 87.

Distance 119km/64M
Gouwzee an additional 18·6km/10M

Bridges 6 opening including Edam and Medemblik.
Locks 3
Tides, heights and soundings
S of Den Oever soundings and heights relate to IJZP (IJsselmeer *zomerpeil* = NAP −0·2m; IJWP, *winterpeil* = NAP −0·4m). In the Noordzeekanaal they relate to *kanaalpeil*. N of Den Oever, in the tidal waters, soundings relate to LLWS (lower low water springs) and heights to MHWS (mean high water springs). Mean spring rates off Den Helder reach 3½kn and it pays to take the ebb on the 12M from Den Oever.

Minimum depths en route
Minimum depths off Marken Point and near Den Oever can be as little as 2m, and 2·2m in the Gouwzee channels. Durgerdam with 1·6m is the shallowest harbour. In the Waddenzee the edges of the Wierbalg and Malzwin channels dry out in places, and the Wierbalg, charted at 1·7m minimum, changes, so it is best to negotiate it near the top of the tide.
Charts
ANWB chart *G* for Amsterdam departure. Dutch small-craft charts *1810, 1811* for majority of route. *Stroomatlas k* for the tidal area.

Route description

AMSTERDAM SIXHAVEN
See Route 13 for detail of facilities.

HET IJ
16·5kph/8·9kn max. Minimum depth 9·5m in channel, 2·5m in places outside. Follow channel E crossing N of IJhaven entrance.

3·7km/2·0M
« **Oranjesluizen**. 3 locks. Traffic lights, loudspeakers. VHF Ch 18. ☎ (020) 360744.
Service hours continuous.
⚓ WV Zuiderzee is 200m NE of locks.

IJsselmeer. Hoek van 't IJ

Buiten IJ

0·5km/0·3M
⚓ **Schellingwouderbrug** (bascule ht 8·9m)
Bridge service hours On the hour and half hr: m-f 0600-0730, 0845-1605, 1800-2200; sa 0600-2200; su/h *1/4-1/11* 0900-1200, 1400-1700, 1830-2000, *1/11-1/4* closed. Closed in winds Force 7 and above.

BUITEN IJ
No speed limit. Greater than 2m depth in buoyed channel, less than 1·5m outside including near southern dam.

⚓DURGERDAM
1·8m-deep narrow channel to harbour. F.R Ldg Lts, leading NNW from E side of GR buoy *P19/D2*. Minimum depth 1·6m in harbour. ZV Het Y (toilets, showers) ☎ (02904) 717; WV Durgerdam, ☎ (02904) 228.

Follow Buiten IJ channel to Hoek van het IJ Lt and the IJsselmeer.

3·5km/1·9M
Hoek van het IJ Lt, Oc.WR.5s18m14/11M.

IJSSELMEER No speed limit.

PAMPUSGEUL CHANNEL
Minimum depth 3m, with 1·5m shoal N of Hoek. Leave channel at about R buoy *P10*, minimum depth 2·2m to Marken Point. Pampusgeul and E shore of Markermeer minimum depth 3m.

13·4km/7·2M
Marken Point. Oc.8s16m9M. Follow G unlit spar buoys NW keeping to their NE side to:

The tiny lighthouse on Marken Point

One of the many spar buoys, difficult to see from a distance, in the Gouwzee

Note A round G over R means *head of channel* buoy to be left to port. R over G means leave to stbd (going inwards).

113

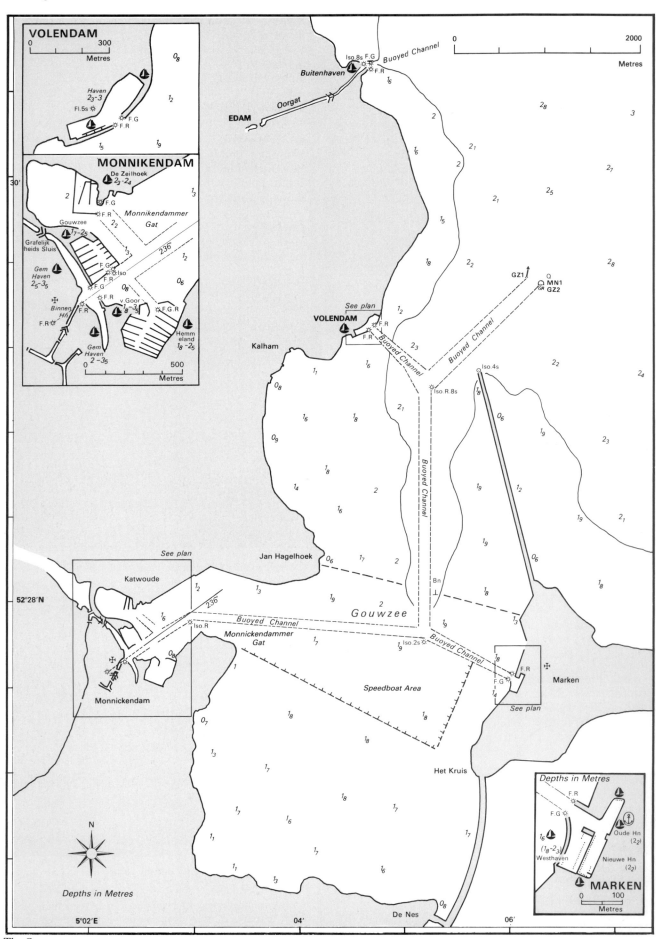

The following are the map labels:

VOLENDAM

0   300
Metres

0_8

Haven
2_3-3
Fl.5s ☼
☼ F.G
☼ F.R
1_2
1_5
1_9

MONNIKENDAM

De Zeilhoek
2_3-2_4
F.G
1_3
2
☼ F.R
Monnikendammer Gat
2_2
Gouwzee
1_7-2_5
236
1_3
1_2
Grafelijk heids Sluis
F.G ☼ Iso
0_8
0_6
Gem Haven
2_5-3_5
F.G
F.R
☼ v.Goor
1_8-3_5
☼ F.G.R
Binnen Hn
F.R ☼
F.R ☼
Hemm eland
1_8-2_5
Gem Haven
2-3_5
0   500
Metres

EDAM   *Oorgat*

Iso.8s F.G   *Buoyed Channel*
Buitenhaven
☼ F.R
1_6

0   2000
Metres

2_8 3
2_1
2
1_6
2_1
2
2_5
1_5 2_1
2_7
1_8 2_2
2_8

GZ1 ⊙ Q MN1
GR ⊙ GZ2

See plan
VOLENDAM   ☼ F.R
☼ F.R
1_2
2_3 *Buoyed Channel*

Kalham
1_1
1_6
0_8
2_1
☼ Iso.R.8s
1_8
⊙ Iso.4s
2_2
2_4

1_6 1_8
0_9
0_6 1_9 2_3

1_8 2 1_9 1_2

1_4 1_9
1_6 1_9 2_1

See plan 0_6
Katwoude 1_2
1_3
236
Jan Hagelhoek 0_6 1_7 2
Bn ⊥ 1_8 1_8
Buoyed Channel
1_6
0_8 ☼ Iso.R
Monnickendammer Gat
2   1_9 *Gouwzee*
1_7 1_3
1_9 ☼ Iso.2s   *Buoyed Channel* 1_8 ☼ F.R
F.G ☼
1_4
Marken
52°28'N
0_8
Monnickendam   *See plan*
0_7 *Speedboat Area*
1_8 1_8
1_3 1 1_8
1_7
1_8 1_7
1_7
1_6 Het Kruis
1_1 1_7
1_7 1_7
1_8
1_6
1_1
1_3

N

Depths in Metres

Depths in Metres
F.R ☼
F.G ☼
1_6
⚓ Oude Hn
(2_2)
(1_8-2_3)
Westhaven   Nieuwe Hn
(2_2)
MARKEN
0   100
Metres

De Nes 0_8

5°02'E   04'   06'

4·8km/2·6M
GR Lt buoy *MN1/GZ2*.

DETOUR INTO THE GOUWZEE
Total distance to and from *MN1* buoy is 18·6km/10M. No speed limit but 8kph/4·3kn in channels near Monnickendam. Minimum depth 2·2m in dredged channels, and generally minimum 1·6m outside, but less than 1m close inshore. Floating spar buoys require keen eyesight.

Channel SW (minimum depth 2·2m) past head of Marken breakwater (Iso.4s6m6M), to:

1·6km/0·9M
G unlit buoy *GZ5*. Channel NW (minimum depth 2·4m) to Volendam entrance. Fl.5s Lt 313° between F.R&G entrance Lts provides leading line. Possible to cut corner between the two channels to Bn *VD1* in depth 2·2m.

0·8km/0·4M
VOLENDAM
Entrance Lts F.R&G
⚓ Moorings along harbour walls. Depth 2·3–3m. Toilets, showers. HrMr ☎ (02993) 64122.

Channel SE (minimum depth 2·4m) to:

0·8km/0·4M
GR unlit buoy *GZ7*[1], and R LtBn *GZ8*. Channel S (minimum depth 2·2m) to:

2·7km/1·5M
GR LtBn *GZ17/MO2*. Channel ESE, minimum depth 2·2m, to Marken entrance. F.W Lt 116° between F.R&G entrance Lts provides leading line.

1·1km/0·6M
MARKEN
Entrance Lts F.R&G
⚓ Free municipal mooring Oude Haven (N arm). WV Marken in Nieuwe Haven (SE arm) and Oude Haven. ZV Het Y in Westhaven, minimum depth 2·2m, but 1·8m in Westhaven. HrMr ☎ (02996) 1636.

Marken. The tiny entrance

1. RGR means port or stbd depending on channel you are entering.

Channel W, minimum depth 2·2m, to Monnickendam entrance. F.R Ldg Lts 236° in the final run of the channel from R LtBn *MO10* to the F.R&G entrance Lts.

4·4km/2·3M
MONNICKENDAM
⚓ Municipal harbour entrance F.R&G, depth 2 to 3·5m. Moorings N and S arms. HrMr ☎ (02995) 1616.
See chart for positions of the yacht harbours below, leading N and S from the channel:
⚓ Jachthaven De Zeilhoek, depth 2·2–2·4m. Toilets, showers, laundrette, 2t crane, ☎ (02995) 1463.
⚓ Municipal yacht haven Hemmeland, depth 2–2·5m, with WV Monnickendam and WV Ark. Toilets, showers, 20t boat-lift, ☎ (02995) 4677.
⚓ Jachthaven Van Goor, depth 2–2·5m. Toilets, showers, 20t boat-lift, ☎ (02995) 2000.
⚓ Watersportcentrum Gouwzee has toilets, showers, 6·5t crane, ☎ (02995) 3751.
Laundrette Wassalon Hoogland, Kalversteeg 1.

Approaching Monnickendam along the Monnickendammergat

Monnickendam. Jachthaven Gouwzee to the N of inner entrance channel

7·2km/3·9M
Return to GR Lt buoy *MN1/GZ2* via the channels.

Total distance of detour 18·6km/10M.

Continue on course for *E1* unlit spar buoy, Edam entrance, keeping clear of coastal shoal and in minimum depth of 2·2m.

2·8km/1·5M
EDAM
E1 G unlit spar buoy.

⚓ Follow spar buoys to Buitenhaven F.R&G entrance Lts, and Iso.8s main Lt behind. Distance 1·1km to entrance Lts. Continue 1·9km to far end of Nieuwe Haven through lock, and bridge serviced by same lock-keeper. Buitenhaven, depth 2·4 to 3·4m, moorings some distance from town. Beyond bridge in town depth 1·8m but edges shallower.

Bridge and lock service hours m-f *16/4-1/6, 1/9-16/10* 0900-1300, 1400-1900, *1/6-1/9* 0800-1300, 1400-2000, *16/10-16/4* 0900-1300, 1400-1700; sa/su/h *16/4-16/10* 0900-1300, 1400-1900, *16/10-16/4* closed.

HrMr ☎ (02993) 71092. 6t crane at Corba Watersport, ☎ (02993) 72451. Laundrette: Loots, Lingerzijde 34, Camping Strandbad.

Course direct to Hoorn entrance, minimum depth 2·5m.

12·6km/6·8M
HOORN
Entrance Lts F.R&G. West pier Lt Iso.4s15m10M. Harbour launch VHF Ch 10, HrMr ☎ (02290) 14012.

⚓ Jachthaven De Nieuwe Haven (depth 2–2·5m) W side from entrance, toilets, showers, laundrette. W Hoogland, 10t crane, ☎ (02290) 16046.

⚓ WV Hoorn N of entrance in Vluchthaven (depth 1·8–2·5m), toilets, showers, ☎ (2290) 13540.

Anchorage in Buitenhaven (depth 2m) NE of entrance, and in Municipal Binnenhaven on walls (depth 2·7m), toilets, showers.

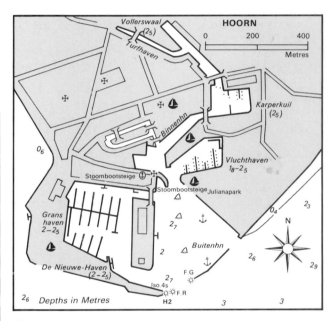

Hoorn

Edam

Edam. Bridge in the Oorgat

Hoorn. The Binnenhaven

4·8km/2·6M
Course direct for G Lt buoy *Nek*. Minimum depth 3m. Follow coast staying in over 2m depth, to:

11·2km/6·0M
KG23 G Lt buoy. Follow channel buoys to Enkhuizen entrance, Broekerhaven lies 1·2km to port of this channel with 3·5m ht fixed bridge. Also sectored Leekerhoek Lt Fl.RW.6s12m11/9M is a long distance mark.

2·6km/1·4M
ENKHUIZEN
F.R&G entrance. To port then stbd round Iso.4s Lt on inner pierhead to the lock.

1·1km/0·6M
≪ ⌂ **Krabbersgatsluizen with drawbridge** (ht 6·3m). VHF Ch 22 *Sluis Enkhuizen*. HrMr ☎ (02280) 12444/13122.
Lock and bridge service hours m-f 0300-2300; sa 1/4-16/10 0300-2300, 16/10-1/4 0300-1900; su/h 1/4-16/10 0800-2000, 16/10-1/4 0900-1700.

Enkhuizen. Entrance to harbour and Drommedaris tower

Krabbersgat channel minimum depth 3·2m, R and G Bns and dammed on E side. Shallow water-ski area on W side. 12kph/6·4kn max Krabbersgat.

4 ⌂ **Drommedarisbrug** (ht 2·6m), also **Keersluis** which stays open, **Wilhelminabrug** (ht 2m), **Blauwpoortsbrug** (ht 2·1m), and **Compagniesbrug** (ht 1·2m) are opening drawbridges.
Service hours m-f 0800-1200, 1300-1800; sa/su/h closed.

See plan for complex of yacht harbours E of lock.
From S to N:
⚓ Spoorhaven, E end, (depth 2–4m) moorings by agreement stationmaster.
⚓ Buyshaven, at the W end of the Spoorhaven, Jachthaven Buyshaven, toilets, showers, ☎ (02280) 15660. Fl.Y Lt on N pier of harbour means keep clear for ferry, all movement forbidden.
⚓ Buitenhaven (depth 2–3·5m), municipal moorings. 2 R Lts on S harbour head mean harbour is full.
⚓ Oude Haven (depth 1·9m) through Drommedarisbrug, municipal moorings.
⚓ Oosterhaven, through Blauwpoortsbrug, moorings W side.
⚓ Jachthaven aan het Krabbersgat (Compagnieshaven) through F.R&G pierhead Lts near exit of Krabbersgat, toilets, showers, laundrette, ☎ (02280) 13353.
Boat-lifts: H.J. van den Berg Bootservice, 30t, ☎ (02280) 13830; Klerk Yacht Service, 20t, ☎ (02280) 13830.

2·0km/1·1M
Krabbersgat exit Bn F.R Lt. Course to De Ven Point, keeping E of G spar buoys marking Kooizand shoal, in 3m minimum depth. At night Iso.G.4s Lt marking S corner of shoal helps.

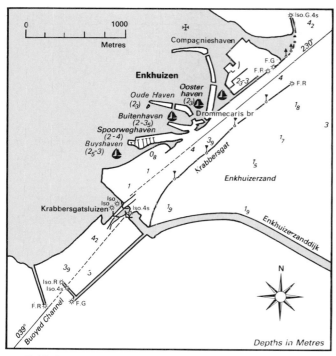

Enkhuizen

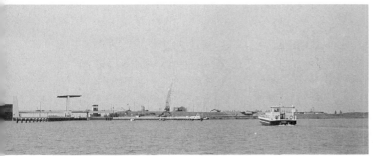

Enkhuizen. Krabbergatsluizen from the NE. In May 1987 the drawbridge was out of action necessitating a 15M detour to Lelystad

4·6km/2·5M

🔻 De Ven Point, Fl.RWG.10s17m11/18M sector Lt. Course for Medemblik, minimum depth 4m but 2·5m near entrance.

ANDIJK

⚓ 6·5km/3·5M along and 1·7km/0·9M S of this track is Andijk/Kerkbuurt, a large isolated marina harbour, 2–3m depth, with Jachthaven Buurtjeshaven (WV De Kreupel), toilets, showers, 10t crane, ☎ (02289) 2350/2227, and Stichting Jachthaven Andijk, toilets, showers, laundrette, 20t crane, ☎ (02289) 3075/1481.

12·0km/6·5M

MEDEMBLIK

F.R&G entrance Lts backed by Oc.5s16m8M Lt on N wall 4·5kph/2·4kn max in harbour.

⚓ Oosterhaven is commercial, Middenhaven has temporary moorings along walls, minimum depth 2·5m. HrMr Oosterhaven, VHF Ch 9, ☎ (02274) 1686/1666.

🔸 Westerhaven must be entered via **Kwikkelsbrug** (drawbridge ht 1·9m).
Bridge service hours 16/4-16/10 m-f 0700-1200, 1300-1800, 1900-2000; sa/su/h 0730-1200, 1300-1800, 1900-2130. *16/10-16/4* m-f 0700-1200, 1300-1700; sa 0800-1200, 1300-1700; su/h closed.
Westerhaven has minimum depth 2·5m throughout with Stichting Jachthaven Medemblik, toilets, showers, laundrette, 3t crane, ☎ (02274) 1861. Medemblik Yacht Service, 25t boat-lift, ☎ (02274) 1769.

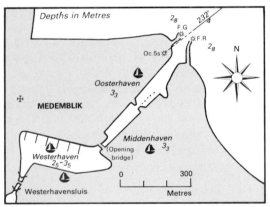

Medemblik

Medemblik entrance

Course to Zeughoek Point minimum depth 3·5m, but 2·5m leaving harbour.

8·1km/4·4M

🔻 Zeughoek Point Lt, Iso.WR.10s17m10/19M sector Lt. Course 1km offshore to Den Oever, channel minimum depth 2·4m, but some shallower patches 1·5 to 2km from the shore.

For deeper-draught yachts a 3 to 7m depth can be followed between Enkhuizen and Den Oever, using the old offshore shipping route.

7·9km/4·3M

DEN OEVER

R Lt buoy *WV8* first of channel buoys (R to stbd). Follow channel carefully, minimum depth 3·4m between G and R unlit spar buoys and one unlit GR buoy (E side of channel). E of channel are shoals, minimum depth 1m.

Entrance F.R&G Lts to Binnenhaven

⚓ Jachthaven Den Oever on each side of 3m depth channel to Stontelersluis. W of entrance. Toilets, showers, 8t crane, ☎ (02246) 1116.

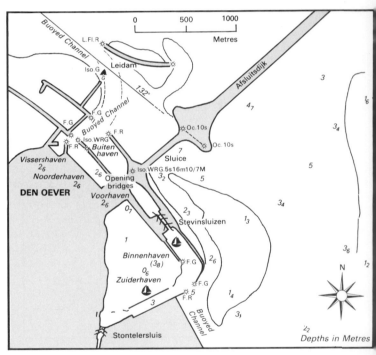

Den Oever

3·2km/1·7M

« 2 🔸 **Stevinsluis and 2 drawbridges** (ht 3m). VHF Ch 20, *Sluis Den Oever*. Lock-keeper ☎ (022 71) 1245.
Lock and bridge service hours m-sa 0500-2100; su/h *1/5-1/10* 0830-1100, 1430-1700, *1/10-1/5* closed.
⚓ Temporary mooring on quaysides of Vissershaven and Noorderhaven, minimum depth 2·6m LLWS, by arrangement HrMr ☎ (02271) 1303. Also 40t crane in shipyard.
MHWS 2·0m, MLWS 0·3m, MHWN 1·9m, MLWN 0·6m.

WADDENZEE

No speed limit. See text above on tides. Stbd beyond lock between F.R&G Lts, keeping in white sector of Iso.WRG.2s Lt astern on wall. Channel minimum depth 2·2m. Then port between channel buoys (R to stbd) on Ldg line of 2 Oc.10s Lts behind on dam.

WIERBALG CHANNEL

1·7m charted minimum depth 1988. Carefully follow winding channel, buoyed, some spars, some lit, and often less than 200m wide. Drying outside channel. Best to take this near the top of the tide, since it is constantly changing and the 1988 chart shows a bar close to LLWS depth at the N end.

11·1km/6·0M

⬎ G Lt buoy *W1*, N end where channel enters the wider Malzwin.

MALZWIN CHANNEL

To port, follow channel (*M* series mainly G buoys, some lit), crossing entrance to Amsteldiep channel. Beware drying S side, Balgzand.

9·3km/5·0M

RG Lt buoy *MH4/M1* off Den Helder entrance.

See Chapter 8 for details of entrance and facilities in Den Helder.

Route 16
Amsterdam to Urk via the Randmeren

Commentary

This route is well protected from the weather, but just to reassure you there are a series of life-saving stations (*Reddingsbrigade* on the chart) at the Hollandse Brug, Huizen, the Stichtsebrug, on the north bank north of the Hardersluis, north bank near Bremerbergse Hoek, and at Elburg. Night sailing is possible since the channel marks include lit buoys and beacons, whilst most entrances are well lit. Do beware of fishing stakes with nets suspended between which are scattered prolifically outside, and often quite close to the edges, of the buoyed channels.

If your air draught is over about 12·5m you will have to enter the Randmeren from the north through the opening Ketelbrug. You will then be able to get as far as the Stichtsebrug (clearance 12·9m) 13km from the western end of the Randmeren.

The route below for yachts within the 12·5m height limit crosses the IJmeer past the strange isolated hump of Pampus island, and follows the old southern shore of the Zuiderzee along the Randmeren channels close to the Flevoland bank. To starboard, across shallows which used to be tidal mudflats, are historic trading and fishing towns on the 'Oude Land' and to port the 'Nieuwe Land'

which emerged from the Zee in 1967 as far as Hardersluis and ten years earlier on the reaches beyond. To port the trees are in neat plantations, the rubbish containers in serried ranks, and there is always a convenient cleat to hand in the yacht harbours and tree-shaded mooring spots, while even the shoreside fishermen sit sedately. To starboard the trees are in clumps, you can skin and eat your *gerokt paling* (smoked eel) straight off the bone from greasy fingers, wander around crowded old market places, or trip over the thick warps of a row of well-preserved *botters* at the quaysides.

Naarden is probably the country's best preserved fortified town, but you will need your bicycle as it is 2km or more from the yacht harbour. Though considered impregnable it was captured and put to the sword by the Spaniards in 1572. The museum is under the ramparts and there is a magnificent Grote Kerk.

On the opposite bank in sharp contrast Almere-Haven is the first stage of Holland's newest new town, an area of residential garden suburbs.

Huizen is a rapidly growing town, with an old fishing harbour, although the western yachting complex is practical rather than picturesque.

Spakenburg is a lovely, narrow, traditional fishing harbour with a fine collection of well preserved, non yacht-converted, old wooden fishing *botters*, and a wide market area.

Nijkerk is 2km or more from the yacht harbour but is another old town with a 15th-century church, and a weigh-house housing the Netherlands Electricity Museum.

Wolderwijd is an artificial yacht harbour near Zeewolde, a new residential and agricultural centre which only got under way in 1982 and is to be developed as a recreational area.

Harderwijk is a 12th-century Hanseatic port and East Indiaman terminal which went into decline in the 18th century due to the silting of the Zuiderzee, rather than the much later opening of the Noord-Hollands Kanaal. Places of interest are the fishing harbour and town walls, dolphinarium, and the Veluwe Museum van Oudheden.

Elburg is another perfectly preserved moated, walled, 13th-century town set out in a square, which you enter from the harbour through the ornate Vispoortbrug. There is a shopping centre and market within the town.

Ketelhaven is primarily a yacht harbour on the 'Nieuwe Land', with the museum of marine archaeology close by (see Chapter 1).

Finally, having passed through the Ketelbrug, Urk is the most fascinating town of all. Together with its neighbour to the east, Schokland, it was originally a fishing island in the Zuiderzee, and was joined to the mainland during the War in 1942 when the North East Polder was drained. The polder was left barren until 1945 and like the Biesbosch formed another perfect retreat for the Dutch Resistance. Schokland was evacuated in 1859 and only the church now remains as a museum. Urk is the only 'hill' in the IJsselmeer. It has a delightful fishing harbour lined with its remaining trawler fleet. On the headland where the women used to watch out for the sails returning there is a monument to those lost at sea, with memorial plaques by vessel and by year with names of skippers, sons, and relatives.

Distance 113km/61M

Bridges 6 opening of which one (Ketelbrug) has 12·9m under fixed span. Additionally 2 fixed bridges with 12·9m clearance.

Locks 4 including 1 major lock (Oranjesluizen).

Tides, heights, and soundings
Soundings and bridge heights refer to IJZP (IJsselmeer *zomerpeil* = NAP −0·2m, *winterpeil* = NAP −0·4m). Non-tidal.

Minimum depths en route
Buoyed fairway in Randmeren dredged to minimum of 3m, beacons mark the 1·3m contour outside the channel. Well over 3m in the Ketelmeer and IJsselmeer near Urk. Depths in most harbours are good; Harderwijk's Vissershaven being shallowest at 1·6m in parts.

Charts
Dutch small-craft chart *1810*. ANWB chart *I* supplements for the Binnen and Buiten IJ out of Amsterdam.

Route description

AMSTERDAM SIXHAVEN
See Route 15 for this part of route.

7·7km/4·2M
Hoek van het IJ Lt, Oc.WR.5s18m14/11M.

IJSSELMEER
No speed limit.

PAMPUSGEUL CHANNEL
Minimum depth 3m. 1·5m shoal N of Hoek but +2·0m generally outside channel. Follow channel to:

3·5km/1·9M
P6/IJM33 GR Lt buoy then stbd and SE, buoyed lit channel towards Hollandse Brug. Minimum depth 3m. Outside channel depths shelve from 2·5m to less than 2m near buoys *16/17* and less than 1m nearer the bridge. If you decide to cut the corner between the two channels in 2m plus of water, then cross N of Pampus Lt, Fl.5s12m6M.

8·1km/4·4M
⊶ **Hollandse Brug** (ht 12·9m, height gauge).

RANDMEREN
16kph max in channel. 9kph outside. Channel is buoyed, lit, minimum depth 3m as far as Ketelmeer. Outside channel, in some cases but not all, RW or GW spar buoys mark 1·3m depth contour. Most shoals are on S and E 'old' side of channel.

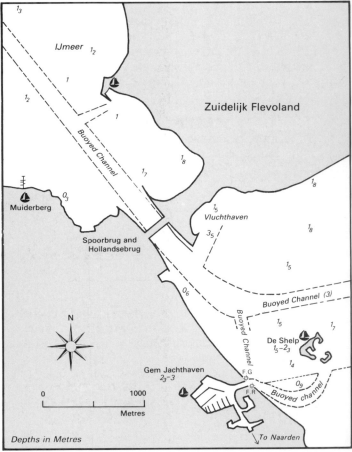

Hollandse Brug and Naarden

1·1km/0·6M
GOOIMEER
Unlit G buoy, *JHN1/GM54*, LtBn close W.

⚓ Channel S bank 800m to municipal Jachthaven Naarden (2·3m depth but the approach channel may be less than this). Toilets, showers, laundrette, 16t crane, ☎ (02159) 42106.

4·9km/2·2M
ALMERE-HAVEN
G LtBn *GM25* N bank.

⚓ Channel, minimum depth 1·8m, runs from W of Bn 400m direct to entrance piers (F.R&G Lts) of WV Almere-Haven (minimum depth 2·5m), toilets, showers, laundrette, 30t crane.

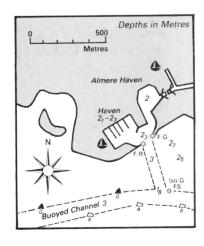

Almere-haven

One of many mooring places on the Randmeren banks

EEMEER

5·9km/3·2M

SPAKENBURG

S bank. GR unlit buoy, *NKN36/JHN1*

⚓ Channel minimum depth 1·9m to Jachthaven Gebr. Nieuwboer, entrance R and G pierhead Lts, distance 0·6km. ☎ (03499) 82306/84389.

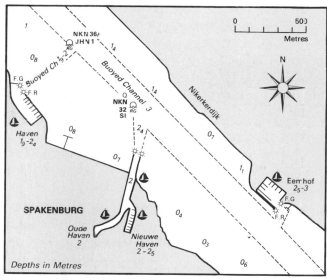

Spakenburg

2·2km/1·2M

HUIZEN

Unlit RG buoy *GM22/H1*, R Lt buoy *20*. S bank. Channel, 1·3km (2·1m depth) to 3 yacht harbours:

⚓ Stichting Jachthaven Huizen/Huizerhoofd, E side, toilets, showers, 10·5t crane, ☎ (02152) 58622.

⚓ Municipal yacht haven, E side near harbour office, toilets, showers, ☎ (2152/59222/57118).

⚓ Huizer Marina, toilets, washing facilities, 20t boat-lift, ☎ (02152) 51159.

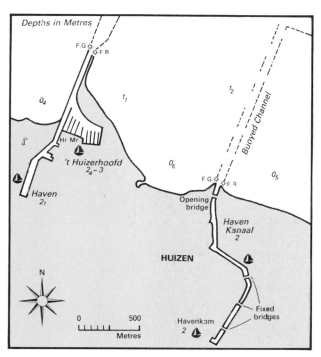

Huizen

4·7km/2·5M

🌉 **Stichtsebrug** (ht 12·9m, height gauge).

Spakenburg has one of the best collections of well preserved fishing boats in Holland

0·9km/0·5M

GR Lt buoy, *NKN32/S1*

⚓ Channel minimum depth 2·1m to Nieuwe Haven, 2–2·5m depth, F.R&G pierhead Lts. Jachthaven WV de Eendracht, toilets, showers, laundrette, 6t crane, ☎ (03499) 81755.

⚓ 500m to Oude Haven, municipal yacht haven, 2m depth, toilets, showers, ☎ (03499) 81782/855-33.

⚓ Jachthaven Eemhof (depth 2·5–3m) N bank just to the E of Spakenburg. Toilets, showers, laundrette, ☎ (03241) 521.

Leaving Spakenburg entrance. End of the W pier

5·8km/3·1M
NIJKERK S bank
GR Lt buoy, *NKN4/NK1*

⚓ Channel minimum depth 3m. 300m to Jachthaven Z & MV De Zuidwal (depth 1·7–2·3m) toilets, showers, 17·5t slipway hoist, ☎ (03494) 53033.

⚓ Open yacht harbour Hameland, depth 1·5–2m, on polderside NW of entrance.

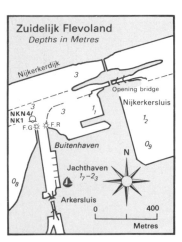

Nijkerk and Nijkerkersluis

Nijkerk entrance

0·5km/0·3M
≪ ✍ Nijkerkersluis lock and opening bridges (ht 7·4m). ☎ (03494) 51278, VHF Ch 18.
Service hours m–sa *1/4–16/10* 0700-1230, 1300-1900, *16/10–1/4* 0800-1230, 1300-1900 (sa to 1800); su/h *1/4–16/10* 1000-1230, 1330-1900, *16/10–1/4* closed.

4·1km/2·2M
NULDERNAUW CHANNEL
F.R&G entrance Lts S bank.

⚓ Jachthaven WV Nulde, only vessels less than 12m. Depth 1·7–3·5m, toilets, showers, 10t boatlift, ☎ (03418) 52732.

4·5km/2·4M
GR unlit buoy, *NN1/JHZ2* W bank.

⚓ 400m distance to Recreatiecentrum Zeewolde, 1·8m depth.

WOLDERWIJD
2·1km/1·1M
GR unlit buoy, *WW31/JHW2* W bank.

⚓ Entrance channel to S of De Zegge Island. Distance 800km, minimum depth 2·6m, to F.R&G Lts entrance Wolderwijd, depth 2–3m. Jachthaven Wolderwijd in the Bonshaven, toilets, showers, laundrette, 20t boat-lift, ☎ (03242) 1220. WV van

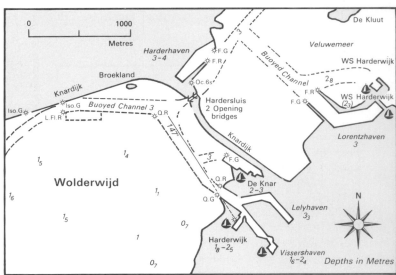

Wolderwijd

Zeewolde lies in the Bolhaven N of entrance, toilets, showers, ☎ (03242) 1583. WV Ark lies in the Pluuthaven.

NULDERNAUW CHANNEL
Follow channel to:

4·6km/2·5M
R and G Lts on polderside, entrance to Harderwijk. Follow channel to:

1·2km/0·6M
Opposite lock there is a channel to stbd towards harbour.

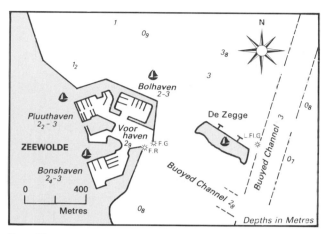

Zeewolde

R beacon marking the beginning of S pier entrance channel to Harderwijk

Harderwijk has a conspicuous domed building, dolphinarium, seen in the approach

DETOUR TO HARDERWIJK

1·7km/0·9M to Vissershaven. Yacht harbours from N to S:

 De Knar, N side of channel, depth 2–3m, showers, toilets, laundrette, 7t crane, ☎ (03410) 23271.

⚓ Zegers (Harderwijk), S side of channel, depth 1·8–2·5m, toilets, showers, 35t boat-lift, ☎ (03410) 13586.

⚓ Vissershaven, S side moorings. Laundrette nearby.

Continue into Hardersluis

« ⚓ **Hardersluis lock and 2 drawbridges** (ht 1·4m) Lock-keeper ☎ (03202) 451.
Bridge service hours m-sa *1/4-16/10* 0700-1230, 1300-1900, *16/10-1/4* 0800-1230, 1300-1800 (sa only 0800-1230); su/h *1/4-16/10* 1000-1230. 1330-1900, *16/10-1/4* closed.

0·8km/0·4M
VELUWEMEER
GR Lt buoy *VM80/IH1* entrance channel to Lorentzhaven and Watersportcentrum Harderwijk.

⚓ 700m along this channel (depth 3m) another buoyed channel branches off to port for 600m to Watersportcentrum Harderwijk, minimum depth 2·3m, toilets, showers, 11t crane, ☎ (03410) 17654.

2·6km/1·4M
GR unlit buoy *VM73/JHF2* N bank.

⚓ Jachthaven Flevostrand, 1·8–2·5m depth, entrance channel between R and G posts. Toilets, showers, laundrette 500m on campsite, 10t crane, ☎ (03202) 457/480.

8·8km/4·4M
⚓ Jachthaven Bremerbergse Hoek, N bank, 1·8–2m depth, toilets.
⚓ Several mooring places on NW bank, but mind the depths.

7·0km/3·8M
⚓ **Elburgerbrug** (drawbridge ht 5·9m).
Service hours See Hardersluis ☎ (05250) 1345.

DRONTERMEER

DETOUR TO ELBURG
1·2km/0·6M to Binnenhaven. Immediately after bridge on S bank, Havenkanaal, depth 2·6m. Yacht harbours from N to S:

⚓ Jachtcentre Elburg, N bank, depth 2·3–3m, toilets, showers, 32t crane, ☎ (05250) 2800.

⚓ Municipal yacht haven on S side of Havenkanaal and in Vissershaven, HrMr ☎ (05250) 2100, 1·5–2m depth.

DRONTERMEER
Continue along it.

⚓ Several mooring places on W bank, but mind the depths.

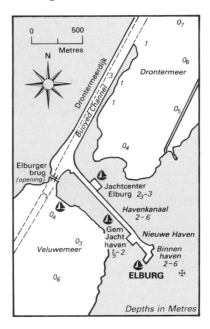

Elburg

Some aggressive looking fishing stakes close to the Drontermeer channel

9·4km/5·1M

GR unlit buoy *DM4/JHR1*, E bank.

⚓ Channel marked by R and G posts, 1·8m depth, to Jachthaven Roggebotsluis, F.R&G entrance Lts, 1·7–2·3m depth, toilets, showers, 8t crane, ☎ (05202) 12402.

0·7km/0·4M

≪ ⟿ **Roggebotsluis lock and drawbridge** (ht 5·6m). *Service hours* See Hardersluis ☎ (03210) 2697.

Roggebotsluis and its drawbridge. This was one of the frequent times when the lock is left open with even levels on each side

VOSSEMEER

⚓ Immediately after the lock, W side, is a pontoon. E side a small yacht haven (1·7–2m depth), taking care to approach from NE, from R buoy *VoM36*, to stay in minimum depth 1·7m.

7·0km/3·8M

⬎ R buoy *VoM6*, Iso.G.2s, Bn *VoM7* on S bank. Channel turns northwards entering entrance to Keteldiep, where it doglegs westwards along buoyed approach channel to the Keteldiep. Beware of heavy barge traffic entering and leaving Keteldiep, as well as the shoal to the S.

0·7km/0·4M

GR unlit buoy *WK9/KH2* at head of channel (2·6m depth) to Ketelhaven.

KETELHAVEN

⚓ Follow channel buoys to E harbour Jachthaven Ketelmeer, distance 0·3km, depth 2·2–2·5m. No entrance Lts to yacht harbour. Toilets, showers, ☎ (03210) 2271.

KETELMEER

Follow channel to *WK1* G Lt buoy, then course to bridge, minimum depth 3m.

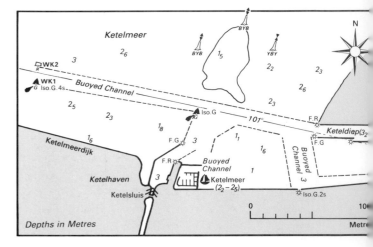

Ketelhaven

Oost Flevoland near Ketelhaven

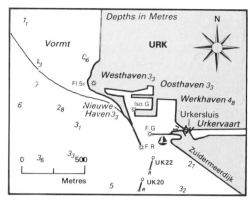

Urk

Jachthaven Ketelmeer at Ketelhaven

Urk. The lighthouse with an enormous fisherman's anchor dredged from the North Sea

8·7km/4·7M

Ketelbrug (ht 9·5m opening part S end, 12·9m fixed part). VHF Ch 18, ☎ (03212) 1607.

Bridge service hours 15/4-15/10 0830-1200, 1330-1600, 1830-2030, *15/10-15/4*[1] 1330-1600. In winds of Force 8 or greater serviced in daylight only.

1. On special request 24hrs in advance ☎ (03200) 61111.

IJSSELMEER

Direct course to Urk harbour entrance, minimum depth 3·5m.

5·9km/3·2M

URK

Entrance F.R&G pierhead Lts. Fl.5s Lt on western point. Horn(3)30s on west pier. HrMr ☎ (05277) 1394.

Jachthaven WV Zuiderzee hard to stbd round G Lt at entrance, S side. Werkhaven (3m max draught, 10m max length). Several boatyards. Temporary moorings in West, Oost and Nieuwe Havens in agreement with HrMr office on N side of Oost Haven. Toilets, showers in hut on pier between Oost and Nieuwe Havens. Scheepswerf Metz (Werkhaven), 2t crane, ☎ (05277) 1741.

Urk. The plaques on the headland show the sea's relentless annual toll of Urk fishing families with vessel numbers from the 19th century onward

Route 17
Amsterdam to Harlingen via east shore of the IJsselmeer

Commentary

Like Route 15 on the other side of the IJsselmeer this is an easy one, but the warnings must be repeated. Avoid strong onshore winds and possible embayment. Winds well offshore with a long fetch create a nasty chop in these shallow waters. Beware of fishing stakes with nets slung between, and look out for those not marked on the chart. Finally take care in the Oranjesluizen where barge traffic is heavy, and particularly at weekends when local yachts are also out in force. Again night sailing is quite feasible as there are good lights at all the prominent places and leading lights into many of the harbours. There are motor lifeboats at Enkhuizen, Hindeloopen, Lemmer and Urk.

Lelystad is worth visiting primarily for the IJsselmeer exhibition at Information Centrum Nieuwe Land (see Chapter 1) south of the lock, and for the Natuurpark Lelystad zoo. WV Lelystad behind the Houtribsluizen is a large and extremely well equipped marina. The new town, although well scattered among trees, is not too inspiring and requires transport. Jachthaven Marina Lelystad to the north is a huge artificial harbour with all yachting facilities, its many pontoons dwarfed by the open spaces and seemingly poised for expansion. For commentary on Urk see Route 16.

Lemmer, one of the entrances to the Frisian canal system has comprehensive yachting facilities, and in sunny weather the town canal (the Zeilroede) with its interesting waterfront and canalside cafés gives the place a Mediterranean atmosphere.

Stavoren is a small but picturesque and more open town spread out between the two harbours, of which the northern is the more photogenic. It was a successful port in the Middle Ages long before the golden age of the western IJsselmeer East Indiaman ports.

Hindeloopen has a similar history, was a prosperous member of the Hanseatic League, and is even more picturesque, with a miniature canal system. The Hidde Nijland museum in the town hall, weigh-house, with its furniture and local costume is worth a visit and the town is well known for its painted furniture and crockery.

Workum close by is equally interesting. Also famous for pottery and in the past for the supply of eels to London. The 17th-century weigh-house, 18th-century town hall, 16th-century St Gertrudiskerk and De Hoop boat-building yard are the places of interest.

Makkum is another Frisian pottery, earthenware, town with a museum devoted to the subject in the weigh-house. The Royal Makkum Pottery and Tile Factory has been operating for at least 300 years, so a conducted tour is well worthwhile.

Finally Harlingen is the largest town en route, ferry port for Terschelling and Vlieland, and with a wealth of gabled buildings and warehouses of the East India Company, particularly round the Noorderhaven where you will probably moor. There is a municipal museum in Hannemahuis and an 18th-century town hall.

Distance 164km/89M

Bridges 7 opening including Stavoren

Locks 4 including Stavoren

Tides, heights and soundings

S of Kornwerderzand soundings and heights relate to IJZP (IJsselmeer *zomerpeil* = NAP−0·2m, IJWP *winterpeil* = NAP −0·4m. In the Noordzeekanaal they relate to *kanaalpeil*. N of Kornwerderzand, in the tidal waters, soundings relate to LLWS (lower low water springs) and heights to MHWS (mean high water springs).

Minimum depths en route

Although this is the deepest water route through the lake with generally 3 to 5m soundings there are a few much shallower patches on the northern shores of the old land (i.e. from Lemmer to Kornwerderzand). The tidal Boontjes channel to Harlingen with drying patches on each side has 1·6m minimum soundings (LLWS) so is best taken well before HW on a rising tide, particularly for deeper draught vessels. Conveniently the flood is northwards towards Harlingen, starting about 5½ hours before and ending at about HW Harlingen. Most harbours and mooring places are 2m and over in depth although Noorderhaven in Harlingen is only 1·1m in places.

Charts

Dutch small-craft charts *1810, 1811*. ANWB chart B. Stroomatlas *k* for the tidal area.

Route description

⚓ AMSTERDAM SIXHAVEN
See Route 15 for this part of route.

7·7km/4·2M
Hoek van het IJ Lt, Oc.WR.5s18m14/11M.

PAMPUSGEUL CHANNEL
Minimum depth 3m, 1·5m shoal N of Hoek but generally over 2m outside channel so it pays to keep out of the way of barge traffic by staying just outside channel.

MARKERMEER
Continue NE past 3 RW safe-water Lt buoys, 2·5–3·5M apart, depths well over 3m to Lelystad.

28·9km/15·6M
LELYSTAD
RW Lt buoy *L/S* off main commercial entrance (F.R&G Lts). Follow wall to the gap/entrance for pleasure craft where wall turns N, just S of lock.

3·9km/2·1M

Stbd through gap (unlit) then SE and hard to port round Iso.G.2s pierhead Lt. Watch out for outgoing traffic.

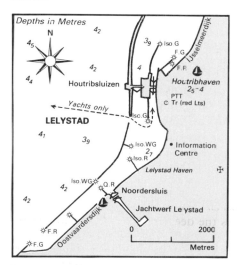

Lelystad

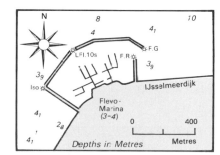

Marina Lelystad

Entrance to the artificial harbour, Marina Lelystad

Marina Lelystad is an artificial yacht harbour with plenty of room for expansion inside

1·4km/0·8M

Houtribsluizen and drawbridge (ht 7·2m). *Service hours* All times.
VHF Ch 20, *Sluis Houtrib*. ☎ (03200) 61111. There are two locks. Contact the control tower and obey the traffic lights. A Fl Lt on either side of a F Lt indicates which lock to use.

⚓ 0·6km to stbd behind E wall of lock round F.G Lt. WV Lelystad in Houtribhaven, depth 2·5–4m, showers, toilets, laundrette, 9t crane, ☎ (03200) 60198.

3km S of the Houtribsluizen is another lock, **Noordersluis**, into the internal canal system of Flevoland (also exits at the Zuidersluis/Vaartsluis further S along the Flevoland coast, and at the Ketelsluis/Kampersluis to the N).

⚓ 500m behind this lock and opening bridge is Jachthaven Scheepskoopers, toilets, showers, 32t boat-lift, ☎ (03200) 60854/60502.
Lock and bridge service hours m-f 0700-1230, 1300-1900 (to 1800 16/10-1/4); sa 0700-1230; su/h closed.

Continue N from the Houtribsluizen between the IJsselmeerdijk and the Houtribdijk. Minimum depth 3·9m.

IJSSELMEER

3·0km/1·6M

⚓ Lt (Iso.R.4s) on the corner of Jachthaven Marina Lelystad. Follow wall past Fl.10s Lt and enter from E between F.R&G pierhead Lts. Jachthaven Marina Lelystad, showers, toilets, laundrette, 50t boat-lift, ☎ (03200) 21000.

Course direct for Urk entrance.

15·2km/8·2M

URK

Long-range Lt on point Fl.5s27m18M. Urk entrance F.R&W Lts. *For details of entrance and facilities in Urk see Route 16.*

Course S and W from entrance, and then N round outer edge of the Vormt shoal (0·6m depth near edges) marked by R buoys (2 lit). Keep well outside 2m depth contour. Continue from R Lt buoy *UK10* in minimum 4m depth direct to round Rotterdamse Hoek.

14·6km/7·9M

Rotterdamse Hoek Iso.WR.10s13m8/5M. Then course NE, 1km offshore following buoys and Bns, one lit, minimum depth 3m, to round Friese Hoek Point.

8·9km/4·8M

Friese Hoek Point Iso.WR.4s12m8/5M. Then course eastwards following R and W Bns of Lemstergeul, minimum depth 3m, 2 sets Ldg Lts 83° (Iso.4s and Iso.8s) and 65° (Iso.G.4s and F.G) to Lemmer.

LEMSTERGEUL

7·7km/4·2M

LEMMER Buitenhaven entrance, F.R Lt.

« Round this R light and follow Buitenhaven channel (4m depth) to **Lemstersluis**. 9kph/4·9kn speed max. There is also an Industriehaven (3–4m depth) and a yacht harbour to the W of the Buitenhaven (2·5m depth).

HrMr/lock-keeper ☎ (05146) 1604/1331.

Service hours 1/5-1/10 m-f 0700-2100, sa 0700-2000, su/h 0830-1200, 1400-1730, 1800-2000; *1/10-15/11* and *15/3-1/5* m-f 0700-2000, sa 0700-1900, su/h closed[1]; *15/11-15/3* m-f 0800-1200, 1300-1700, sa 0800-1200, su/h closed.

1. Open 0900-1100 and 1600-1800 last 2 Sundays in April and first 2 Sundays in October.

Main facilities before entering the lock:

⚓ Jachthaven Friese Hoek (behind entrance Lt), 2–3m depth, toilets, showers, laundrette, 30t boat-lift, ☎ (05146) 1650.

⚓ Jachthaven International Nautic Centre (S end of Industriehaven), 2·5–3m depth, 40t boat-lift, ☎ (05146) 2100.

⚓ Jachtwerf Maronier (Industriehaven), toilets, showers, 12t boat-lift, ☎ (05146) 3300.

⚓ Jachtwerf Maritiem (Industriehaven), toilets, showers, 12t boat-lift, ☎ (05146) 1500.

⚓ Municipal yacht harbour directly W of the Lemstersluis, toilets, showers, ☎ (05146) 3343.

⚓ Jachthaven Slump, E of the Lemstersluis, ☎ (05146) 2725.

There are at least 3 other yards in the Industriehaven.

Main facilities inside the Lemstersluis and in or near the Zijlroede (depth 2·1m):

3 ⛵ There are 3 opening drawbridges over the Zijlroede, (E to W) **Oudesluisbrug** (ht 1·82m), **Flevobrug** (ht 0·74m) and **Zijlroedebrug** (ht 0·85); same service hours as Lemstersluis.

⚓ Moorings along the sides of the Zijlroede.

Laundrette, Wasserette Helen near Zijlroedebrug.

⚓ Municipal yacht harbour, S side W of bridges, ☎ (05146) 1979.

⚓ Jachthaven Iselmar, S side at end of Zijlroede, toilets, showers, laundrette, ☎ (05146) 2924.

⚓ WS Tacozijl at end of Zijlroede in Stroomkanaal, toilets, showers, laundrette, ☎ (05146) 2003.

⚓ WS Caravanpark Lemmer on Stroomkanaal and the Grote Brekken, toilets, showers, laundrette, 12t boat-lift, ☎ (05146) 2115.

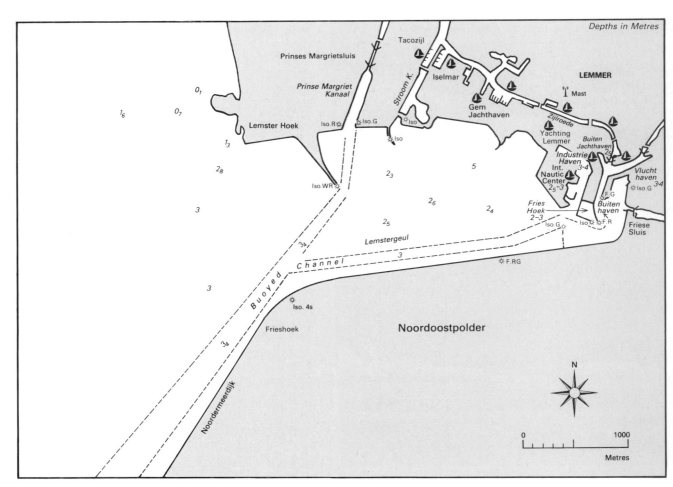

Lemmer

LEMSTERGEUL
Leave Buitenhaven and follow Lemstergeul (see above).

8·9km/4·8M
Friese Hoek Point Iso.WR.4s12m8/5M. Continue W, following *SB* and *VZ* series of R buoys, some lit (keep to their S) and rounding Vrouwezand shoal turning northwards. Shoal 1·3m and less depth and fishing stakes and traps on landward side of buoys, to R Lt buoy *VZ2*.

24·2km/13·0M
R Lt buoy *VZ2*.

Course NE (along Ldg Lts 030° in Stavoren) direct for Stavoren.

STAVOREN
S entrance. 9kph/4·9kn max.

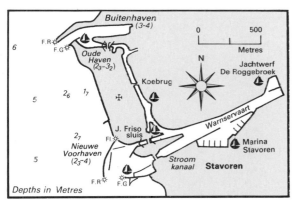

Stavoren. Entrance to the northern harbour, the Oude Haven, to the right

Stavoren

4·3km/2·3M
Pierheads F.R&G Lts. Municipal HrMr ☎ (05149) 1766/1757.

⚓ Nieuwe Voorhaven depths 2·5–4m. Uncomfortable pontoons off S harbour wall.

⚓ ⛵ Stbd to **Johan Frisosluis lock and opening bridge** (ht 1·90m).
Lock and bridge service hours m-sa *1/5-1/10* 0600-0700[1], 0700-2100 (sa to 2000) *1/10-15/11*, *15/3-1/5* 0600-0700[1], 0700-1900, 1900-2000[1] (sa 0600-0700[1], 0700-1800, 1800-1900[1]), *15/11-15/3* 0600-0700[1], 0700-1700, 1700-2000[1] (sa 0600-1900[1]); su/h *May and September* 0900-1200, 1400-1800, *1/6-1/9* 0900-1200, 1400-1700, 1800-2000, *April and October* 0900-1100, 1600-1800, *1/11-31/3* closed.
1. By arrangement Prov. Waterstaat Friesland ☎ (058) 925888/122422.

⚓⚓ Municipal moorings inside immediately N behind lock wall and along town canal; toilets, showers. 600m along canal to stbd is Marina Stavoren with toilets, showers, laundrette, 2t crane, 24t boat-lift, ☎ (05149) 1566.

The Johan Friso Kanaal (3·5m depth channel) is an alternative entrance to the Frisian waterway system (see Route 19) joining the Prinses Margriet Kanaal.

N entrance to Buitenhaven and Spoorhaven. State HrMr ☎ (05149) 1216. Long-range Lt, Iso.4s15m 12M near root of N wall.

⚓ Entrance between R and G pierhead Lts. Moorings to SE at W end of Oude Vissershaven (depth 2·3–3·2m).

Departure off Buitenhaven entrance then course direct for GR *H2/W1* offing Lt buoy for Hindeloopen and Workum channels.

8·5km/4·6M
GR Lt buoy *H2/W1* (possible to cut corner before this buoy, see below).

HINDELOOPEN
Oc.3s9m8M on W pierhead. Entering Hindeloopen in daylight, it is possible to cut corner into the buoyed channel at G unlit buoy *H1*, keeping minimum depth 2m, SE along buoyed channel (1·9m depth), distance 9 cables/1·7km from *H2* and 3 cables/600m from *H1* to entrance yacht harbours.

Hindeloopen Point

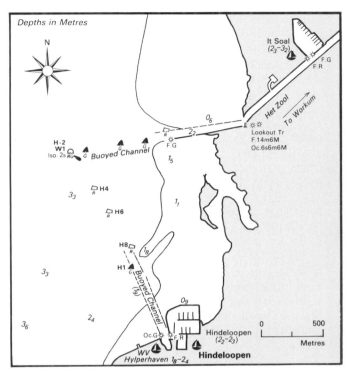

Hindeloopen-Workum

Workum, looking of the S breakwater of the entrance channel towards Hindeloopen church. Note the bird life on one of the IJsselmeer's few remaining beaches

Workum in 1987 new moorings were being laid in the N end of Het Zool

To port inside entrance is Jachthaven Hindeloopen, 2·2–3m depth, toilets, showers, laundrette, 30t crane, ☎ (05142) 1238/1866. To stbd inside entrance is WV Hylper Haven, toilets, showers, ☎ (05142) 2009/2437.

WORKUM

Follow channel buoys and Bns (G on the S wall which is sometimes covered) E from *H2*. Channel is 35–50m wide only, and there is a small lookout building with a tower like a church at the root of the channel where Het Zool leads off NE. Very difficult to pick up coming from N, when it is essential to keep off the shallows (under 1m) to the N of the channel. Minimum depth 2·2m. Het Zool, the channel beyond is 1·7–1·9m depth.

⚓ Jachthaven It Soal/Het Zool 2·2km from entrance between F.R&G Lts on N bank, depth 2·3 to 3·2m, toilets, showers, laundrette, 40t crane, ☎ (05151) 2927/1222.

⚓⚓ Beyond Het Zool, along the N bank as far as the lock are a considerable number of new moorings, and another marina, Jachthaven Anne Wever B.V., toilets, showers, 30t crane, ☎ (05151) 2361.

This is another (1·7m depth) entrance to the Frisian canals and lakes. Beyond the **lock and opening bascule bridge** are **4 opening bridges**, and 4 yacht havens all with showers and toilets, and from just S of the **Noorderbrug** round to the Klitrak these are:

⚓ Jachthaven Schaap, 6t crane, ☎ (05151) 1728.

⚓ Jachthaven T. Bouma, 8t crane, ☎ (05151) 1797.

⚓ Jachthaven Bouwsma, 20t boat-lift, ☎ (05151) 2004.

⚓ Workumer Jachthaven, 20t boat-lift, ☎ (05151) 1855.

Lock and bridge (most bridges) service hours m-sa *1/5-1/10* 0800-0930, 1000-1200, 1300-1500, 1530-1700, 1800-2000, *1/10-15/11* and *15/3-1/5* 0800-0930, 1000-1200, 1300-1500, 1530-1800 (sa to 1700), *15/11-15/3* 0800-1800 (sa to 1700) but only on special request, ☎ (05151) 1241; su/h April and October 0900-1100, 1600-1800, May and Sept 0900-1200, 1400-1500, 1530-1800, *1/6-1/9* 0900-1200, 1400-1500, 1530-1700, 1800-2000, *1/11-1/3* closed.

Course from *H2* buoy NNW for Y Lt buoy *V21*.

5·0km/2·7M
Y Lt buoy *V21*. Course NNW keeping out of fishing stakes area to E marked by Y buoys.

4·4km/2·4M
G Lt buoy *VF5* first of G channel buoys to Kornwerderzand. Course NE to Makkum.

2·5km/1·3M

⚓ ⚓ MAKKUM

G̲ Lt buoy *MA7*, first of Makkumerdiep channel buoys. There is a shoal (0·6m depth) to the S marked by a RW unlit spar buoy with topmark. Follow channel Bns (between F.R&G Lts en route) and S wall of Makkumerdiep, minimum depth 4·3m, Ldg Lts 92° (F.R&G, the G on the weigh-house) to T-junction, with the F.R Lt on wall. 9kph/4·9kn max. Stbd into Vissershaven. Quayside and pontoon moorings at end. Toilets, showers. HrMr ☎ (05158) 1450, (05128) 2127. 30t boat-lift, Jachtwerf Bloemsma, ☎ (05158) 1789. Ship repair yards Het Kolkje, 15t crane, and Eduard de Boer, 25t crane. There are also pontoon moorings in the Industriehaven (3–4m depth) to the W of the Vissershaven, and at Jachthaven WV Makkum on the S side of the entrance channel.

Course direct to Kornwerderzand locks.

KORNWERDERZAND

Locks entrance, F.R&G pierhead Lts.
MHWS 2·2m, MLWS 0·3m, MHWN 1·9m, MLWN 0·5m.
《 2 ⚓ **Lorentzsluizen with 2 opening bridges** (ht 4·20m) serviced at all times. VHF Ch 18 *Sluis*

Makkum. NE extremity of IJsselmeer. The lock into the Zijlroede

Kornwerderzand. HrMr ☎ (05177) 441. No customs (Harlingen for clearance). Moorings each side in Binnenhaven and Voorhaven, but vessels must always be attended.

3·0km/1·6M
⚓ Exit pierhead Lts (F.G&R)

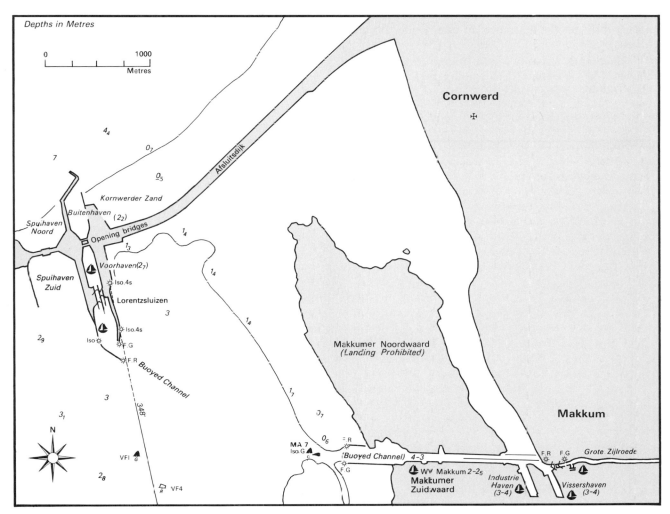

Kornwerderzand-Makkum

WADDENZEE
No speed Limit. See text above on tides. Head NE along 100–150m wide channel. *KZ1* G Bn to port. *KZ4* R Bn to stbd. Round N side of N cardinal Lt buoy *BO11/KZ2* and follow buoyed channel E and N.

BOONTJES CHANNEL
Follow channel buoys and beacons (some lit). Drying patches each side. Narrow channel at southern neck. Minimum depth 2·5m for 6km, then less than 2m (minimum 1·6m) for approximately 4km, deepening to 6m off Harlingen.

12·0km/6·5M
HARLINGEN
Iso.5s entrance Lt on W pierhead.
MHWS 2·2m, MLWS 0·2m, MHWN 1·9m, MLWN 0·4m
No entry signals. VHF Ch 11 manned m 0000 to sa 2200. HrMr ☎ (05178) 12512.
Customs Zuiderhaven 73, ☎ (01578) 18750.
Entrance Lts Iso.R.4s narrow sector Lt marks the dangerous N side of the Pollendam, and Ldg Lts 112° Oc.6s (rear), Iso.4s (front) mark the safe course to the harbour along the S side of the Pollendam.
Entrance In 1987 a new eastern pier was constructed and 2 R Lt buoys marked the obstructed E side of channel into harbour. Enter between W wall and these buoys (which will eventually be removed) then dogleg NE to the entrance to the Oude Buitenhaven.
≪ ⌒**Keersluis** usually open unless tidal rise is above NAP +1·1m (LLWS +2·28m). **Keersluisbrug** (double swing bridge ht 4·5m).

⌒ Then direct across to **Prins Hendrikbrug** (bascule ht 1·6m) into the Noorderhaven. Temporary waiting posts.
Service hours both bridges m-sa 0600-2200 on the hr and ½hr except 0900, 1400, 1900 (and 0800, 1300 sa); su/h *1/4-1/10* 0730-0800, 0930-1000, 1130-1200, 1300-1330, 1530-1600, 1730-1800, 1930-2000, 2130-2200, *1/10-1/4* only by contacting Jachthaven Noorderhaven.
⚓ Open Jachthaven Noorderhaven, depth 1·1m, toilets, showers, laundrette, ☎ (05178) 15666. 10t crane Fa. Th. W. Nauta, Noorderhaven 21.

There are at least 3 other yacht havens with toilets and showers in other parts of the town:
⚓ Binnenjachthaven of Harlinger WV, 9t crane, ☎ (05178) 16898, on the Noordergracht.
⚓ Atlantic, 20t boat-lift, ☎ (05178) 17658.
⚓ Harlinger Jachtbouw, 10t crane, ☎ (05178) 14053. The latter 2 are on the Harlinger/Franekertrekvaart. There are also several boatyards.

AVOID
"ATLANTIC" is OK

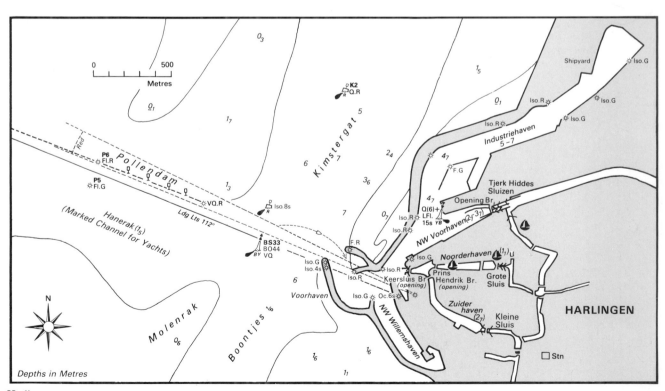

Harlingen

11. Friesland and Groningen Rivers, lakes and canals

Route 18
Harlingen to Delfzijl by canal

Commentary

Given the distance and numbers of bridges and locks, you need to be a committed canal cruising enthusiast to take the whole of this route. Alternatively you may be making passage to the German Frisian islands and avoiding the very shallow tidal offshore passages through the Waddenzee of Routes 20 and, above all, 21. You can probably scrape through the whole of this canal route with a draught of 6 feet, and you do not need to lower your mast. The scenic part of the route is as far as Groningen along winding rivers, across the Lauwersmeer and through ancient towns and villages, whilst the final wide pencil-straight Eems Kanaal leading to the industrial port of Delfzijl is an easy passage chore.

For commentary on Harlingen see Route 17. Franeker university was suppressed by Napoleon but he left alone Holland's oldest student tavern, the De Bogt Fan Gune which is worth visiting. Coopmanhuis, once a professor's house, is the town museum, and there is a weigh-house, a Renaissance town hall, and an 18th-century clockwork-powered planetarium.

Leeuwarden is the thriving capital of Friesland. There are two museums, the Frisian and the Princessehof, an 18th-century town hall, 16th-century weigh-house, and the leaning Oldehove tower of a cathedral which was never completed.

At Dokkum the bridgekeeper cycles between the three bridges and collects *bruggeld* via a clog suspended from a fishing rod. Originally a port built on a group of *terpen*, the town was headquarters of the Frisian Admiralty until this moved to Harlingen when the approaches silted up. There are moats, ramparts, a 17th-century town hall, 18th-century weigh-house, two excellent windmills, and a museum housed in 17th-century Admiralty House.

The Expo-Zee exhibition at Lauwersoog looks at the history of the Waddenzee and the enclosing of the Lauwersmeer, and is worth a visit if you make the diversion northwards or are travelling offshore along Route 21. The ferry from here to Schiermonnikoog used to start from Oostmahorn, which is a strange little walled harbour with a large nearby marina, now enclosed in the Lauwersmeer, and of Erskine Childers and *Riddle of the Sands* fame. An interesting cycle trip is into the land of the *terpen* behind the coast west of Lauwersoog.

Groningen is the capital of the province and retains its old university. With access to the sea along the Reitdiep it was another Hanseatic League member and has many preserved buildings, including the 100m high 15th-century Martinitoren (must

be climbed!), medieval almshouses or *hofjes*, an 18th-century town hall, and no less than six museums. Delfzijl is a large port evidenced by the towering North Sea rigs moored in its harbour. The town has rapidly developed since the discovery of natural gas and salt in the area, but apart from a windmill standing on the old ramparts there is not a great deal of tourist interest.

Distance 138km/74M. See Route 19 for southern diversion to the Frisian lakes and Lemmer. Overall distances from Lemmer: Harlingen 89km/48M, Delfzijl 177km/96M.

Bridges 49 opening. These are clustered: 5 in Leeuwarden, 3 in Dokkum, and 13 in Groningen, leaving 28 spread elsewhere. 1 railway bridge.

Locks 3 locks, 2 open sluices.

Tides, heights and soundings
Non-tidal except for harbours of Harlingen and Delfzijl outside the sea-locks. Heights and soundings relate to standard (usually summer) canal and lake levels: Fries *zomerpeil*, Lauwersmeer *zomerpeil*, Westerkwartierpeil, and Winschoterpeil.

Minimum depths en route
2·1m in Leeuwarden and 1·95m in the Dokkumergrootdiep are the shallowest passage depths, but care of course should be taken to avoid shallower depths in some of the bank-side mooring places and yacht harbours.

Charts
ANWB charts *B* (a good scale but Harlingen to Leeuwarden only) and *A* (somewhat small scale) adequate for whole route, but Dutch small-craft charts *1811, 1812* help for Harlingen, the Lauwersmeer and Delfzijl.

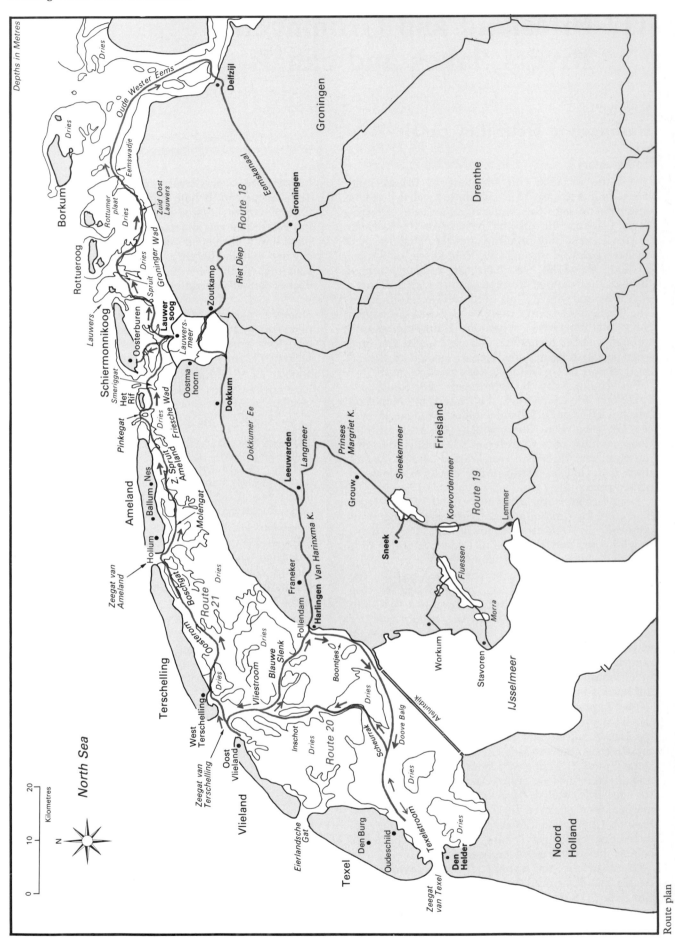

Route plan

Route description

HARLINGEN NOORDERHAVEN
See Route 17 for details of entrance and facilities.

Harlingen. The Noorderhaven

Harlingen, looking seawards through Tsjerk Hiddessluizen and its open bascule bridge. This is the entrance to the van Harinxmakanaal into Friesland

0·9km/0·5M

≪ ◈ Tsjerk Hiddessluizen lock and bascule bridge (ht 6·60m).
Lock and bridge service hours m-sa *1/5-1/10* 0500-2100 (sa to 2000), *1/10-1/4* 0600-2100 (sa to 1900); su/h *1/5-1/10* 0900-1000, 1400-1500, 1800-1900. *1/10-1/5* closed.

VAN HARINXMAKANAAL
12·5kph/6·7kn max, depth 3–4m.

1·6km/0·9M

◈ Koningsbrug (bascule 5·3m)
Bridge service hours m-sa *1/5-1/10* 0600-0700[1], 0700-2100 (sa to 2000), *1/10-15/11* and *15/3-1/5* 0600-0700[1], 0700-1900, 1900-2000[1] (sa 0600-0700, 0700-1800, 1800-1900), *15/11-15/3* 0600-0700, 0700-1700, 1700-2000 (sa 0600-1900); su/h throughout year closed.
1. By arrangement Prov. Waterstaat Friesland, ☎ (053) 925888.

4·3km/2·3M

◈ Kiesterzijl swing bridge (ht 5·3m)
Bridge service hours See Koningsbrug

2·0km/1·7M

FRANEKER
6kph/3·2kn max speed in town.
⚓ Franeker WV, entrance N bank. 10t crane at T. Bodewes ☎ (05170) 5200.

W side of Franeker. Yacht haven off the N bank of the van Harinxmakanaal

1·1km/0·6M

◈ Stationsbrug (drawbridge ht 0·75m)
Bridge service hours[1] *1/5-1/10* m-f 0500-2100, sa 0500-2000, su/h 0830-0930, 1900-2000; *1/10-1/5* m-f 0600-2100, sa 0600-1900, su/h closed.
1. Can be limited during train arrivals at the nearby station.

6·8km/3·7M

⌐ **Dronrijp bascule bridge** (ht 5·3m)
Bridge service hours See Koningsbrug

6·2km/3·3M

⌐ **Deinum bascule bridge** (ht 5·3m)
Stbd van Harinxmakanaal
Bridge service hours See Koningsbrug

0·8km/0·4M

⌐ **Ritzumazijl bascule bridge** (ht 5·3m)
Bridge service hours See Koningsbrug

HARLINGERTREKVAART
0·7km/0·4M

⌐ Harlingertrekvaart to port.

0·9km/0·5M

⌐ T-junction. Stbd to town.

LEEUWARDEN
9kph/4·8kn max in town. Depth 2·1m. HrMr ☎ (058) 131441.

0·4km/0·2M

⌐ **Railway bridge** permanently open, unused spur line.

⌐ **Hermesbrug** (ht 1·07m)
Bridge service hours m-f 0600-0715, 0830-1215, 1330-1600, 1730-2030 (*1/10-1/4* to 1930); sa 0730-1215, 1330-1830 (*1/10-1/4* to 1700); su *May, Sept* 0900-1100, 1600-1800, *1/6-1/9* 0900-1100, 1800-2000, *1/10-1/5* closed; h closed.

⌐ **Verlaatsbrug** (ht 1·07m). To port along Westerstadsgracht (Zuiderstadsgracht is to stbd).
Bridge service hours See Hermesbrug

The leaning tower of Leeuwarden. Oldhove Toren overshadowing Vrouwenpoortsbrug on the Westerstadsgracht

WESTERSTADSGRACHT
⚓ Municipal quays E bank, toilets. Because of the fixed bridges, in order to visit the yacht harbours on the E side of town off the Widje Greuns it is necessary to make a long detour back along the Harlingertrekvaart and S round the van Harinxmakanaal through opening bridges. The Nieuwe Leeuwarder Jachthaven has showers and a 10t crane but is on the Widje Greuns.

2·1km/1·1M

⌐ **Vrouwenpoortsbrug** (ht 1·85m)
Bridge service hours See Hermesebrug

NOORDERSTADSGRACHT
⚓ Municipal quays E bank
⌐ **Noorderbrug** (ht 1·35m)
Bridge service hours See Hermesbrug

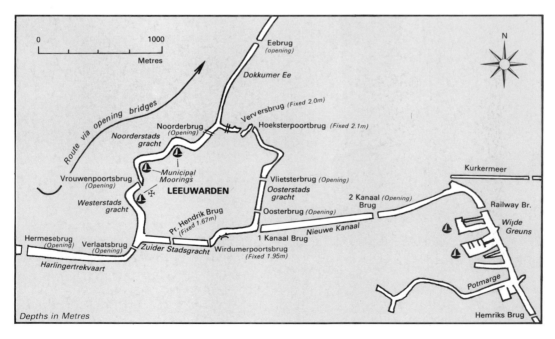

Leeuwarden

1·0km/0·5M
DOKKUMER EE
⚓ To port is Dokkumer Ee. 9kph/4·9kn max. Minimum depth 2·1m.

0·8km/0·4M
⚓ **Eebrug** (ht 1·3m)
Bridge service hours See Hermesbrug

11·0km/5·9M
⚓ **Van Steenhuizenbrug** (ht 1·4m)
Bridge service hours m-sa *1/5-1/10* 0700-0800, 0830-1200, 1300-1700, 1800-2000, *1/10-15/11*, *15/3-1/5* 0700-0800, 0830-1200, 1300-1800 (sa to 1700), *15/11-15/3* 0700-1800 (sa to 1700)[1]; su/h *May, Sept* 1000-1200, 1500-1700, *1/6-1/9* 1000-1200, 1700-1900, *1/10-1/5* closed.
1. By arrangement, Prov. Waterstaat Friesland ☎ (058) 925888/122422.

0·5km/0·3M
⚓ **Birdaard Nieuwe Brug** (drawbridge, ht 1·5m)
Bridge service hours As for Steenhuizenbrug

4·0km/2·2M
⚓ **Klaarkampsterbrug** (ht 1·47m)
Bridge service hours As for Steenhuizenbrug

4·1km/2·2M
DOKKUM
⚓ **Eebrug** (bascule bridge, ht 0·8m)
Bridge service hours *1/5-1/10* m-sa 0700-0800, 0830-1200, 1300-1615, 1715-1800, 1830-2000 (sa to 1900); *1/10-1/5* m-sa 0700-0800, 0900-1200, 1300-1615, 1715-1800 (sa to 1700); su/h *May, Sept* 0900-1200, 1400-1700, *1/6-1/9* 0900-1200, 1400-1700, 1800-2000. *1/10-1/5* closed.

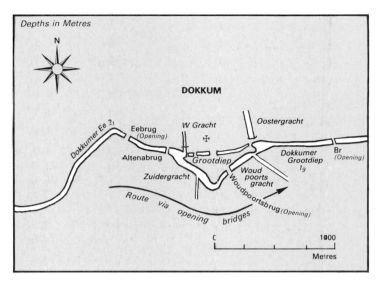

Dokkum

Dokkum. Altenabrug with the windmills on the Zuidergracht in the background

⚓ **Altenabrug** (drawbridge, ht 0·9m)
Bridge service hours See Eebrug

⚓ Stbd to Zuidergracht.

ZUIDERGRACHT
⚓ Quayside moorings. Toilets and showers near the sports complex on the N side of the Dokkumergrootdiep, E of Halvemaanspoortbrug.

⚓ **Woudpoortsbrug** (drawbridge, ht 1m)
Bridge service hours See Eebrug

2·5km/1·4M
DOKKUMERGROOTDIEP
⚓ Stbd to Dokkumergrootdiep. Minimum depth 1·9m.
⚓ N bank WV Dokkum, ☎ (05190) 4088. Toilets, showers at camping site E of yacht harbour. 20t lifting facilities at Watersportbedrijf F. v.d. Zwaag.

Dokkum. Woudpoortsbrug

6·8km/3·7M

⚓ **Brug te Ee/Ir.D.F. Woudabrug** (ht 1·67m).
Bridge service hours m-sa *1/5-1/10* 0700-0800, 0830-1200, 1300-1730, 1800-2000 (sa to 1900), *1/10-1/5* 0700-0800, 0830-1200, 1300-1800 (sa to 1700, sa *1/12-1/3* on special request); su/h *May, Sept* 0900-1200, 1400-1700, *1/6-1/9* 0900-1200, 1400-1700, 1800-2000, *1/10-1/5* closed.

2·7km/1·5M

⚓ **Brug te Engwierum** (ht 1·28m)
Bridge service hours m-sa *1/5-1/10* 0700-800, 0830-1200, 1300-1700, 1800-2000, *1/10-15/11, 15/3-1/5* 0700-0800, 0830-1200, 1300-1800 (sa to 1700); *15/11-15/3* m-f 0700-1800[1]; sa 0700-1700[1]. su/h *May, Sept* 0900-1200, 1400-1700, *1/6-1/9* 0900-1200, 1400-1700, 1800-2000, *1/10-1/5* closed.
1. ☎ (058) 925888/122422.

1·2km/0·6M

≪ ⚓ **Dokkumer Nieuwezijlen, Nieuwe Sluis lock and drawbridge** (ht 4·29m) S side of entrance to Dokkumerdiep.
Service hours As Brug te Engwierum except: su/h *May, Sept* 0900-1200, 1400-1800.

DOKKUMERDIEP

No speed limit. Depth 2·3–4m. Channel marked with port/stbd withies (unbound E side) and buoys (R, E side). Withies normally mark the 1·3m contour.

⚓ Jachthaven Lunegat, S bank outside lock. Depth 1·8–2·4m. HrMr ☎ (05112) 303. Toilets, showers, 4t crane.

3·5km/1·9M

⚓ Stbd. E side Senneroog Island.

2·8km/1·5M

⚓ *DD2-S1* GR unlit buoy. Turn SE close S of this buoy.

LAUWERSMEER

Follow Slenk E keeping N of stbd (bound) withies. Depth 4–5m.

⚓ At this point there is the alternative of visiting Oostmahorn Jachthaven 2·2km N, or Lauwersoog (Jachthaven Noordergat) 6·5km N. See also Route 21.

2·1km/1·1M

⚓ Stbd fork at G beacon. Zoutkamperril channel buoys and withies (bound and R to port). Depth 2·6–4·5m.

ZOUTKAMP

⚓ Jachthaven Hunzegat, N bank before lock. Toilets, showers.

7·2km/3·9M

≪ ⚓ **Keersluis and Reitdiepbrug** (ht 3·5m), in middle one of three channels. Sluice gates are usually open.

Bridge service hours m-sa 0700-1200, 1300-1800 (*1/6-1/9* to 1900); su/h *1/5-1/10* 0800-0900, 1800-1900, *1/10-1/5* closed.

REITDIEP

Depth 2·4m. 9kph/4·9kn max.

⚓ N bank next to lock, Oude Binnenhaven, toilets, showers. Jachtwerf Gruno, 20t crane ☎ (05956) 2057. D. Bouma 30t crane ☎ (05956) 2182/1828.

⚓ Jachthaven Electra. S bank just before Electrasluis and drawbridge.

5·0km/2·7M

≪ ⚓ (ht 1·3m). **Electrasluis**, sluice gates are usually open. Toilets, showers, ☎ (05949) 266.
Bridge service hours m-sa *1/6-1/9* 0700-1200, 1300-1900, *1/9-1/6* 0700-1200, 1300-1800; su/h closed except *16/5-16/9* 0830-1200, 1400-1600, 1830-2000.

5·5km/3·0M

⚓ **Roodehaanbrug** (drawbridge, ht 0·9m)
Service See Electrasluis
6kph/3·2kn max speed from here to Groningen.

7·2km/3·9M

⚓ **Garnwerdbrug** (drawbridge, ht 1·8m)
Service See Electrasluis

⚓ Jachthaven Garnwerd S of bridge. Toilets, washing facilities.

3·4km/1·9M

⚓ **Brug te Adorp** (ht 2·4m)
Service As for Electrasluis, except su/h closed.

1·2km/0·6M

⚓ **Opening bridge** (ht 3·68m)
Service As for Electrasluis, except su/h closed.

⚓ Cross van Starkenborghkanaal

0·5km/0·3M

≪ ⚓ **Bridge and Sluis te Dorkwerd** (ht 3·9m)
Service As for Electrasluis except su/h closed.

GRONINGEN

Minimum depth 2·75m. 6kph/3·2kn max speed in town canals. HrMr ☎ (050) 120306/125777. Convoys through the bridges between Pleiadenbrug and Museumbrug are organised on Sundays and holidays from *16/5-16/9*: Pleiadenbrug 1005, 1405, 1805; Museumbrug 0900, 1300, 1700.

3·4km/1·8M

⚓ **Plataanbrug** (ht 4·75m)
Bridge service hours m-sa 0600-0745, 0845-1200, 1400-1700, *1/6-1/9* also 1800-1900; su/h closed.

⚓ **Pleiadenbrug** (ht 0·9m). *Service* See Plataanbrug

⚓ **Railway bridge** (ht 0·9m). *Service hours* Average 1 to 2 times per hr m-sa 0630-1150, 1430-1900 (*1/9-1/6* to 1740); su/h closed. See *Openingstijden Spoorbruggen*.

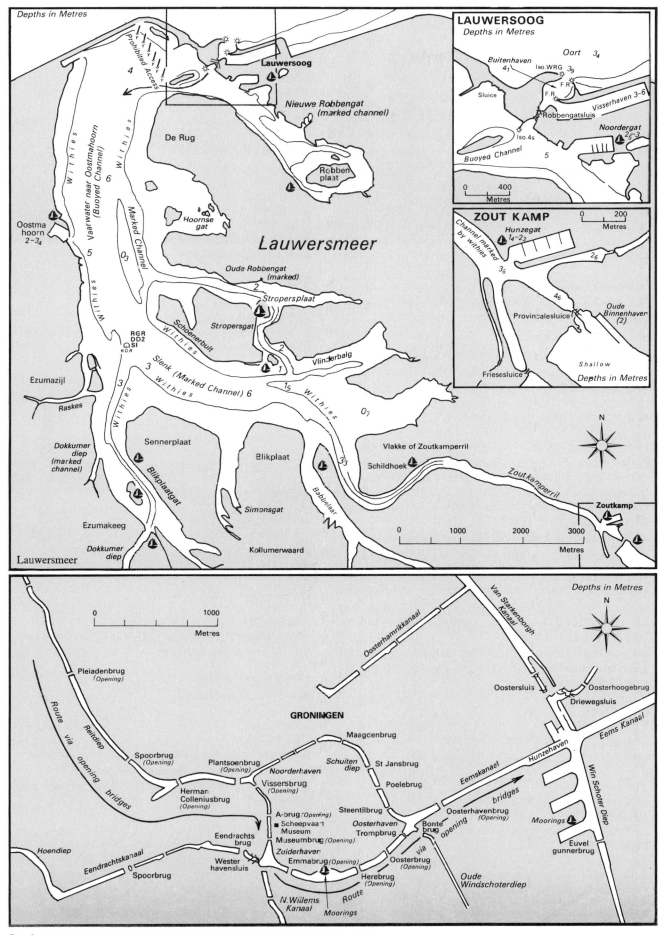

Depths in Metres

Prohibited Access

Lauwersoog

Nieuwe Robbengat
(marked channel)

LAUWERSOOG
Depths in Metres

Oort 3₄

Buitenhaven
4₁   Iso.WRG 3₉
Sluice   F.R
          F.R
Robbengatsluis   Visserhaven 3·6

Iso.4s

Noordergat 2₅·3

Buoyed Channel   5

0   400
Metres

ZOUT KAMP   0   200
                   Metres

Channel marked by withies

Hunzegat 1₄·2₂

3₆

2₆

4₆

Provincialesluice

Oude Binnenhaven (2)

Friesesluice   *Shallow*
                Depths in Metres

De Rug

Withies   *Withies*

Vaarwater naar Oostmahoorn (Buoyed Channel)

Marked Channel

Robben plaat

Hoornse gat

Lauwersmeer

Oostma hoorn 2·3₄

Withies

5   0₃

6

Oude Robbengat (marked)

2   *Stropersplaat*

Stropersgat

RGR DD2 SI
RGR

Schoenerbult *Withies*

2   Vlinderbalg

Slenk (Marked Channel) 6   1₉   *Withies*

Ezumazijl

Raskes

3   3   *Withies*

1   0₇

Dokkumer diep (marked channel)

Sennerplaat

Blikplaat

Vlakke of Zoutkamperril

Schildhoek

N

Ezumakeeg

Blikplaatgat

Simonsgat

Babbelaar

3·3

Zoutkamperril

Zoutkamp

Dokkumer diep

Kollumerwaard

0   1000   2000   3000
Metres

Lauwersmeer

Depths in Metres

Oosterhamrikkanaal

Van Starkenborgh Kanaal

N

Pleiadenbrug
(Opening)

Route via opening bridges

Reitdiep

Spoorbrug
(Opening)

Oostersluis   Oosterhoogebrug

Driewegsluis

GRONINGEN

Eems Kanaal

Maagcenbrug

Plantsoenbrug
(Opening)

Noorderhaven

Schuiten diep   St Jansbrug

Vissersbrug
(Opening)

Poelebrug

Eemskanaal   Hunzehaven

Herman Colleniusbrug
(Opening)

Steentilbrug

Oosterhavenbrug
(Opening)

opening bridges

Win Schoter Diep

Moorings

A-brug *(Opening)*
Scheepvaart Museum
Museumbrug *(Opening)*

Oosterhaven Trompbrug

Bonte brug

via opening

Euvel gunnerbrug

Hoendiep

Eendrachtskanaal

Eendrachts brug

Zuiderhaven
Emmabrug *(Opening)*

Wester havensluis

Oosterbrug
(Opening)

Herebrug
(Opening)

Oude Windschoterdiep

Spoorbrug

N.Willems Kanaal

Moorings

Route

Groningen

Groningen. Two masted barge negotiating the bend in the Zuider Haven

Eems Kanaal. Typical stretch

◿ **Herman Colleniusbrug** (ht 1·2m)

◿ **Plantsoenbrug** (ht 1·4m). *Service* See Plataanbrug

⬐ Stbd into Zuider Haven.

◿ **Vissersbrug** (ht 1·6m). *Service* See Plataanbrug

◿ **A-Brug** (ht 1·8m). *Service* See Plataanbrug

◿ **Museumbrug** (ht 1·1m). *Service* See Plataanbrug

⬐ Port into Verbindingskanaal

◿ **Emmabrug** (ht 3·2m). *Service* See Plataanbrug

⚓ Moorings N quay. Groninger MBC pontoons, toilets and showers. Laundrettes: Was-O-Net at Rademarkt 25 and Ged. Zuiderdiep 125; Fa. Lefferts at Meeuwerderweg 30, Nieuwe Boteringestraat 46 and Bedumerweg 14.

◿ **Herebrug** (ht 4·1m). *Service* See Plataanbrug

◿ **Oosterbrug** (ht 3·2m). *Service* See Plataanbrug

◿ **Trompbrug** (ht 3m). *Service* See Plataanbrug

◿ **Oosterhavenbrug** (ht 3·8m). *Service* See Plataanbrug

6t crane in Hunzehaven: Gemeentelijk Havenbedrijf, ☎ (050) 120306/125757.

⚓ Jachtwerf Groeneveld, 700m detour S of Hunzehaven, moorings on N side of Finsehaven off W side of Winschoterdiep.

6·2km/3·3M
EEMSKANAAL
15kph/8·1kn max. Depth 4·5–5·2m.

⬐ Cross van Starkenborghkanaal

1·3km/0·7M
◿ **Driebondsbrug** (ht 6·8m)
VHF Ch 18 or ☎ (050) 410097.
Service hours m 0400-2400, tu-f 0000-2400, sa 0000-2000, su/h closed.

1·5km/0·8M
◿ **Borgbrug** (ht 1·75m). VHF Ch 18.
Bridge service hours See Driebondsbrug except *1/5-1/10* m-f 0700-0830, 1600-1800 once per ½hr.

9·3km/5·0M
◿ **Bloemhofbrug** (ht 1·75m). VHF Ch 10.
Service See Driebondsbrug

Bloemhofbrug on the Eems Kanaal

7·3km/3·9M
◿ **Woldbrug** (ht 1·75m). VHF Ch 10.
Service See Driebondsbrug.

3·0km/1·6M
⬐ Stbd to Eemskanaal

2·5km/1·3M
DELFZIJL
⬐ To port past the Oosterhorn Kanaal entrance.
《 2 ◿ **Lock and 2 opening bridges**.
VHF Ch 11, ☎ (05960) 12092. 24hr service except su/h closed.

2·3km/1·2M
⚓ Balkenhaven, ZV Neptunus, NW of the sea lock, minimum depth 3·5m. HrMr ☎ (05960) 15004/ 19260.

See Route 21 for plan and details of facilities and offshore entrance.

140

Route 19
Lemmer to Leeuwarden via the Frisian lakes

Commentary

This is definitely sailing country. The distances are short and there are many wide lakes, providing you have shallow draught. If you do not wish to strike inland as far as Leeuwarden you can easily loop westwards at the northern end of the Koevordermeer along the Johan Friso Kanaal, through the lakes (Heegermeer, Fluessen and Morra) and out into the IJsselmeer again at Stavoren. Yachting facilities are extremely plentiful, and this is the place *par excellence* where a wide variety of traditional Dutch sailing craft can be seen cruising and racing.

For commentaries on Lemmer and Harlingen see Route 17. Sneek is another extremely pretty town with first-class yachting facilities. It has a number of 15–18th-century buildings, including the twin-spired Waterpoort (water gate), Martinikerk, the town hall and a Frisian maritime museum. Again like Lemmer it can have a Mediterranean atmosphere in summer when moored or rafted alongside one of the town streets.

Distance 64km/35M. See Route 18 for continuations to Harlingen or Delfzijl. Overall distances from Lemmer: Harlingen 89km/48M, Delfzijl 177 km/96M.

Bridges 19 opening (detours: additional 4) including 3 railway.

Locks 1 and 1 open sluice.

Tides, heights and soundings
Non tidal. Soundings and heights to local summer canal level: Fries *zomerpeil*.

Minimum depths en route
2·1m in Lemmer's Zijlroede. 1·5m to 1m or less outside the buoyed channels in the lakes (Grote Brekken, Koevordermeer, Sneekermeer) and 1·65m in parts of the Sneek yacht harbours. Care also needs to be taken when going alongside walls and banks.

Charts
ANWB chart *B*; chart *A* also includes chart of Leeuwarden. Dutch small-craft chart *1810* includes chart of Lemmer.

Route description

LEMMER (entrance)
See Route 17 for entrance and facilities in Lemmer.

ZIJLROEDE
9kph/4·9kn max. Depth 2·1m.
⚓ Moorings N of lock on each side.

Lemmer. Entrance to the Buiten Jachthaven outside and on the W side of lock

0·8km/0·4M
⚓ **Oude Sluisbrug** (ht 1·82m)
Service See Lemstersluis (Route 17).
⚓ Moorings both banks.

0·5km/0·3M
⚓ **Flevobrug** (ht 0·74m)
Service See Lemstersluis (Route 17).
⚓ Moorings N bank.

0·4km/0·2M
⚓ **Zijlroedebrug** (ht 0·85)
Service See Lemstersluis (Route 17).
⚓ Municipal yacht harbour S bank, washing facilities, ☎ (05146) 1979.
⚓ Jachthaven Iselmar S bank, toilets, showers, laundrette, ☎ (05146) 2924.

1·0km/0·5M
⚓ Stbd enter Stroomkanaal.

STROOMKANAAL (depth 3·1m)
⚓ S of the junction, the yacht haven on N side of canal is Watersportcentrum Tacozijl, toilets, showers, laundrette, ☎ (05146) 2003. N of yacht haven on E side stretching as far as the Grote Brekken is Watersportcentrum Caravanpark Lemmer, toilets, showers, laundrette, ☎ (05146) 2115.

1·0km/0·5M
⚓ Stbd enter Grote Brekken.

GROTE BREKKEN
12·5kph/6·7kn max in channel, 9kph/4·9kn outside channel. Minimum depth 3m in channel, 1·5m over most of lake. Follow R and G channel buoys (some lit).

4·0km/2·2M
GR unlit buoy (Fl.G Lt on stbd bank). Enter Prinses Margriet Kanaal.

PRINSES MARGRIET KANAAL
12·5kph/6·7kn max, depth 3·6m.

1·7km/0·9M
⌐ **Spannenburgerbrug** (bascule, ht 7·3m)
Service hours m-sa *May, Sept* 0600-0800[1], 0800-
2000, *1/6-1/9* 0600-0800[1], 0800-2100 (sa to 2000),
1/10-15/11, *15/3-1/5* 0600-0800[1], 0800-1900,
1900-2000[1] (sa 0600-0800[1], 0800-1800, 1800-1900[1]),
15/11-15/3 0600-0800[1], 0800-1200, 1300-1700,
1700-2000[1] (sa 0600-1900[1]); su/h *May, Sept* 0900-
1200, 1400-1800, *1/6-1/9* 0900-1200, 1400-1700,
1800-2000, *1/10-1/5* closed.
1. On request from Prov. Waterstaat Friesland, ☎ (058)
   925888.

Prinses Margriet Kanaal. Spannenburg bascule bridge

2·5km/1·3M
⬎ Enter Koevordermeer

KOEVORDERMEER
9kph/4·9kn in channel, 12kph/6·5kn max outside.
Depth 3·5m channel, 1m and less over much of
lake. Follow R and G channel buoys, some lit.
⚓A 1·5km detour E, along the Idskenhuistermeer
(buoyed unlit) and its feeder channel (depth 1·5m,
6kph/3·2kn max), leads to Recreatiepark Idsken-
huizen at the S end of the lake; toilets, showers,
laundrette.
⚓ Jachthaven De Koevoet on E bank of Koevordermeer past entrance, toilets, showers, laundrette.

3·4km/1·8M
⬎ G Lt to stbd. Re-enter Prinses Margriet Kanaal.

PRINSES MARGRIET KANAAL
12·5kph/6·7kn max, depth 3·6m.

2·2km/1·2M
⬎ Stbd to E side of island, follow buoyed channel
into Westerbrugsloot.

2·3km/1·2M
WESTERBRUGSLOOT (Prinses Margriet Kanaal)
⌐ **Uitwellingergabrug** (bascule, 7·3m)
Service See Spannenburgerbrug above.

UITWELLINGERGA DETOUR
Short detours N and S in branch canals off Westerbrugsloot lead to:
⚓ Watersportbedrijf Cantecleer, toilets, showers, 9t
crane.
⚓ Jachthaven Krekt oer't Wetter, toilets, showers,
5t crane, ☎ (05153) 244.
⚓ Jachthaven WSC/Bomotel Hart van Friesland,
toilets, showers, laundrette.
⚓ Jachthaven De Horse Watersport, toilets, showers, 15t boat-lift, ☎ (05153) 356.

Continue along Prinses Margriet Kanaal.

2·7km/1·5M
⬎ To port is junction with the Houkesloot.

DETOUR INTO SNEEK
Municipal HrMr ☎ (05150) 85555.
Maximum speeds: Houkesloot 12·5km/6·7kn,
Zomerrak 6kph/3·2kn, rest 9kph/4·9kn.

● **Detour of 8·4km/4·5M round trip**
To port and follow the Houkesloot
⬎ To stbd (3·5km). Follow Burg de Hoop Kanaal.
⬎ To port (0·5km).
Jachthavens De Domp Nos I and II (0·2km to E),
showers, toilets, ☎ (05150) 12559. No. II Mendes
de Jong B.V., 25t boat-lift, 5t crane, ☎ (05150)
19025. To stbd, Sneeker Jachthaven (0·2km to W)
☎ (05150) 13089.

Sneek Waterpoort

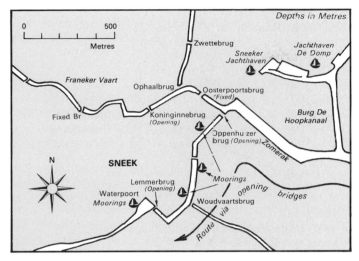

Sneek

● **Detour of 10·4km/5·6M round trip**
To port and follow the Houkesloot.

➤ To port (3·5km). Follow Zomerrak. Moorings below are mainly temporary for 24 hours.

➤ To port (0·8km) (quayside moorings to the N on Oosterkade).

3 ⌫ Follow town canal (Stadsgracht) through 3 opening bridges to the yacht moorings, Waterpoort (0·9km). Moorings alongside throughout this stretch and in the Waterpoort. Laundrettes: Gebr. Bakker B.V. at Woudvaart, Tante Sidonia and Kleinzand 54.

3 ⌫ ⚓ In sequence: **Oppenhuizerbrug** (ht 0·78m), **van Harinxmabrug** (ht 1·24m), and **Lemmerbrug** (ht 1·09m).
Service hours m-sa *1/4-1/11* 0700-0800, 0900-1200, 1300-1700, 1800-2000 (*1/6-1/9* to 2100), *1/11-1/4* on request, ☏ (05150) 13658/12323; su/h *May, Sept* 0800-0900, 1200-1300, 1800-2000, *1/6-1/9* 0800-0900, 1400-1700, 1800-2000, *1/10-1/5* closed.

Return from detour by same route to:

➤ GR unlit buoy *HO1/PM72*. Then to port (keeping buoy to port) into Sneekermeer.

SNEEKERMEER
12·5kph/6·7kn max in channel, 9kph/4·9kn outside. 3kph/1·6kn in small junction channels into the *poelen* (pools). Lakes mostly navigable up to 1·2m draught; deeper draught yachts must follow buoyed channel, or take local advice if entering *poelen*. R and G channel buoys some lit.

⚓ Pontoons on Starteiland E bank. Paviljoen Sneekermeer 400m to port 1·2km along channel, toilets, showers, laundrette, 3·5t crane, ☏ (015150) 13955.

4·1km/2·2M
⪡ **Terhornstersluis.** Sluice gates usually left open.

DETOUR INTO TERHORNE
➤ Stbd after sluice following channel buoys into and through Nieuwe Zandsloot opening bridge. Oude Zandsloot bridge to the S is no longer in yacht harbour's service.

⚓ Jachthaven van Sjerp de Vries, toilets, showers. Jachthaven Oksewiel 10t crane ☏ (05668) 277. Jachtwerf Rijpkema 10t crane ☏ (05668) 340. W. Dam 2t crane ☏ (05668) 538. Watersportbedrijf De Horne 2·5t crane ☏ (05668) 264.

⚓ Moorings S bank of Zandsloot, E of old bridge, and in the Terhornster and Terkaplester Poelen.

Zandsloot drawbridge (ht 2·45m)
Service hours m-sa *1/5-1/10* 0700-0800, 0830-1200, 1300-1730, 1800-2100, (sa to 2000), *1/10-15/11, 15/3-1/5* 0700-0800, 0830-1200, 1300-1730, 1800-1900 (sa to 1800). *15/11-15/3* m-f 0700-1200, 1300-1700. On m-f 0600-0700 and 1700-2000 and sa 0700-1700 only on request, ☏ (058) 925888/122422. su/h *1/5-1/6, 1/9-1/10* 0900-1200, 1400-1800, *1/6-1/9* 0900-1200, 1400-1700, 1800-2000, *1/10-1/5* closed.

Continue along Nieuwe Wetering.

NIEUWE WETERING (Prinses Margriet Kanaal)
12kph/6·5kn max. Minimum depth 3·6m.

4·4km/2·4M
⌫ **Oude Schouw** (bascule bridge ht 7·3m)
Service See Spannenburgerbrug above.

2·2km/1·2M
2 ⌫ **Grouw railway bridge** (ht 4·85m) and **road bridge** (ht 5·3m).
Service hours m 0400-2400, t-f 0000-2400; sa 0000-2000; su/h *5/5-1/10* 0830-2000, *1/10-5/5* closed. Waiting time 20 to 40 minutes, see clock on bridge office for next opening. (VHF Ch 18 *Spoorbrug te Grouw*).

2·0km/1·1M
Fl.G Lt to stbd, entrance to Pikmeer.

PIKMEER
Minimum depth 3·6m channel, generally 1·8m Pikmeer and Grouw. Follow G and R channel buoys. Fl.G Lt to stbd N end entrance channel to Biggemeer.

GROUW
⚓ WV Grouwster Watersport, toilets, showers. Variety of municipal and private pontoons in the town and to N and W in approaches to Rechte Grouw and the Nauwe Galle. Jachtwerf De Polle B.V. 20t crane, A.E. Wester en Zn 4t boat-lift ☏ (05662) 1335.

0·8km/0·4M
G unlit buoy.

0·8km/0·4M
BIGGEMEER
G buoy to stbd.

0·3km/0·2M
➥ Between R buoy and G LtBn. Keep to E of island.

0·8km/0·4M
➥ Port branch re-entering Prinses Margriet Kanaal.

4·8km/2·6M
PRINSES MARGRIET KANAAL/NW KANAAL
➥ Cross Rogsloot.

DETOUR INTO WARTENA
6kph/3·2kn speed max.
⚓ Jachthaven Wartena to port and 500m up Rogsloot, 3·5m depth, on N side. Toilets, showers, ☎ (05105) 1870.

2·8km/1·5M
⌒ **Fonejachtbrug** (bascule bridge ht 7·3m)
Service See Spannenburgerbrug above.

0·7km/0·4M
➥ To port into Schalke Diep.

SCHALKE DIEP
Depth 3·95m. Keep N of 2 G unlit buoys 1km W of entrance.

4·9km/2·6M
➥ To stbd into Lang Deel.

LANG DEEL
Depth 2·15–3·95m

LEEUWARDEN
HrMr ☎ (058) 131441. 9kph/4·9kn max in town canals. Fixed-masted yachts must make long detour to W of town entering along Harlingertrekvaart to avoid fixed bridges.

1·7km/0·9M
➥ Port branch van Harinxmakanaal.

1·2km/0·6M
➥ Cross the Nauwe Greuns.

DETOUR TO LEEUWARDEN YACHT HAVENS

⌒⚓ 1·3km N off the E side of the Wijde Greuns and through opening bridge is Jachthaven Leeuwarder Watersport, and Nieuwe Leeuwarder Jachthaven, toilets, showers. **Hemriksbrug or Greunsbrug** (opening bridge 2·52m and fixed bridge 3·08m height).
Service hours m-f 0600-0715, 0830-1215, 1400-1730, 1815-2015 (*1/10-1/4* to 1915); sa 0830-1215, 1330-1630, 1800-1915 (except *1/10-1/4*); *1/5-1/10* su 0930-1115, 1800-1900, h 0800-1000, 1930-2030, *1/10-1/5* su/h closed.

VAN HARINXMAKANAAL
12·5kph/6·7kn max, depth 3·95m.

1·4km/0·8M
⌒ **Drachtsterbrug** (ht 5·3m)
Bridge service hours m-sa *1/5-1/10* 0600-0700[1], 0700-2100 (sa to 2000), *1/10-15/11* and *15/3-1/5* 0600-0700[1], 0700-1900, 1900-2000[1] (sa 0600-0700[1], 0700-1800, 1800-1900[1]), *15/11-15/3* 0600-0700[1], 0700-1700, 1700-2000[1] (sa 0600-1900[1]). su/h closed.
1. On request to Prov. Waterstaat Friesland, ☎ (058) 925888.

1·5km/0·8M
2 ⌒ **Overijsselse Brug** (double bascule ht 5·3m)
Service See Drachtsterbrug

1·5km/0·8M
2 ⌒ **Footbridge and railway bridge** (ht 5·3m)
Service hours See Drachtsterbrug, but due to trains waiting times of over an hour are possible. See ANWB *Openingstijden spoorbruggen*.

0·8km/0·4M
➥ Cross Zwettehaven

0·7km/0·4M
⌒ **Railway bridge** (ht 5·3m)
Service hours See Drachtsterbrug, but due to trains waiting times of over an hour are possible. See ANWB *Openingstijden spoorbruggen*.

0·8km/0·4M
➥ To stbd turning sharp E into Harlingertrekvaart.

0·9km/0·5M
➥ T-junction, stbd to town.

LEEUWARDEN
See Route 18 for bridges and facilities in Leeuwarden.

2·5km/1·3M
Vrouwenpoortsbrug (end of route).

12. The Frisian Islands and the Waddenzee

Route 20
A circular tour of the southern
Waddenzee (*See page 134 for route plan*)

Commentary

This area provides the deepest water cruising in the Waddenzee and you will see many fascinating large traditional Dutch barge yachts as well as deep-draught modern vessels in the harbours. It is generally well protected from weather with winding channels and a multitude of drying areas, particularly at low water. However, the two *zeegats* can be extremely uncomfortable in strong westerly to northerly conditions, and with wind against ebb since the streams sluice out between the islands.

The islands are sand dunes, with pasture land and coniferous plantations usually at their eastern leeward ends. To the town dweller there is the relaxing novelty of seeing and, above all, hearing so few cars, since non-resident vehicles are discouraged. Bicycles can be hired in most of the islands.

Texel teems with bird life primarily on the west coast requiring you to have transport. Oudeschild is a pleasant village with two churches, and a lifeboat museum near the windmill which overlooks the harbour. In May 1987 the yacht moorings were on a string of pontoons stretching from the northern end of the harbour, and although shown on the charts, the eastern basin area was cleared but had not yet been excavated, as if completion was some time away. Den Burg the capital of Texel is half an hour's cycle ride away through pasture land towards the middle of the island. It is another leafy town built in circles around the shopping centre which also has a museum.

Oost Vlieland is the jewel of the islands, with a small harbour a short walk from a long tree-lined main street with restaurants and small shops, backed by forested dunes with a small lighthouse emerging above the trees. Visitors' cars are banned and there are special cycle tracks winding through the woods and to the beaches on the northern side. Try the cranberry wine, a specialty of the island.

Terschelling is a much larger island but with similar woodlands, heaths, dunes and beaches if you travel far enough from the main town near the harbour which has a good selection of restaurants and a small museum. *For commentary on Harlingen see Route 17.*

Distances 153km/82M. Four stages: Harlingen to Texel 26M, Vlieland 31M, West Terschelling 7M, and Harlingen 19M.
Bridges 2 opening in Harlingen.
Locks 1 open *keersluis* in Harlingen.

Tides, heights and soundings
Tidal throughout. Soundings, as on the Dutch small-craft chart, relate to LLWS (lower low water springs). Although the range is small, 1·4m neaps to 2·0m springs, streams in the deeper channels can average up to 3½kn and more nearer the *zeegats*, so on the three longer legs it pays to use them.

Harlingen to Texel (26M): the shallow Boontjes channel is best taken on the last of the flood and the ebb taken out from Kornwerderzand to Texel.

Texel to Vlieland (31M): by starting at about half tide rising the ingoing tide can be taken up the Scheurrak and the ebb down the Inschot, Vliestroom, motoring if necessary for the last mile against the stream along the Vliesloot.

Vlieland to West Terschelling (7M): the *zeegat* is best crossed nearer slack water and for depth around HW is preferable.

West Terschelling to Harlingen (19M): can be conveniently taken on a flood tide.

Minimum depths en route
The Boontjes channel with drying patches on each side has 1·6m soundings (LLWS) and is best taken on a rising tide, near the top of the tide for deeper draught yachts. Depths are over 2m throughout the rest of this route.

Charts
Dutch small-craft chart *1811*, together with *Stroomatlas k*.

Route description

⚓ HARLINGEN NOORDERHAVEN
See Route 17 for entrance and facilities in Harlingen.

No traffic signals. Pass out of harbour between the R Lt buoys marking construction work on E side of entrance and W wall, then round W pierhead. Minimum depth near entrance 3·2m.

1·5km/0·7M
N cardinal Lt buoy *BS33/BO44* off Harlingen entrance. Turn S into channel keeping buoy to stbd.

BOONTJES
Follow channel buoys and Bns, some lit, on rising tide. 6m minimum depth off Harlingen, then for 4km less than 2m depth (minimum 1·6m), then for 6km minimum depth 2·5m. Channel is narrow with

Harlingen. Keersluis double swing bridge at the entrance to the Oude Buitenhaven. The Keersluis usually remains open

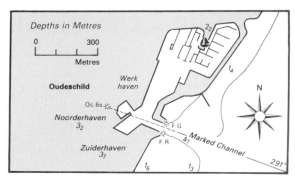

Oudeschild

drying patches on each side. Follow channel across N of Kornwerderzand lock entrance. Note that here the S side of channel is deepest and 2m contour encroaches into channel from N.

14·6km/7·9M

W cardinal Lt buoy *KWZ*, keep to stbd and turn to port into buoyed channel heading SW.

DOOVE BALG

Channel is buoyed, many lit. Minimum depth 4·4m.

19·4km/10·4M

GR Lit buoy *D2/SO1*. Keep to its S. Continue W and SW round to N of Burgzand into the Texelstroom.

TEXELSTROOM

Channel buoyed, many lit. Minimum depth 5m in fairway.

Oudeschild entrance

OUDESCHILD

MHWS 1·8m, MHWN 1·5m. LLWS NAP −1·2m.
Den Helder
MHWS 1·8m, MLWS 0·2m, MHWN 1·6m, MLWN 0·5m.

12·8km/6·9M

⚓ Entrance to harbour. 2F.R and 2F.G on pierheads. Fog signal S pierhead Horn(2)30s, 0600-2200 only. Oc.6s Lt kept between pierhead Lts gives 291° Ldg line. R Lt buoy 350m ESE of entrance channel with two entrance buoys. Depth of commercial harbour 3·2–4·2m. N end of harbour is Jachthaven Oudeschild, with a newly constructed section, depth 2·2m and WV Texel (toilets, showers), ☎ (02220) 3608.
HrMr VHF Ch 9, ☎ (02220) 2710/ 2709. No customs facilities, clearance only at Den Helder.

TEXELSTROOM

Return eastwards along buoyed lit channel (above).

Oudeschild Zuiderhaven

12·8km/6·9M

GR Lt buoy *D2/SO1*. Keep to its N. Turn ENE into Scheurrak channel.

SCHEURRAK, OMDRAAI, OUDE VLIE CHANNELS

Channel buoys, unlit. Daylight route. Winding, minimum depth 3m between drying edges, narrows less than 200m at N end.

20·4km/11·0M
G unlit buoy *IN19* (close). Port into Inschot channel. Beware drying spits each side of entrance. Note buoyage changes, G to port, R to stbd.

INSCHOT
Channel buoyed, many lit. Minimum depth 3m in fairway. Follow channel buoys around W side of Wolfshoek drying bank at N end of the channel.

10·4km/5·6M
GR Lt buoy *BS1/IN2*. Either side N into Vliestroom.

VLIESTROOM
Channel buoyed, many lit. Minimum depth 7m in fairway. Follow round N side of Richel Island to entrance of Vliesloot channel at the E end of Oost Vlieland.

11·9km/6·4M
R unlit buoy *VS4* and GR Lt buoy *ZS13/VS2*. Enter channel between two buoys. Spit to E.

VLIESLOOT
Channel buoyed lit, G unlit buoys on E side are somewhat confusing and depths changing so keep to W side of channel near G buoys on Vlieland side and round the G LtBn on its E side. Minimum depth 3·8m.

2·6km/1·4M
OOST VLIELAND
MHWS 2·3m, MLWS 0·2m, MHWN 2·0m, MLWS 0·5m
⚓ Entrance F.R&G Pierhead Lts. Official HrMr ☎ (05621) 1563. Jachthaven HrMr ☎ (05621) 1729.
Customs (1 May to 1 Nov) NW end of yacht harbour.
⚓ Minimum depth (N end) 1·8m, Werkhaven 2·4m. Moorings in each basin. Can be crowded in season so anchoring in channel may be necessary with long dinghy trip to harbour. Showers, toilets, 10t crane.

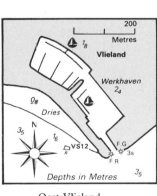

Oost Vlieland

West Terschelling

VLIESLOOT
Return E and N along buoyed lit channel (above).

2·6km/1·4M
R unlit buoy *VS4* and GR Lt buoy *ZS13/VS2*.
From position between two buoys, direct course to GR Lt buoy *VL2/SG1*, crossing **GRONDEN VAN STORTEMELK**, in the *zeegat*.

4·0km/2·2M
GR Lt buoy *VL2/SG1*. Keep close to N of buoy to enter channel.

SCHUITENGAT
Channel buoyed, beaconed and lit. Minimum depth 2·6m, very narrow. Follow channel buoys NE.

4·3km/2·3M
G LtBn *SG11*. Keep close to its N and then head direct for harbour entrance G Lt buoy *SG15* opposite side of channel to entrance. Ldg Lts 053° along deep channel to entrance; west pierhead F.WR, and F.W 1·1M behind on dyke.

WEST-TERSCHELLING
MHWS 2·2m, MLWS 0·1m, MHWN 1·9m, MLWN 0·5m.
VHF Ch 2 *Kustwacht*

1·4km/0·8M
⚓ Entrance F.WR (sector Lt) and Horn 15s on west pierhead. F.G on E pierhead. Follow harbour wall, F and Fl Lts on E side. Minimum depth 4·1m S end, 2·6m N end. Moorings at N end of harbour in Dellewal, the new visitors' harbour. 2·6m depth, toilets, showers, laundrette, HrMr ☎ (05620) 2235. *Customs* (1 May to 1 Nov) Willem Barentszkade 34, ☎ (05620) 2884.

West Terschelling. On the W side of the harbour there is some space for visitors

1·4km/0·8M
G LtBn *SG11*. Keep close to its N and then follow Schuitengat channel SW.

SCHUITENGAT
Return SW along buoyed lit channel.

4·3km/2·3M

GR Lt buoy *VL2/SG1*. Round buoy to its E to leave channel then southwards.

VLIESTROOM

Return southwards along buoyed lit channel.

9·3km/5·0M

GR Lt buoy *BS1/IN2* and R Lt buoy *BS2*. Between these buoys turn to port into Blauwe Slenk.

BLAUWE SLENK

Follow winding channel buoyed, some lit. Minimum depth 3m. Steep drying edges.

10·9km/5·9M

R Lt buoy *BS28* and G Lt buoy *BS27*. It is critical to approach S side of Pollendam from between these buoys.

POLLENDAM

Harlingen Iso.R.4s sector Lt indicates dangerous N side of dam. Follow S side of Pollendam on 112°, same bearing as Ldg Lts on black and white masts; front Iso.4s, rear Oc.6s, 112°. R Bns (some lit) close together along N side. G LtBns widely spaced S side. Very narrow. Minimum depth Harlingen entrance 3·2m.

HANERAK

This is a shoal-draught alternative channel, minimum depth 1·5m, S of the Pollendam channel between closely spaced unlit R and G buoys.

6·9km/3·7M

GR Lt buoy *BS33/BO44* off harbour entrance. Pass close N of buoy.

1·5km/0·8M

⚓ HARLINGEN NOORDERHAVEN (see above).

Route 21
The northern Waddenzee. Following the withies from Terschelling to Delfzijl

Commentary

Whilst this route ends at Delfzijl it is more likely that readers will be using it to reach Borkum only, continuing on the more popular route via the German islands to the Elbe, the Kiel Canal and Scandinavia. The tricky tidal planning is dealt with below.

The channels are all well marked with brightly painted buoys at the deep-water ends and with withies in between. The buoys are lettered according to the name of the channel and numbered (e.g. *ZSA9*, Zuider Spruit Ameland channel, 9th). As the buoyage system tends to overspill eastwards across the watersheds the red and green buoys in the higher reaches of the channels on the eastern sides of the islands are sometimes on the 'wrong' side relative to the tidal flow. It is essential to examine the charts, which are marked with the red outlines of large arrows in the direction of the buoyage; often in opposition to the flood tide.

Similarly the withies, which are closely spaced, are predominantly port hand with branching crowns and with red fluorescent tapes on their stems. These are only occasionally helped by starboard withies, branches bound downwards and with green fluorescent tapes. The withies overflow into the channels on the eastern sides of the islands to provide continuous lines along the northern sides of the channels. These withies mark the low-water edges of the channels.

To maximise the length of time you can use a channel during a tide it is a useful rule to stay in the deepest water by keeping a distance from the withies when you start at the wider and deeper end of the channel at low water, and as the tide rises move progressively closer to the withies near the top of the watershed (the *wantij*, in Dutch) where the channel is narrower. Follow the withies and marks on the ground rather than the contours on the charts which may be out of date.

For commentary on Terschelling see Route 20.

Ameland, once dependent on the whaling industry is now dependent on tourism. The eastern end of the island is pasture with few trees and a bird sanctuary, Natuurmuseum Ameland, not far from Nes. After settling on the firm bottom against the harbour wall, a trip on hired bicycles is called for to visit the three villages of Ballum, Hollum and Buren, two with old churches. Hollum has a small museum in one of the many old 'Captains' houses'. The remains of a dyke join Ameland with the mainland. Mentioned by Erskine Childers in *Riddle of the Sands*, this was built towards the end of the 19th century in an abortive hope of creating a low-water causeway.

For commentary on Lauwersoog see Route 18.

Schiermonnikoog is another fascinating smaller island with a yacht harbour which can only be described as a water hole surrounded by baffle walls at the end of a causeway from the island across the sand. Again visiting cars are banned and coniferous woods, pasture land, dunes and a bird sanctuary on the east end of the island call for a healthy ride on hired bicycles.

For commentary on Delfzijl see Route 18.

Distances 164km/88M. Three stages: West Terschelling to Nes 26M, Lauwersoog 20M, and Delfzijl 43M.

Lock 1 lock entrance to Lauwersoog.

Tides, heights and soundings

Tidal throughout, except in the detour into the Lauwersmeer where heights and soundings are to LZP (Lauwersmeer *zomerpeil* NAP−0·9m). Elsewhere soundings are to LLWS and heights to MHWS.

Minimum depths en route

Tidal ranges gradually increase northeastwards in the Waddenzee. Spring/neap ranges are: West Terschelling 2·1/1·4m, Harlingen 2·0/1·5m, Nes 2·5/1·8m, Lauwersoog 2·5/1·7m, Schiermonnikoog 2·6/1·8m, Borkum (W Germany) 2·7/2·0m, Delfzijl 3·2/2·5m. On the highest watersheds (*wad or wantij* in Dutch) along this route minimum depths are around 1·5m at MHW, ranging between about 1·2 and 1·8m, and drying at an average 0·7m above LLWS. Even with a 1·25m/4·1ft draught boat it is advisable to make passage near to springs, and a 1·1m/3·6ft draught is more comfortable, whilst centreboarders of 0·5m draught are common in the area. It is certainly advisable to be able to take the ground flat and to have a good powerful engine to make up time.

The only way to make passage on this route is to start at the earliest possible time on the flood and take a 'nudging' tidal approach across the watersheds, using the engine and anchoring and waiting for 'lift-off' each time the vessel grounds. This also often means that the tide is still flooding into the next *zeegat* and into the next harbour. On the West-Terschelling to Nes (26M) leg this is easily achieved and, of course, as Nes dries out arrival at or up to say an hour after HW is ideal. Nes to Lauwersoog (20M) is a little, but not much, more difficult since it is not possible to get out of Nes until some time after LW, unless you leave on a falling tide and anchor and wait outside in the channel. Lauwersoog to Delfzijl (43M) is more difficult since not only is there a 26M passage over several watersheds to the Eems, but there is the problem of the last 17M up the Eems when you need to motor hard against the ebb, difficult at springs. On both counts therefore a powerful engine helps. However a normal auxiliary engine is adequate since if there is in any doubt of reaching Delfzijl it is easy to run into Borkum, the West German island at the mouth of the river, and leave the passage to Delfzijl for another day.

Charts

Dutch small-craft charts *1811, 1812. Stroomatlassen k, l and m.*

Route description

⚓ WEST-TERSCHELLING

MHWS 2·2m, MLWS 0·1m, MHWN 1·9m, MLWN 0·5m
See Route 20 for entrance and facilities.

Depart turning eastwards at entrance.

OOSTEROM

Channel buoys and Bns unlit, daylight passage. Keep close N of N cardinal wreck-marker buoy, 3km/1·6M E of entrance. At RG unlit Bn *O15/NB14* dogleg S to G unlit buoy *NB5* (**NOORDER BALGEN** channel) keeping it close to port, then E back into Oosterom keeping R buoys close to port. Passage between 2 pairs of Y spar buoys (X top-

marks) which mark crossing of submarine pipelines. Continue following R buoys keeping them to port even though now across watershed. Watershed dries above LLWS. Depth at MHW approximately 1·5m.

26·7km/14·4M

R unlit buoy *O60*. Port into channel.

BOSCHGAT

Channel buoyage changes here. Keep R unlit buoys *O62* and *O64* close to port, but then also keep G unlit buoys close to port near to Terschelling's steep-to shore. Minimum depth 2·5m in channel.

Note An alternative short cut at HW across the spit between Blauwe Balg and Borndiep is marked by R buoys, series *BB*, close N of the nature reserve.

4·3km/2·3M

G unlit buoy *WG13*. Close N of buoy turn stbd into Borndiep.

BORNDIEP

Channel steep-to each side. Ameland LtHo to E (see Chapter 8). Minimum depth 5m. Buoyed, unlit except for a single Y LtBn on Ameland drying edge, and a GR Lt buoy *WG31/VH50* at the S end of the channel.

9·1km/4·9M

R unlit buoy *MG2*. Stbd round S side of buoy and NE along Molengat.

MOLENGAT AND BRANDGAT CHANNELS

R unlit buoys N side. Iso.R.4s Bn approaching N bend off the Leidam. G unlit buoys S side and Fl(5)Y.20s Bn N side of channel approaching Nes entrance, minimum depth 2·4m.

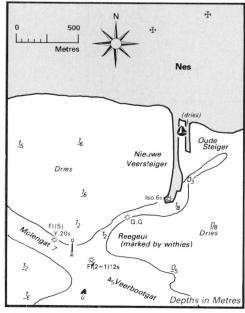

Nes

7·6km/4·1M

NES

MHWS 2·7m, MLWS 0·2m, MHWN 2·4m, MLWN 0·6m
RG Bn Fl(2+1)R.12s, *VA2/R1*. Entrance channel to W following withies; unbound to port, bound to stbd. G LtBn on S side of E bend. Iso.6s Lt on pierhead.

⚓ Drying moorings against E wall at N end, with permission of HrMr ☎ (05191) 2304/4305/2729; toilets, showers. Anchoring for deep-keel yachts in Brandgat and mouth of entrance.

VEERBOOTGAT

Channel buoys (1 lit), R to port (N of channel), G to stbd. Minimum depth 3m.

1·5km/0·8M

RG unlit buoy *ZSA1/KG14*. Keep to its N and then N of G buoy *ZSA3*. There is a drying spit S of this.

ZUIDER SPRUIT AMELAND

Keep close to buoys, R to port, G to stbd going eastwards. Two sets of Y spar buoys (X topmarks) mark entrance and exit of a pipeline area which is also crossed by the remains of the old dyke; channel passes through gap in the dyke between two pairs of R and G buoys, *ZSA8/ZSA17* and *ZSA10/ZSA19*. At R buoy *ZSA16* follow close to the port-hand unbound withies eastwards. Very winding channel across watershed. Dries above LLWS; depth at MHW approximately 1·5m.

10·7km/5·8M

S cardinal buoy *ZSA/HB*. Leave to port turning E.

HOLWERDERBALG

Unlit channel buoys, *HB* series, continue in E direction, R to port G to stbd, out to deep channel (depth 2·2m minimum). It is not recommended to navigate the continuing unmarked channel out into the Friesche Zeegat.

7·2km/3·9M

N cardinal unlit buoy, Pinkegat. Turn to stbd round N side of buoy into Pinkegat channel.

PINKEGAT

Channel unlit, mainly G buoys to stbd, one R to port. Slightly deeper than drying (LLWS).

2·6km/1·4M

S cardinal unlit buoy, *Smeriggat*. Close S of this buoy double back N still keeping G buoys to stbd.

SMERIGGAT

Channel unlit G Bns (keep to stbd). Y LtBn near end of winding channel. Slightly deeper than drying (LLWS).

3·7km/2·0M

RG unlit buoy *WG13/SG2*. Stbd into Westgat.

WESTGAT AND ZOUTKAMPERLAAG

Channels buoyed, lit. Minimum depth 2·9m, steep edges of fairway. Approach harbour from N of G unlit *Z15* buoy.

10·8km/5·9M

LAUWERSOOG

MHWS 2·9m, MLWS 0·4m, MHWN 2·6m, MLWN 0·9m
≪ Entrance Buitenhaven. F.R&G Lts on pierheads. Fog signal Horn(2)30s W pierhead. Cross entrance to Vissershaven past F.R Lt on N pierhead. No customs office (see lock-keeper). VHF Ch 22 *Robbengatsluis*. Ch 9 *Vissershaven*.

Lock service hours m-f *1/5-1/10* 0700-1200, 1300-2000, *1/10-1/5* 0700-1200, 1300-1800; sa *1/5-1/10* 0700-1200, 1300-1900, *1/10-1/5* 0700-1200, 1300-1700; su/h *1/5-1/10* 0900-1200, 1400-1830, *1/10-1/5* closed.

⚓ Pleasure craft may anchor in Buitenhaven to wait for lock.

⚓ Through lock to E of entrance is Jachthaven Noordergat, toilets, showers, laundrette, 15t boat-lift, ☎ (05193) 9040.

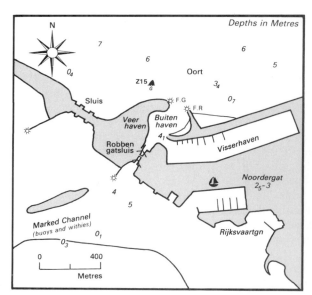

Lauwersoog

Lauwersoog entrance at low water

Lauwersoog. Seaward side of the locks with opening bridge

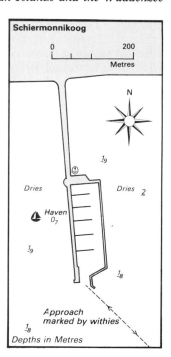

Schiermoonnikoog

DETOUR TO OOSTMAHORN

S from Lauwersoog. From lock gate or marina eastwards keeping S of island. Direction of buoyage, beacons, towards E and S down Lauwersmeer; R and unbound withies to port, G and bound withies to stbd. Follow Vaarwater naar Oostmahorn to W side of lake to entrance. Distance 3·9km from lock to entrance of yacht harbour on W side of lake.

⚓ Jachthaven Oostmahorn, minimum depth 2·5m, toilets, showers, laundrette, ☎ (05193) 1445/1880.

Schiermonnikoog. The small deep-water yacht haven pool is out on a limb at the end of a long causeway across the sand

Oostmahorn. Entrance to the ferry harbour

Schiermonnikoog. The entrance to the yacht haven. The channel is lined with port and starboard withies

DETOUR TO SCHIERMONNIKOOG

N from Lauwersoog.

MHWS 2·8m, MLWS 0·2m, MHWN 2·4m, MLWN 0·6m
VHF Ch 5, working Ch 16 and 67 *Kustwacht Schiermonnikoog.* HrMr ☎ (05195) 1544. Busy in season so contact HrMr in advance for berth (office open *1/5-1/10*). NW from entrance cross **ZOUT-KAMPERLAAG** to RG Lt buoy *Z12/BZ13.* Fol-

low **GEUL VAN BRAKZAND** channel (minimum depth close to drying and with approximately 1·4m at half tide) N keeping unlit G buoys to port (buoyage direction is S). Cross **GAT VAN SCHIER-MONNIKOOG** to G Lt buoy *GVS5.* Head W of N to G buoy *R3* (leave to stbd) and follow withies across drying area (unbound to port, bound to stbd) over the Siegewal drying area to entrance. No entrance Lts. Total distance 8·6km/4·6M. Requires top end (say 2½ hours) of tide, preferably rising, both inwards and outwards in order to visit village; i.e. 2 days for round trip from Lauwersoog.

⚓ Jachthaven De Oude Veerdam has 0·7m minimum depth LLWS. Floating pontoons, toilets, showers.

Continue from Lauwersoog heading E for Oort channel.

OORT CHANNEL
Buoyed, 2 G Lt buoys (keep them to stbd). Minimum depth 2m.

5·0km/2·7M
G Lt buoy *O11*, stbd round N side of buoy then follow buoys.

LUTJEWAD
Unlit channel buoys *LW* series, R to port, G to stbd. Continue across S end of Eilanderbalg channel keeping to the S of RG buoy *LW12/EB1* to S. Channel close to drying (LLWS).

4·6km/2·5M
R unlit Bn *LW16* to port.

HORNHUIZERWAD
Continue E along winding withied channel (unbound, keep them to port). Dries above LLWS, depth at MHW approximately 1·5m.

3·5km/1·9M
R unlit buoy *SP2* to port.

SPRUIT
Follow channel, port buoys R, stbd buoys G, series *SP*. Close to drying (LLWS) then deepens to 8m.

The winding drying channel across the **PIETERBUREN WAD** to the S is not to be recommended and is not much shorter. Minimum depth at MHW is approximately 1·2m.

7·0km/3·8M
N cardinal unlit buoy *SP/ZOL*. Keep it to stbd and double SE into Zuidoost Lauwers.

ZUIDOOST LAUWERS
Follow *ZOL* series buoys (direction as above). Shoals 6m to drying.

16·2km/8·8M
R unlit Bn *ZOL52* close to port.

UITHUISERWAD/EEMSWADJE
Follow S side of unbound withies to R unlit Bn *R2*, then follow buoys, keeping R to port and G to stbd. Watershed dries above LLWS, depth at MHW is approximately 1·5m.

6·9km/3·7M
RW unlit buoy *VR*. Keep to stbd and turn SE.

OUDE WESTEREEMS
Channel minimum depth 6m in fairway. Follow G buoys (some lit) keeping close S and outside shipping channel past entrance to Eemshaven (closed to pleasure craft, in emergency VHF Ch 14 *Havendienst Eemshaven*).

DOEKEGAT AND OOSTFRIESCHE GAATJE
Follow G buoys (some lit) keeping just outside shipping channel. Beware of shoals beyond the channel to the S. Minimum depth 3·2m towards Delfzijl entrance. Keep N of GR Lt buoy *PS3/BW26* to approach square into entrance.

BOCHT VAN WATUM CHANNEL is not to be recommended owing to a changing bar across the N end, and in any case it is not a significant short cut.

31·1km/16·8M
DELFZIJL
MHWS 3·4m, MLWS 0·2m, MHWN 3·1m, MLWN 0·6m
Entrance F.R&G pierhead Lts. Fog signal Horn15s E pierhead. HrMr VHF Ch 14 *Havendienst Delfzijl*, ☎ (05960) 14966.
Customs De Vennen, ☎ (05960) 15060.

Stbd into Zeehavenkanaal, minimum depth 5m. Stbd at N end into Balkenhaven.

5·0km/2·7M
⚓ Balkenhaven. Minimum depth 3·5m. ZV Neptunus. ☎ (05960) 15004/19260. Lifting facilities, both at Handelskade West, are H.S. Hunfeld (15t crane) ☎ (05960) 13446, and Havenschap Delfzijl (30t) ☎ (05960) 14966. Laundrette 1km from harbour, H.K. Kleinhuis, Oranjestraat5, ☎ (05960) 12795.

Delfzijl. Yacht in Zeehavenkanaal waiting to enter the locks

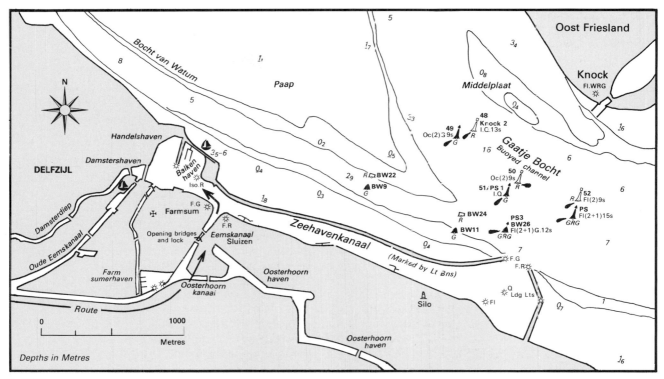

Delfzijl

Delfzijl. Pontoons of ZV Neptunus in the Balkenhaven, with
North Sea platforms moored around

Appendix

I. Sea and waterway charts and tidal atlases

Admiralty charts

To be used in conjunction with booklet *5011, Symbols and Abbreviations used on Admiralty Charts*.

Chart	Title	Scale
110	Oosterschelde – Westkappelle to Goeree	75,000
112	Terschellinger Gronden and approaches to Harlingen	50,000
120	Westerschelde – Flushing to Zandvlietsluis	50,000
	Terneuzen	30,000
122	Approaches to Europoort and Hoek van Holland	50,000
	Scheveningen	15,000
124	Noordzeekanaal incl. IJmuiden, Zaandam and Amsterdam	20,000
	Continuation of Noordzeekanaal	15,000
132	Nieuwe Waterweg and Europoort, Hoek van Holland to Vlaardingen	20,000
133	Nieuwe Maas and Oude Maas Vlaardingen to IJsselmonde and Dordrecht	20,000
137	Dordtsche kil, Hollandsche Diep and Volkerak, Krammer	25,000
139	Westerschelde – Valkenisse to Antwerp	25,000
191	Zeegat van Texel	50,000
	Den Helder Nieuwediep harbour	12,000
192	Oosterschelde	40,000
	Wemeldinge	10,000
	Tholen – Bergen op Zoom	25,000
325	Westerschelde – Oostende to Westkapelle	50,000
	Flushing	25,000
1405	Texel to Helgoland	300,000
1406	Dover and Calais to Orfordness and Scheveningen	250,000
1408	Harwich to Terschelling and Cromer to Rotterdam	300,000
2182A	North Sea – southern sheet	750,000
2322	Goeree to Texel	150,000
2593	Zeegat van Texel to Friesche zeegat	150,000
3371	Gabbard and Galloper banks to Europoort	150,000
3509	Approaches to Die Ems	50,000
3510	Die Ems – Dukegat to Pogum	25,000
	Emden	15,000
	Groningen	40,000
	Pogum to Papenburg	50,000
3761	Friesche zeegat to Die Jade	150,000

Imray charts

Chart	Title	Scale
C25	Harwich to River Humber and Holland Oudeschild, Scheveningen, IJmuiden, Den Helder	343,000
C30	Thames to Holland and Belgium Harwich and North Foreland to Hoek van Holland and Calais. Dunquerque, Oostende, Zeebrugge, Vlissingen, Nieuwpoort, Breskens, Blankenberge.	182,000

Dutch small-craft charts

Chart	Title	Scale
1801	Noordzeekust. Oostende tot Den Helder 8 charts, 7 plans	375,000 to 15,000
1803	Westerschelde. Vlissingen tot Antwerpen 9 charts, 6 plans	250,000 to 10,000
1805	Oosterschelde, Veerse Meer en Grevelingenmeer 9 charts and 17 plans	250,000 to 10,000
1807	Zoommeer, Volkerak, Spui, Haringvliet, Hollandsch Diep 9 charts and 21 plans	250,000 to 25,000
1809	Nieuwe Waterweg, Nieuwe/Oude Maas, Spui en Noord, Dordtsche Kil, Brielse Meer 10 charts, 5 plans	250,000 to 10,000
1810	IJsselmeer met Randmeren 6 charts, 34 larger-scale plans	210,000 to 30,000
1811	Waddenzee (Westblad) en Aangrenzende Noordzeekust 9 charts, 8 larger-scale plans	250,000 to 5,000
1812	Waddenzee (Oostblad) en Aangrenzende Noordzeekust, 9 charts, 8 plans	200,000 to 7,500

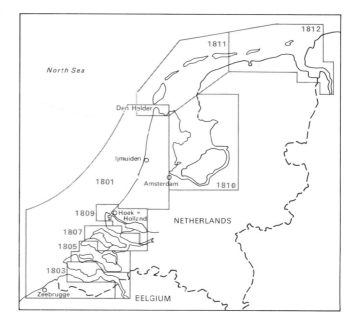

Dutch small-craft charts

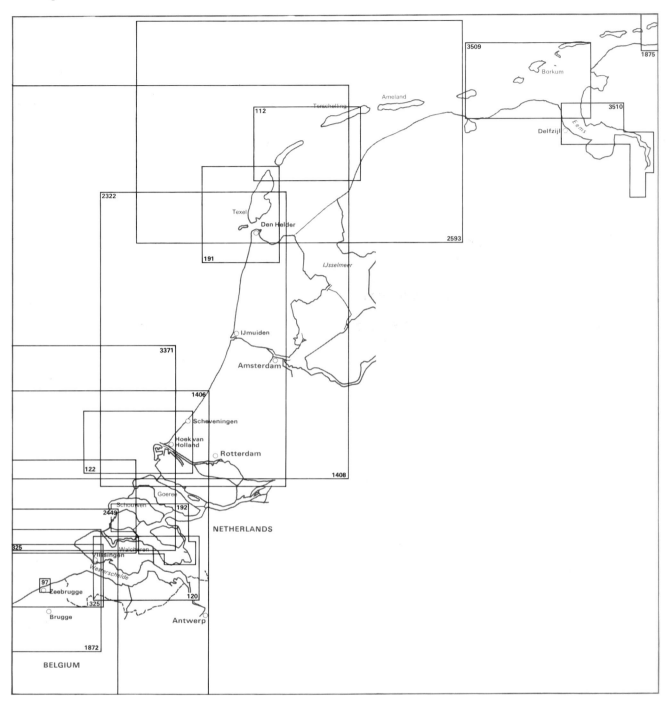

Admiralty charts

Dutch sea charts

To be used in conjunction with booklet *Tekens en afkortingen No. 1* (symbols and abbreviations).

Chart	Title	Scale
1014	Noordzee Zuidblad	750,000
1035	Noordzee. Dungeness en Cap Gris Nez tot Doggersbank en Terschelling	375,000
1037	Noordzee. Texel tot die Elbe en Lister Tief	375,000
1349	Noordzee. West Hinder en Outer Gabbard tot Vlissingen en Noordwijk	150,000
1350	Noordzee. Nederlandse Kust. Goeree tot Texel	150,000

Chart	Title	Scale
1351	IJsselmeer 1 chart, 16 plans	100,000 to 10,000
1352	Noordzee. Texel tot Borkum	150,000
1442	Noordzee. Belgisch-Nederlandse Kust. Monding van Westerschelde 3 plans	60,000 to 15,000
1443	Westerschelde. Van Vlissingen tot Antwerpen met Kanaal van Terneuzen naar Ghent 2 plans.	50,000 to 25,000
1448	Noordzee. Westkapelle tot Stellendam en Maasvlakte 2 plans	75,000 to 40,000

Chart	Title	Scale
1449	Noordzee. Aanloop Europoort en Hoek van Holland	50,000
1450	Noordzee. Aanloop Scheveningen en IJmuiden	50,000
	1 plan	to 1,000
1454	Waddenzee. Den Helder tot Harlingen. Toegangen tot het IJsselmeer	50,000
	3 plans	to 15,000
1456	Noordzee. Terschellinger Gronden tot Harlingen	50,000
	1 plan	to 15,000
1458	Noordzee. Bornrif tot Monden van de Eems	50,000
	1 plan	to 25,000
1460	Noordzee. Monden van de Eems	50,000
1533	Rede Vlissingen	25,000
1538	Dordtsche Kil, Hollandsch Diep tot Noordschans	25,000
1540	Nieuwe Waterweg en Europoort. Hoek van Holland tot Vlaardingen	20,000
1541	Nieuwe Maas en Oude Maas. Vlaardingen tot IJsselmonde en Dordrecht	20,000
1543	IJmuiden, het Noordzeekanaal en havens van Zaandam en Amsterdam	20,000 to 15,000
1546	Noordzee. Zeegat van Texel en Rede Den Helder	30,000
	1 plan	to 15,000
1555	Eems en Dollard. Doekegat tot Delfzijl en Emden	40,000
	1 plan	to 25,000

ANWB Waterkaarten

Chart	Title	Scale
A	Groningen–Noord Friesland	125,000
B	Friese Meren	50,000
C	Noordwest–Overijssel	50,000
D	Gelderse IJssel	25,000
E	Randmeren	50,000
F	Alkmaar–Den Helder	50,000
G	Amsterdam–Alkmaar	50,000
H	Hollandse Plassen	50,000
I	Vechtplassen	50,000
J	Grote Rivieren, westblad (Hoek to IJsselmonde)	50,000
K	Grote Rivieren, middenblad (IJsselmonde to Wijke bij Duurstede)	50,000
L	Grote Rivieren, oostblad (Wijk bij Duurstede to Lobith	50,000
M	Limburgse Maas	50,000
N	Biesbosch	25,000
O	Veerse Meer	25,000
P	Vinkeveense Plassen	10,000
R	Loosdrechtse Plassen	15,000
S	Grevelingenmeer	25,000

Dutch stroomatlassen

Figures in brackets below show depth beneath surface for which average tidal effect has been measured.

Atlas	Title
a	Westerschelde (0–5m)[1]
c	Oosterschelde (0–2m)[2]
d	Benedenrivieren (0–10m)[1, 3]
f	Aanloop Hoek van Holland (0–5m)[1]
j	Zeegat van Texel, Aanlopen IJmuiden[1] en Scheveningen (0–5m)
k	Waddenzee, Westlijk deel (0–5m)
l	Waddenzee, Oostlijk deel (0–5m)
m	Eemsmonding (0–10m)
n	Noordzee, Zuidelijk deel[4]

Notes

1. Available also in 0–10m and (in some cases) 0–15m for deeper draught vessels.
2. New edition incorporating Oosterschelde works, published 1987.
3. Nieuwe and Oude Maas and Hollands Diep.
4. Southern North Sea from Dover Strait to Denmark and Northumberland.

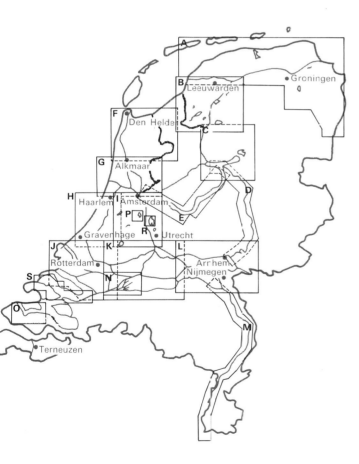

ANWB Waterkaarten

II. Chart data on inland waterways

THE 'STILL' WATERS

Lauwersmeer

Lauwersmeer *zomerpeil* = NAP −0·9m (Dutch small-craft charts), *winterpeil* = NAP −1m.

Friesland waterways

Fries *streefpeil* = NAP −0·66m (ANWB chart *B*), Fries *zomerpeil* = NAP −0·51m.

Rietdiep

Westerkwartierpeil +0·83m (summer, ANWB chart *A*).

Groningen/Eems Kanaal

Winschoterpeil = NAP +0·62m (ANWB chart *A*)

IJsselmeer

IJsselmeer *zomerpeil* = NAP −0·2m (Dutch small-craft charts), *winterpeil* = NAP −0·4m.

Noord-Holland

Referentiepeil (ANWB chart *F*) possible variations of + or − 0·3 metres. Tide gauges at all locks and some bridges. Canal depths are usually given in ranges, e.g. D35–45 (decimetres) on the Noordhollands Kanaal.

Grevelingenmeer

NAP −0·2m (Dutch small-craft charts).

Veerse Meer

Zomerpeil = NAP (Dutch small-craft charts). Sept-Oct level = NAP −0·3m, and Nov-Apr = NAP −0·7m.

Volkerak

Volkerakpeil = NAP (Dutch small-craft charts).

Other ANWB charts

In other 'still' waters behind the weirs the depths and bridge heights are charted to local KP (*kanaalpeil*), SP (*stuwpeil, weirpeil*), or PP (*polderpeil*) with varying NAP heights.

Note

Whilst making a waterway passage it is useful to check charted depths and bridge heights at specific positions with your own soundings and the height scales (*hoogteschaals*), to estimate any significant difference from the chart's datum level on that particular day, to give you confidence in interpreting the more marginal depths and bridge clearances you will be negotiating.

THE SEMI-TIDAL WATERS AND FLOWING RIVERS

On the ANWB charts of the semi-tidal waterways and those subject to the effect of the Haringvliet sluicing programme the datum for bridge and other heights is MHW (Mean High Water) and for soundings MLW (Mean Low Water). MHW and MLW levels are based on mean tidal levels for a mean stream flow on the Upper Rhine. The tidal range progressively reduces inland along the Rhine and its tributaries as it is gradually overcome by the strength of the downstream current. The NAP differences for MHW and MLW are printed in boxes on the chart near selected reaches of the rivers. Moving inland along each waterway illustrates this.

Location	NAP difference MHW metres	MLW metres	Range metres
Nieuwe Waterweg			
Hoek Van Holland	+0·9	−0·7	1·6
Vlaardingen	+1·0	−0·6	1·6
Rotterdam/IJsselmonde	+1·0	−0·5	1·5
Lek (E from Rotterdam)			
Streefkerk	+1·0	−0·3	1·3
Langerak	+1·2	0·0	1·2
Vianen	+1·4	+0·3	1·1

Weir and lock at Hagestein above which datum is *stuwpeil* = NAP +2m to +3m.

Noord, connecting Lek to Dordrecht

Location	MHW	MLW	Range
N of Papendrecht	+1·1	−0·4	1·4

Oude Maas, Merwede, Waal (E from Vlaardingen)

Location	MHW	MLW	Range
Hoogvliet	+1·1	−0·5	1·6
Oud-Beijerland	+0·7	−0·2	0·9
Zwijndrecht	+1·0	+0·1	0·9
Werkendam	+0·9	+0·6	0·3
Herwijnen	+1·4	+1·0	0·4
Heesselt	+3·5	+3·3	0·2

Spui, connecting Oude Maas to Haringvliet

Location	MHW	MLW	Range
Nieuw-Beijerland	+0·6	+0·1	0·5

Dordtse Kil, connecting Oude Maas near Dordrecht to Hollands Diep

Location	MHW	MLW	Range
Halfway point (approx)	+0·8	+0·3	0·5

Haringvliet and Hollands Diep

This waterway is virtually non-tidal, and levels are kept constant by the sluicing programme. However, since sluicing can only take place near LW there can be a twice daily 'apparent' tide. Soundings in the Haringvliet on small-craft chart *1807* are based on NAP, and heights from MHW (NAP +0·7m). The apparent tide can vary at extremes from NAP −0·5m to NAP +1·55m, but is mainly in the range NAP +0·25 to +0·5m, so the data are 'safe' ones.

Amer, Nieuwe Merwede, and Maas (E from Hollands Diep).

Like the Haringvliet/Hollands Diep this is virtually non-tidal.

Location	NAP difference MHW metres	MLW metres	Range metres
As far as Huisden	+0·7	+0·5	0·2
In the Biesbosch	+0·5	+0·4	0·1
Near Kessel	+1·1	+1·0	0·1

Above the weir at Lith the datum is *stuwpeil* = NAP +5.

Notes

1. Using the appropriate tidal range (listed above) taken from the chart and the appropriate charted bridge clearance or depth it is possible to quickly obtain an average LW or HW height or sounding.

2. To obtain the approximate times of HW and LW on the appropriate reach of the northern rivers as far as Hagestein on the Lek or Heesselt on the Waal, there is a plan in the *Getijtafels*, just before the table for Hoek van Holland, showing time differences at half-hourly intervals of HW and LW based on Hoek van Holland. The plan does not cover the Haringvliet, Hollands Diep and Maas because of the less significant range.

III. Netherlands lifeboat stations

In addition to a coastguard service operated by the State Pilotage Board which has watch posts at or near most of the main light locations, the Netherlands Life-saving Service, run by two societies, has a network of inshore and offshore lifeboats. The whole system is triggered on VHF Ch 16. There are 23 lifeboat locations around the outer coast, with 10 offshore vessels and 18 for inshore work which of course are more mobile in terms of launching place. From S to N along the outer coasts lifeboats are stationed as listed below; the inshore are in medium typeface, *offshore in italics*, and both **inshore and offshore in bold**.

1. Cadzand, near Belgian border
2. **Breskens**
3. **Burghsluis, inside N end Oosterschelde barrier**
4. **Stellendam, Buitenhaven outside Goereesesluis**
5. Ouddorp, inside N end of Brouwersdam
6. *Hoek van Holland*
7. Ter Heijde, N of Hoek
8. *Scheveningen*
9. Katwijk aan Zee
10. Noordwijk aan Zee
11. Zandvoort
12. **IJmuiden**
13. Wijk aan Zee
14. Egmond aan Zee
15. **Den Helder**
16. Eierland, 8 cables SE of LtHo
17. Vlieland harbour
18. *West Terschelling*
19. N coast Terschelling, 2·6M NW of W Terschelling
20. *Harlingen*
21. Hollum, Ameland
22. Oosterburen, Schiermonnikoog
23. *Lauwersoog*

Netherlands lifeboat stations

IV. Bibliography

Almanacs
Almanak voor watertoerisme, deel 1, reglementen en vaartips (regulations and navigation tips); *deel 2 vaargegevens* (navigation data), Koninklijke Nederlandse Toeristenbond ANWB.

The Macmillan & Silkcut Nautical Almanac, Macmillan Press Ltd.

Practical Boat Owner Cruising Almanac, Practical Boat Owner.

Reed's Nautical Almanac, Thomas Reed Publications Ltd.

Hydrographer of the Navy
Admiralty List of Lights and Fog Signals
Vol B, Southern and eastern sides of the North Sea, NP 75.

Admiralty List of Radio Signals
Vol 1 Part 1, Coast Radio Stations in Europe, Africa, & Asia, NP 281(1).

Vol 2, Radio Navigational Aids. Radio Direction-Finding Stations, Radiobeacons, Radar Beacons, NP 282.

Vol 6, Part 1, Port Operations, Pilot Services, and Traffic Management, NP 286(1).

Diagrams relating to Port Operations, Pilot Services and Traffic Management, NP 286(a).

Admiralty Notices to Mariners – small craft edition (4 times per year), NP 246

Dover Strait Pilot, NP 28.

North Sea (East) Pilot, NP 55.

Symbols and abbreviations used on Admiralty charts, NP 5011.

Chef der Hydrografie, 's-Gravenhage, Netherlands
Catalogus van Nederlandse zeekarten en andere hydrografische publikaties

Chart *1970, Mariners' Routeing Guide, Southern North Sea; Passage Planning Chart*. Scale 550:000. This is an eastern extension of British Admiralty Chart *5500* showing the new separation schemes round the Netherlands.

Getijtafels voor Nederland (Netherlands tide tables).

Waterstanden en Stromen, HP 33. Ministerie van Verkeer en Waterstaat

Bridge opening times
Bedieningstijden spoorbruggen, Rijkswaterstaat, dienst Verkeerskunde.

Bedieningstijden van sluizen en bruggen, Rijkswaterstaat, dienst Verkeerskunde.

Openingstijden spoorwegbruggen, ANWB.

Pilots and Guides
Brackenbury, Mark, *Frisian Pilot*, Stanford Maritime Ltd.

Bristow, Philip, *Through the Dutch Canals*, A. & C. Black/Nautical Books Ltd.

The Cruising Association, *Cruising Association Handbook*.

Levison, Henry, *Dutch Inland Sailing Pilot*, Stanford Maritime Ltd.

Navin, Brian, *North Sea Passage Pilot*, Imray, Laurie, Norie & Wilson Ltd.

Oliver, John, *Holiday Cruising in the Netherlands*, David & Charles Ltd.

Werner, Jan, *Holland mit dem Boot, Fuhrer fur Sportschiffer*, Delius Klasing Verlag.

Tourism

Chester, Carole, *Welcome to Holland Belgium & Luxembourg*, Collins.

Constance, Pat and Hazel, *The Visitor's Guide to Holland*, Moorland Publishing Co. Ltd, Hunter Publishing Inc.

Netherlands Board of Tourism, *Holland Watersports Paradise*. Also wide-ranging leaflets including tourist attractions, cycling, traditional sailing, boat-hire, flowers, bird sanctuaries, fishing.

VVV provincial offices each publish at least one tourist leaflet on each provincial area. See Introduction for addresses.

Royal Yachting Association

Planning for Going Foreign, Vol 1 (Belgium, N and W France, Holland, UK).

V. Glossary

ENGLISH TO DUTCH AND GERMAN

English	Dutch	German
aft	achter/achterschip	achtern/hinten
anchor	anker	Anker
anchorage	ankerplaats	Ankerplatz
anchoring prohibited	verboden ankerplaats	ankern verboten
attendance	bediening	bedienung
bacon	spek	Speck
baker	bakker	Bäcker
batten	zeillat	Latte
beacon	baken	Bake
beef	rundvlees	Rindfleisch
bell	mistklok/bel	Glocke
binoculars	verrekijker	Fernglas
black	zwart	schwarz
block	blok	Block
blue	blauw	blau
boat	boot	Boot
boom	giek	Baum
bow	boeg	Bug
bread	brood	Brot
breadth (beam)	breedte	Breite
bridge	brug	Brücke
brown	bruin	braun
bulkhead	schot	Schott
bunk/berth	kooi	Koje
buoy	ton, boei	Tonne, Boje
butcher	slager	Metzger
butter	boter	Butter
cabin	kajuit	Kajüte
chain	ketting	Kette
channel, fairway	vaargeul, vaarwater	Fahrwasser, Fahrrinne
chart	zeekaart/waterkaart	Seekarte/Wasserkarte
cheese	kaas	Käse
chemist	apotheek	Apotheke
clew	schoothoorn	Schothorn
closed	gesloten	geschlossen
cockpit	kuip	Cockpit
current	stroom	Strom
customs	douane	Zoll
cutter	kotter	Kutter
dentist	tandarts	Zahnarzt
depth	diepte	Tiefe
diesel engine	dieselmotor	Dieselmotor
dinghy	bijboot, jol	Beiboot, Dingi

English	Dutch	German
dolphin	dukdalf/meerpaal	Dalbe
draught	diepgang	Tiefgang
drawbridge	ophaalbrug	Zugbrücke
east	oost	Ost, Osten
ebb	eb	Ebbe
echo sounder	echolood	Echolot
eggs	eieren	Eier
ferry	veer, pont	Fähre
fish	vis	Fisch
fishing harbour	vissershaven	Fischereihafen
fishmonger	vishandel	Fischhändler
fixed bridge	vaste brug	feste Brücke
flood	vloed	Flut
fog	mist	Nebel
foot (sail)	onderlijk	Unterliek
fore	voor	vordere
forecastle	vooronder	Vorschiff
foresail	voorzeil	Vorsegel/Focksegel
gale	storm	Sturm
genoa	genua	Genua
grease	smeer	Schmiere
green	groen	Grün
greengrocer	groente man	Gemüsehändler
grocer	kruidenier	Krämer
halyard	val	Fall
ham	ham	Schinken
harbour	haven	Hafen
harbour master	havenmeester	Hafenmeister
hatch	luik	Luke
head (of sail)	top	Kopf
headroom	doorvaarthoogte	Durchfahrtshöhe
high water	hoogwater	Hochwasser
horn	nautofoon	Nautofon
hospital	ziekenhuis	Krankenhaus
immigration	passpoortkontrole	Passkontrolle
inner	binnen	Binnen
insurance	verzekering	Versicherung
jam	jam	Marmalade
keel	kiel	Kiel
leech	lijk	Liek
lifting bridge	hefbrug	Hubbrücke
light float	lichtvlot	Leuchtfloss
light vessel	lichtschip	Feuerschiff
lighthouse	vuurtoren	Leuchtturm
lights	lichten	Lichten
lock	sluis	Schleuse
locker	opbergruimte	Schrank/fach
low water	laagwater	Niedrigwasser
luff	loef	Luv
mainsail	grootzeil	Gross-segel
mast	mast	Mast
mean, average	gemiddeld	Durchschnitt
meat	vlees	Fleisch
milk	melk	Milch
mist	nevel/mist	Dunst, Nebel
mooring buoy	meerboei	Festmacheboje
mooring place	aanlegplaats	Liegeplatz
mooring prohibited	verboden aan te leggen	Anlegen verboten
motor sailer	motorzeiljacht	Motorsegler
movable bridge	beweegbare brug	bewegliche Brücke
mutton	schapenvlees	Hammelfleisch
neap tide	doodtij	Nippzeit
no	nee	nein
no, none	geen	kein
north	noord	Nord, Norden
office	kantoor	Büro

English	Dutch	German
officer	beamte	Beamter
oil	olie	Öl
open	open	geöffnet
outer	buiten	Aussen
petrol engine	benzinemotor	Benzinmotor
pork	varkensvlees	Schweinefleisch
port	bakboord	Backbord
post office	postkantoor	Postamt
prohibited	verboden	verboten
propeller	schroef	Propeller, Schraube
pulpit	preekstoel	Bugkorb
pump	pomp	Pumpe
pushpit	hekstoel	Heckkorb
radio telephone	marifoon	Radio Telefon
radiobeacon	radiobaken	Funkfeuer/Radiobake
range (tide)	verval	Tidenhub
red	rood	rot
reed	mistfluit	Zungenhorn
rope	touw, koord	Tau, Seil, Strick
rudder	roer	Ruder
sailmaker	zeilmaker	Segelmacher
sausages	worstjes	Wurstchen
schooner	schoener	Schoner
shackle	sluiting	Schäkel
shop	winkel	Geschäft, Laden
shrouds	want	Wanten
siren	mistsirene	Sirene
sloop	sloep	Slup
south	zuid	Sud, Suden
speed	snelheid	Schnelligkeit
spinnaker	spinnaker	Spinnaker
spring tide	springtij	Springtide
starboard	stuurboord	Steuerbord
station (railway)	station	Bahnhof
stay	stag	Stag
stem	voorsteven, boeg	Vordersteven, Bug
stern	achtersteven, hek	Achtersteven, Heck
supermarket	supermarkt	Supermarkt
swing bridge	draaibrug	Drehbrücke
tack	hals	Hals
tiller	helmstok	Ruderpinne
toilet	WC	Toilette
tower	toren	Turm
vegetables	groenten	Gemüse
water	water	Wasser
water level	waterstand	Wasserstand
watt or watershed	wantij	Wattenhoch
west	west	West, Westen
whistle	mistfluit	Pfeife
white	wit	weiss
withies	steekbaken, pricken	Pricken, Baken
yacht	jacht	Jacht
yacht chandler	scheepsleverancier	Jachtausrüster
yawl	yawl	Yawl
yellow	geel	gelb
yes	ja	ja

DUTCH TO ENGLISH AND GERMAN

Dutch	English	German
achter/achterschip	aft	achtern/hinten
aanlegplaats	mooring place	Liegeplatz
achtersteven, hek	stern	Achtersteven, Heck
anker	anchor	Anker
ankerplaats	anchorage	Ankerplatz
apotheek	chemist	Apotheke
Bakboord	port	Backbord

Dutch	English	German
baken	beacon	Bake
bakker	baker	Bäcker
beamte	officer	Beamter
bediening	attendance	Bedienung
benzinemotor	petrol engine	Benzinmotor
beweegbare brug	movable bridge	bewegliche Brücke
bijboot, jol	dinghy	Beiboot, Dingi
binnen	inner	Binnen
blauw	blue	blau
blok	block	Block
boeg	bow	Bug
boot	boat	Boot
boter	butter	Butter
breedte	breadth (beam)	Breite
brood	bread	Brot
brug	bridge	Brücke
bruin	brown	braun
buiten	outer	Aussen
diepgang	draught	Tiefgang
diepte	depth	Tiefe
dieselmotor	diesel engine	Dieselmotor
doodtij	neap tide	Nippzeit
doorvaarthoogte	headroom	Durchfahrtshöhe
douane	customs	Zoll
draaibrug	swing bridge	Drehbrücke
dukdalf/meerpaal	dolphin	Dalbe
eb	ebb	Ebbe
echolood	echo sounder	Echolot
eieren	eggs	Eier
fluit	whistle	Pfeife
geel	yellow	gelb
geen	no, none	kein
gemiddeld	mean, average	Durchschnitt
genua	genoa	Genua
gesloten	closed	geschlossen
giek	boom	Baum
groen	green	grün
groente handelaar	greengrocer	Gemüsehändler
groenten	vegetables	Gemüse
grootzeil	mainsail	Gross-segel
hals	tack	Hals
ham	ham	Schinken
haven	harbour	Hafen
havenmeester	harbourmaster	Hafenmeister
hefbrug	lifting bridge	Hubbrücke
hekstoel	pushpit	Heckkorb
helmstok	tiller	Ruderpinne
hoogwater	high water	Hochwasser
ja	yes	ja
jacht	yacht	Jacht
jam	jam	Marmalade
kaas	cheese	Käse
kajuit	cabin	Kajüte
kantoor	office	Büro
ketting	chain	Kette
kiel	keel	Kiel
kooi	bunk/berth	Koje
kotter	cutter	Kutter
kruidenier	grocer	Krämer
kuip	cockpit	Cockpit
laagwater	low water	Niedrigwasser
lichten	lights	Lichten
lichtschip	light vessel	Feuerschiff
lichtvlot	light float	Leuchtfloss
loef	luv	Liek
los steekbaken	withies	Pricken
luik	hatch	Luk
marifoon	radio telephone	Radio Telefon

Dutch	English	German
mast	mast	Mast
meerboei	mooring buoy	Festmacheboje
melk	milk	Milch
mist, nevel	fog	Nebel
mistfluit	reed	Zungenhorn
mistklok/bel	bell	Glocke
mistsirene	siren	Sirene
motorzeiljacht	motor sailer	Motorsegler
nautofoon	horn	Nautofon
nee	no	nein
nevel	mist	Dunst, Nebel
noord	north	Nord, Norden
olie	oil	Öl
onderlijk	foot (sail)	Unterliek
oost	east	Ost, Osten
opbergruimte	locker	Schrank/Fach
open	open	geöffnet
ophaalbrug	drawbridge	Zugbrücke
passpoortkontrole	immigration	Passkontrolle
pomp	pump	Pumpe
postkantoor	post office	Postamt
preekstoel	pulpit	Bugkorb
radiobaken	radiobeacon	Funkfeuer/Radiobake
roer	rudder	Ruder
rood	red	rot
rundvlees	beef	Rindfleisch
schapenvlees	mutton	Hammelfleisch
scheepsleverancier	yacht chandler	Yachtausrüster
schoener	schooner	Schoner
schoothoorn	clew	Schothorn
schot	bulkhead	Schott
schroef	propeller	Propeller/Schraube
slager	butcher	Metzger
sloep	sloop	Slup
sluis	lock	Schleuse
sluiting	shackle	Schäkel
smeer	grease	Schmiere
snelheid	speed	Schnelligkeit
spek	bacon	Speck
spinnaker	spinnaker	Spinnaker
springtij	spring tide	Springtide
stag	stay	Stag
station	station (railway)	Bahnhof
steekbaken, pricken	withies	Pricken, Baken
storm	gale	Sturm
stroom	current	Strom
stuurboord	starboard	Steuerbord
supermarkt	supermarket	Supermarkt
tandarts	dentist	Zahnarzt
ton, boei	buoy	Tonne, Boje
top	head (of sail)	Kopf
toren	tower	Turm
touw, koord	rope	Tau, Seil, Strick
vaargeul, vaarwater	channel, fairway	Fahrwasser, Fahrrinne
val	halyard	Fall
varkensvlees	pork	Schweinefleisch
vaste brug	fixed bridge	feste Brücke
veer, pont	ferry	Fähre
verboden	prohibited	Verboten
verboden aan te leggen	mooring prohibited	Anlegen verboten
verboden ankerplaats	anchoring prohibited	Ankern verboten
verrekijker	binoculars	Fernglas
verval	range (tide)	Tidenhub
verzekering	insurance	Versicherung
vis	fish	Fisch

Dutch	English	German
vishandel	fishmonger	Fischhändler
vissershaven	fishing harbour	Fischereihafen
vlees	meat	Fleisch
vloed	flood	Flut
voor	fore	Vordere
vooronder	forecastle	Vorschiff
voorsteven, boeg	vordersteven, bug	Stem
voorzeil	foresail	Vorsegel/Focksegel
vuurtoren	lighthouse	Leuchtturm
WC	toilet	Toilette
want	shrouds	Wanten
wantij	watt or watershed	Wattenhoch
water	water	Wasser
waterstand	sea level	Wasserstand
west	west	West, Westen
winkel	shop	Geschäft, Laden
wit	white	weiss
worstjes	sausages	Wurstchen
yawl	yawl	Yawl
zeekaart/waterkaart	chart	Seekarte/Wasserkarte
zeillat	batten	Latte
zeilmaker	sailmaker	Segelmacher
ziekenhuis	hospital	Krankenhaus
zuid	south	Sud, Suden
zwart	black	Schwarz

GERMAN TO DUTCH AND ENGLISH

German	Dutch	English
achtern/hinten	achter/schip	aft
Achtersteven, Heck	achtersteven, hek	stern
Anker	anker	anchor
Ankern verboten	verboden ankerplaats	anchoring prohibited
Ankerplatz	ankerplaats	anchorage
Anlegen verboten	verboden aan te leggen	mooring prohibited
Apotheke	apotheek	chemist
Aussen	buiten	outer
Backbord	bakboord	port
Bäcker	bakker	baker
Bahnhof	station	station (railway)
Bake	baken	beacon
Baum	giek	boom
Beamter	beamte	officer
Bedienung	bediening	attendance
Beiboot, Dingi	bijboot, jol	dinghy
Benzinmotor	benzinemotor	petrol engine
bewegliche Brücke	beweegbare brug	movable bridge
Binnen	binnen	inner
blau	blauw	blue
Block	blok	block
Boot	boot	boat
braun	bruin	brown
Breite	breedte	breadth (beam)
Brot	brood	bread
Brücke	brug	bridge
Bug	boeg	bow
Bugkorb	preekstoel	pulpit
Büro	kantoor	office
Butter	boter	butter
Cockpit	kuip	cockpit
Dalbe	dukdalf/meerpaal	dolphin
Dieselmotor	dieselmotor	diesel engine
Drehbrücke	draaibrug	swing bridge
Dunst, Nebel	nevel	mist
Durchfahrtshöhe	doorvaarthoogte	headroom

German	Dutch	English
Durchschnitt	gemiddeld	mean, average
Ebbe	eb	ebb
Echolot	echolood	echo sounder
Eier	eieren	eggs
Fähre	veer, pont	ferry
Fahrwasser, Fahrrinne	vaargeul, vaarwater	channel, fairway
Fall	val	halyard
Fernglas	verrekijker	binoculars
feste Brücke	vaste brug	fixed bridge
Festmacheboje	meerboei	mooring buoy
Feuerschiff	lichtschip	light vessel
Fisch	vis	fish
Fischereihafen	vissershaven	fishing harbour
Fischhändler	vishandel	fishmonger
Fleisch	vlees	meat
Flut	vloed	flood
Funkfeuer/ radiobake	radiobaken	radiobeacon
gelb	geel	yellow
Gemüse	groenten	vegetables
Gemüsehändler	groenteman	greengrocer
Genua	genua	genoa
Geöffnet	open	open
geschlossen	gesloten	closed
Geschäft, Laden	winkel	shop
Glocke	mistklok/bel	bell
Gross-segel	grootzeil	mainsail
grün	groen	green
Hafen	haven	harbour
Hafenmeister	havenmeester	harbourmaster
Hals	hals	tack
Hammelfleisch	schapenvlees	mutton
Heckkorb	hekstoel	pushpit
Pfeife	fluit	whistle
Hochwasser	hoogwater	high water
Hubbrücke	hefbrug	lifting bridge
ja	ja	yes
Jacht	jacht	yacht
Kajüte	kajuit	cabin
Käse	kaas	cheese
kein	geen	no, none
Kette	ketting	chain
Kiel	kiel	keel
Koje	kooi	bunk/berth
Kopf	top	head (of sail)
Krämer	kruidenier	grocer
Krankenhaus	ziekenhuis	hospital
Kutter	kotter	cutter
Latte	zeillat	batten
Leuchtfloss	lichtvlot	light float
Leuchtturm	vuurtoren	lighthouse
Lichten	lichten	lights
Liegeplatz	aanlegplaats	mooring place
Liek	lijk	leech
Luk	luik	hatch
Luv	loef	luff
Marmalade	jam	jam
Mast	mast	mast
Metzger	slager	butcher
Milch	melk	milk
Motorsegler	motorzeiljacht	motor sailer
Nautofon	nautofoon	horn
Nebel	mist	fog
nein	nee	no
Niedrigwasser	laagwater	low water
Nippzeit	doodtij	neap tide
Nord, Norden	noord	north

German	Dutch	English
Öl	olie	oil
Ost, Osten	oost	east
Passkontrolle	passpoortkontrole	immigration
Postamt	postkantoor	post office
Pricken, Baken	steekbaken, pricken	withies
Propeller	schroef	propeller
Pumpe	pomp	pump
Radio Telefon	marifoon	radio telephone
Rindfleisch	rundvlees	beef
rot	rood	red
Ruder	roer	rudder
Ruderpinne	helmstok	tiller
Schäkel	sluiting	shackle
Schinken	ham	ham
Schleuse	sluis	lock
Schmiere	smeer	grease
Schnelligkeit	snelheid	speed
Schoner	schoener	schooner
Schothorn	schoothoorn	clew
Schott	schot	bulkhead
Schrank/fach	opbergruimte	locker
schwarz	zwart	black
Schweinefleisch	varkensvlees	pork
Seekarte	zeekaart	chart
Segelmacher	zeilmaker	sailmaker
Sirene	mistsirene	siren
Slup	sloep	sloop
Speck	spek	bacon
Spinnaker	spinnaker	spinnaker
Springtide	springtij	spring tide
Stag	stag	stay
Steuerbord	stuurboord	starboard
Strom	stroom	current
Sturm	storm	gale
Sud, Suden	zuid	south
Supermarkt	supermarkt	supermarket
Tau, Seil, Strick	touw, koord	rope
Tidenhub	verval	range (tide)
Tiefe	diepte	depth
Tiefgang	diepgang	draught
Toilette	WC	toilet
Tonne, Boje	ton, boei	buoy
Turm	toren	tower
Unterliek	onderlijk	foot (sail)
Verboten	verboden	prohibited
Versicherung	verzekering	insurance
Vordere	voor	fore
Vordersteven, Bug	voorsteven, boeg	stem
Vorschiff	vooronder	forecastle
Vorsegel/Focksegel	voorzeil	foresail
Wanten	want	shrouds
Wasser	water	water
Wasserstand	waterstand	sea level
Wattenhoch	wantij	watt or watershed
Weiss	wit	white
West, Westen	west	west
Wurstchen	worstjes	sausages
Yachtausrüster	scheepsleverancier	yacht chandler
Yawl	yawl	yawl
Zahnarzt	tandarts	dentist
Zoll	douane	customs
Zugbrücke	ophaalbrug	drawbridge
Zungenhorn	mistfluit	reed

VI. Conversion tables

metres–feet

m	ft/m	ft
0.3	1	3.3
0.6	2	6.6
0.9	3	9.8
1.2	4	13.1
1.5	5	16.4
1.8	6	19.7
2.1	7	23.0
2.4	8	26.2
2.7	9	29.5
3.0	10	32.8
6.1	20	65.6
9.1	30	98.4
12.2	40	131.2
15.2	50	164.0
30.5	100	328.1

centimetres–inches

cm	in/cm	in
2.5	1	0.4
5.1	2	0.8
7.6	3	1.2
10.2	4	1.6
12.7	5	2.0
15.2	6	2.4
17.8	7	2.8
20.3	8	3.1
22.9	9	3.5
25.4	10	3.9
50.8	20	7.9
76.2	30	11.8
101.6	40	15.7
127.0	50	19.7
254.0	100	39.4

metres–fathoms–feet

m	fathoms	ft
0.9	0.5	3
1.8	1	6
3.7	2	12
5.5	3	18
7.3	4	24
9.1	5	30
11.0	6	36
12.8	7	42
14.6	8	48
16.5	9	54
18.3	10	60
36.6	20	120
54.9	30	180
73.2	40	240
91.4	50	300

kilometres–nautical miles

km	M/km	M
1.9	1	0.5
3.7	2	1.1
5.6	3	1.6
7.4	4	2.2
9.3	5	2.7
11.1	6	3.2
13.0	7	3.8
14.8	8	4.3
16.7	9	4.9
18.5	10	5.4
37.0	20	10.8
55.6	30	16.2
74.1	40	21.6
92.6	50	27.0
138.9	75	40.5
185.2	100	54.0
463.0	250	135.0
926.0	500	270.0
1852.0	1000	540.0

kilograms–pounds

kg	lbs/kg	lbs
0.5	1	2.2
0.9	2	4.4
1.4	3	6.6
1.8	4	8.8
2.3	5	11.0
2.7	6	13.2
3.2	7	15.4
3.6	8	17.6
4.1	9	19.8
4.5	10	22.0
9.1	20	44.1
13.6	30	66.1
18.1	40	88.2
22.7	50	110.2
34.0	75	165.3
45.4	100	220.5
113.4	250	551.2
226.8	500	1102.3
453.6	1000	2204.6

litres–gallon

l	gals/l	gals
4.5	1	0.2
9.1	2	0.4
13.6	3	0.7
18.2	4	0.9
22.7	5	1.1
27.3	6	1.3
31.8	7	1.5
36.4	8	1.8
40.9	9	2.0
45.5	10	2.2
90.9	20	4.4
136.4	30	6.6
181.8	40	8.8
227.3	50	11.0
341.0	75	16.5
454.6	100	22.0
1136.5	250	55.0
2273.0	500	110.0
4546.1	1000	220.0

Index